Everything but the Script

Professional Writing in the Entertainment Industry

Everything but the Script

Professional Writing in the Entertainment Industry

Jason Davids Scott

Arizona State University

cognella®

SAN DIEGO

Bassim Hamadeh, CEO and Publisher
Jennifer McCarthy, Field Acquisitions Editor
Amy Smith, Project Editor
Christian Berk, Production Editor
Jess Estrella, Senior Graphic Designer
Sara Schennum, Licensing Associate
Natalie Piccotti, Senior Marketing Manager
Kassie Graves, Vice President of Editorial
Jamie Giganti, Director of Academic Publishing

Cover image copyright © 2017 iStockphoto LP/Kjekol.
copyright © 2018 iStockphoto LP/PrathanChorruangsak.

Printed in the United States of America.

3970 Sorrento Valley Blvd., Ste. 500, San Diego, CA 92121

Brief Contents

Detailed Contents

Acknowledgments

A number of people have provided me with consistent guidance and support in my career, and have shared with me many lessons, techniques, and stories that inform my expertise in this subject. Thanks specifically to my mentors and colleagues Cara White, Harry Clein, Mary Lugo, Teri Kane, Janice Roland, Shannon Treusch, Steve Beeman, Jeff Hill, Jeremy Walker, Bumble Ward, Rob Harris, Sheryl Main, Claudia Gray, Dave Fulton, Lori DeWaal, and the gone but not forgotten Gary Hill and Marc Urman, all from the world of publicity and marketing; and Dana Jackson, Stephen Moore, Paul Cremo, Connie Tavel, Curtis Burch, Lauren Williams, Jackie Levine, and Vanessa Livingston from the world of management, acquisitions, and development. My colleagues at Arizona State University who have encouraged me to pursue this as a signature topic include my current director Tiffany Ana Lopez, and my former superiors in the film program F. Miguel Valenti and Greg Bernstein. Fellow faculty members Joe Fortunato, Gene Ganssle, Chris LaMont, Gregg Maday, Stephani Etheridge Woodson, Lance Gharavi, and Tamara Underiner have also provided encouragement and cheerleading when required. Thanks too to my editor at Cognella, Amy Smith, who patiently navigated some unexpected life turns on my part and provided efficient and appropriate feedback.

My mother, Ingrid, and father, Richard, both taught me the value of good writing. I learned as much about technical writing and editing from my mother as I did about the history of movies and the practice of publicity from my father, so I see this book as an equal reflection of my parents' own life works and their passion for sharing their talent and skills with me. Sadly, the week after I signed the contract for this book, my father left the world of the living and retired to the great double feature in the sky. While I regret that he is not able to cast his living eyes upon these particular fruits of my labor, he is present in spirit in every word, and I am blessed to be able to share what he shared with me with a wide audience of readers who, it is hoped, love the movies and TV just as much as he did.

Preface

Learning From a Show Business Life

I was fortunate enough to be raised by parents who were, for much of my childhood, employed as professional writers of one sort or another. My mom and dad met in journalism school at the University of Missouri, one of the most respected "j-school" programs in the country; they later earned master's degrees in English (mom) and creative writing (dad) at the University of Iowa. After marrying and relocating to the West Coast, they both worked as college instructors of journalism and English, freelance magazine writers, and copy editors for a number of years.

My father eventually landed a job doing public relations for Disneyland, then moved into the mainstream studio system via Walt Disney Studios, ultimately working for more than 15 years as a publicist and executive for several major studios and firms. My mother coauthored a book and made extra money as a copy editor before eventually returning to school to get advanced degrees in social work and psychology. So my formative years were spent hearing the distinctive click-click-click of their electric typewriters, a sound that soothed me as I examined their giant wall of textbooks and great works of literature. I promised myself that one day I would be able to type faster than my parents, because typing seemed like such a "grown-up" thing to do.

As my dad nurtured his career as a movie studio executive, I got to tag along to various events, or spend a day or two with him at his office every year, where the sheer amount of paperwork, files, and memoranda showed me the decidedly unheroic and unglamorous side of the business. Yes, at lunch we got to walk around the set of "The Dukes of Hazzard" or snoop through the private Disney animation library, but most of the day was spent watching my dad and all those around him bang away on typewriters. They'd look at posters for upcoming movies and pitch tag lines to one another, then my dad would type the best ones into a memo and "cc" ("carbon copy" and distribute) to four or five people above him, including the heads of all the marketing departments and the studio president. My dad and his colleagues would meet and discuss which stars and stories to "pitch" to a weekly magazine like *People* to support a film's release. He would then go to his office and type a letter to an editor or writer at *People*. In the pre-digital age, his assistants would then make copies; distribute them to all parties concerned; messenger, mail, or fax them to their intended recipients; and file their own copies into folders stashed away in filing cabinets.

The kind of work my dad was doing was, in its way, very creative. He had earned his graduate degree at the University of Iowa Writer's Workshop, where he studied under author Kurt Vonnegut, who was on my dad's MFA committee. My dad had grown up loving movies and wanting to be a writer, and even cowrote an episode of "Gunsmoke" that aired in 1971. But he had trained as a journalist and had a skill for writing "feature" copy—he had his own humorous opinion column in his high school and college newspapers, and loved the deadlines and structure of professional journalism. Historically, those in the field of publicity had been called "press agents," and many of the older people my dad worked with were good storytellers with lively imaginations.

As a child, I first saw that passion and creativity in his work when he began working for Disneyland, in 1975, and was put in charge of the hoopla surrounding Disney's Bicentennial Celebrations, and also the editing of all Disney trade/travel magazines. From the perspective of my first-grader self, the important part of my dad's job was that he actually knew Mickey Mouse, who existed in our lives as a kind of real person. (Mickey and I even exchanged letters, with my dad as the "mailman.") As the executive in charge of planning events for Mickey Mouse's 50th birthday in 1978, my dad proposed a nationwide "whistle-stop" train tour, ending in Washington, DC, on Mickey's actual birthday (November 18) and an opening of an exhibit at the Library of Congress.

It was also my dad's idea to get Mickey Mouse a star on the Hollywood Walk of Fame (the first animated or fictional character to earn this public accolade), and he showed me the letter he wrote to the Walk of Fame committee (on behalf of Disney Studios, of course) that ultimately secured this honor. He even took me to Hollywood Boulevard and asked me to help him pick out which star would be Mickey's—reminding me that it had to be someplace where a big press event could be held. We found a star on the northwest corner of Hollywood and Wilcox that we deemed appropriate. But a few days after our decision, the Chinese Theatre agreed to add new space for a star right outside the legendary venue, where Mickey would add his autograph and hand and footprints in cement. I was disappointed, but you have to admit the new site was much, much more befitting for Mickey!

When I was a teenager—having finally learned to type, and avidly reading the trade papers my father brought home from work every day—my dad struck out on his own for a few years, first producing electronic press kits (EPKs, which we'll get to later in this book), and later freelancing for several studios and distributors. He found himself working a lot with Warner Brothers International Television; short-staffed, it needed someone to write plot synopses for all of the TV shows it wanted to sell in other global markets. As much as my dad liked to write, he was overwhelmed with this rather boring "piecemeal" work, while still trying to do bigger and more lucrative projects and consulting. Fortunately, in me, he had a willing and eager apprentice, who far preferred typing for a living to shredding cheese and sweeping up at the local pizza parlor.

So my dad allowed me to do some of his grunt work, such as generating multiple synopses for sitcoms, including *Family Matters*, *Head of the Class*, and *Just the Ten of Us*, and late-night dramas such as *Falcon Crest* and *Knots Landing*. My dad received a script for each show—usually about five or six at a time—and would hand most of them off to me. I would read each script and then write a one-page synopsis of what occurred in the episode. My dad would proofread and then send everything back to Warner Brothers. TV comedy scripts aren't very long, so it didn't take long for me to get this process down to about 90 minutes per script, for which I was paid $30.

I had ambitions of studying film and running a movie studio one day, but I didn't realize that these specific writing skills would define my professional life after college. Sure, I was grateful for the experience and the money, but I was under the mistaken impression that *everyone* in Hollywood had these skills—after all, my dad had them, as did most of his coworkers. I now realize, of course, that my father and his friends were exceptions: in many offices, in many departments, a solid "professional" writer is too rare of a thing.

This became especially evident to me shortly after I graduated from New York University and was fortunate enough to have a good friend and colleague from film school (Dana Jackson) leave Manhattan and move to Los Angeles—thus leaving an open position as an assistant at a boutique public relations firm. That company, Clein + White, with offices in New York and Los Angeles, specialized in the marketing of independent, foreign, and documentary films. This was in the "heyday" of the film festival and indie revolution of the early 1990s, and the company worked on the earliest films by such now-iconic directors as Richard Linklater, Gus Van Sant, Todd Haynes, Jim Jarmusch, Sally Potter, Stephen Soderbergh, the Coen Brothers, Pedro Almodóvar, and Quentin Tarantino. There were some very good writers on the staff of Clein + White, but there was always a lot of writing to be done, and the account executives were generally much more valued for their in-person and on-phone pitching skills than their writing abilities. After all, writing takes a certain amount of private time, and publicists are, by definition, supposed to be available to anyone who needs to reach them.

Later, after I relocated to Los Angeles, my friend Dana came through again, this time offering me freelance work as a story analyst (or "reader") at Castle Rock Entertainment, where she was a junior executive in feature film development. Although I had never worked in that part of the industry (aside from a brief internship in college), I knew I had the ability to write a synopsis, and was confident enough in my critical abilities to be able to write effectively about the strengths and weaknesses of a script. Eventually, I became Dana's assistant; our office was responsible for supervising all of the freelance and in-house readers, and for managing the studio's script library. Later, we moved to help actress Helen Hunt and producer Connie Tavel set up a production deal at Sony, working with writers and producers all over town on a variety of projects through various stages of the acquisition and development process. (One of our projects was *Then She Found Me*, a feature film that Helen eventually directed and starred in with Bette Midler and Matthew Broderick.)

When I chose to return to graduate school to pursue my advanced degrees and begin my teaching career, I continued to work as a freelance script reader to supplement my meager grad student income. I had maintained my contacts in public relations, continuing to work for publicity firms on both coasts on an as-needed basis. Writing press kits, in particular, helped keep me directly connected to filmmakers, studio executives, actors, and others who were navigating their careers just as the world of on-demand and streaming entertainment began to change the marketplace. Although the content of the projects remained the same—feature films, documentaries, dramatic and comedic television series, and various charity events or one-off announcements—the way in which these projects were seen and sold was (and is) rapidly evolving. Learning new skills such as writing for social media, connecting publicity to promotions, and pitching entrepreneurs such as famous chefs, designers, and architects as "entertainment" properties have allowed me to evolve my work alongside the expanding industry.

So to a great extent, what I offer in this book is a reflection of the values and skills I have learned in this lifelong career far behind the scenes. But it's important to point out that just because I have managed to make a good living by engaging my fingers with a computer keyboard, it does not mean that writing is the only skill necessary for someone to succeed. It's best to think about writing as a skill that is absolutely essential for some in the business, and a strong "bonus" superpower for most others.

CHAPTER 1

The Not-So-Sexy Secret of Show Biz Success

U nless you grew up in a family that works in show business, you very likely would have a somewhat romantic view of a career in the entertainment industry. That's not to say that some of your more romantic notions are incorrect: people who make films and television for a living often rub elbows with the glamourous, rich, and famous. There are red carpet premieres, festival accolades, critical praise, and golden statue ceremonies that publicly affirm the value of one's work, and there is the deep satisfaction of being paid to work in the world of creative imagination. For most people, this romantic view of the industry usually means identifying with people who emerge as artistic champions—actors, directors (in film), writers and producers (in television), or possibly less well-known but no less important cinematographers, editors, animators, effects artists, or other highly skilled craftspeople who are driven by their artistic vision and unique abilities.

But if you're reading this book, you've probably long since realized that this romantic view of "Hollywood" is, at best, only partially accurate. You know that making a movie is more than just pointing a camera toward a group of actors, shouting "action!" and pressing a button. You know that taking a project from really amazing idea to an actually makeable thing is a laborious and slow process that requires cooperation and collaboration. You may have learned these things by practicing your own filmmaking, or because you have immersed yourself in the behind-the-scenes stories of your favorite movies and television shows. If you are reading this book, it's because you've decided to embrace a career in show business even knowing what you know about the hard work, elusive lucky breaks, and steep odds against becoming the next industry legend.

And yet, it's still quite likely that you will hang on to that romantic ideal of the artistic champion—that somehow you will succeed, and your projects will succeed, if and only if you can establish yourself as a creative powerhouse. Of course, having a strong creative voice is an asset to every project, but creative vision and a passionate imagination are not any guarantee of success. The industry (and the world at large) is filled with great ideas, and great people who are theoretically capable of bringing those ideas to life. So what allows one person to beat the odds and turn their idea into the next bingeworthy Netflix series, while hundreds of others barely make it to an infrequently updated YouTube channel? Why does one film dazzle the audience at Sundance and get the unknown filmmaker a deal with a studio, while a dozen other equally good films go ignored (and a hundred others don't even make it to Sundance)?

And this is where our understanding of the industry becomes distinctly *un*-romantic. Because the secret element that gets someone's creative notion from "what a great idea for a movie" to "your cousin Courtney can buy tickets to see your film at the multiplex in Fargo" isn't power, or money, or sex appeal, or even simple blind luck.

The secret element is writing.

To be more specific—*not* creative writing. At least, not creative writing in the sense of being a good screenwriter, having an ear for dialogue, or knowing how to suggest subtlety of character through the counterpoint between intentions and obstacles. Those are all good skills to have, just as being a director who knows how to make actors feel comfortable, a cinematographer who understands the power of color and composition, or an editor with an instinct toward rhythm will give anyone in those positions a leg up on their competition.

No, the writing I refer to here is what we might call "technical" writing. It's often done by people who mostly work far from the actual set of the movie—the work they do is usually anonymous, and often subject to being rewritten by others without their permission. And, unless they really look for it, people such as your cousin Courtney in Fargo never see this technical writing, because it's not generally made available directly to the public.

But these technical materials are essential in ensuring the project gets made and seen. Just as movie trailers, billboards, television commercials, banner ads, and promotions help "sell" a film to the general public, the technical writing that is the subject matter of this book—such as script coverage, story notes, production notes, pitch letters, and other marketing-related materials—are absolutely essential in "selling" a film to the key players who are less visible to the general public.

Who reads these materials? Producers, agents, managers, studio and network executives, journalists, critics, editors, talk-show bookers, distributors, and promotional partners—in other words, the people whose support and belief in a project help ensure that more people will seek out and pay attention (and give time and money) to that project. This is the "secret sauce" of Hollywood success, a key ingredient that can be just as important as having a shrewd business instinct, a strategic manager, the right "insider" contact, a hot property, and a big star.

Savvy producers, filmmakers, and professionals know that the common career skill that supports success throughout the process of acquisition, development, marketing, and distribution is the ability to write effectively. As much as Hollywood regularly pays deserved respect and lots of money to screenwriting and screenwriters, industry success absolutely requires the hard work and imagination of the technical and professional writers who go to work after the screenplay is finished.

If you are an aspiring filmmaker or screenwriter, this book will offer insight into how technical writing determines the way in which your creative work is understood, talked about, and "processed" as a potential sale or green light.

Let me explain: If you compare your script or film to a baby, then that baby is usually going to be "raised" and nourished by other people. The "clothes" that baby wears are the written elements that go alongside the script, or "dressing it up." Knowing how technical writing in development and publicity works will give you more control and understanding of the decisions others are making about your project—about how they are dressing up your beautiful, perfect baby.

If you are a would-be producer, this book is an opportunity to learn the value of technical writing, which will allow you to shepherd your properties and clients from idea to green light to market success. If you can master these abilities, you'll instantly be a "working" producer with an all-too-rare skill that allows you to participate, execute, and manage throughout all phases of production. To continue the metaphor from above, you're the point person in charge of actually putting the outfit on that million-dollar baby. The better you are at that part of the job, the more likely everyone is to be successful—and the more likely you are to be indispensable and in demand.

If you are hoping to specialize further and become an agent or manager, a casting director, or an executive in advertising, publicity, promotion, marketing, or social media, this book will give you the experience and help you create a writing portfolio that will make you a top-of-the-pile candidate for every job listing. Almost everyone in show business is selling something. Good writers are as essential to that process of suggesting and concluding a sale as commercial artists, data analysts, distribution specialists, and content creators.

HOW TO GET THE MOST OUT OF THIS BOOK

This book is set up for most effective use in a classroom setting. Some chapters are longer and feature more writing exercises than others, so whether you are a teacher using this as an instructional resource, or a self-taught learner who is working on your own, you might want to take some time to review each chapter and determine what kind of schedule might work best for you. The book is divided into two main sections that mirror the traditional industrial process: the first section covers acquisition, development, and preproduction; the second is devoted to production, distribution, and exhibition.

For writers and directors, this book will help you to specifically understand the work of your career from the perspective of the technical writer, and encourage you to develop the following skills:

- Creating an effective synopsis based on a screenplay or other submitted property (teleplay, novel, article, etc.).
- Creating effective critical comments to accompany a "first read" report (coverage).
- Crafting and refining story notes designed to help a writer or writers move from draft to draft.
- Write effective pitch letters regarding a property to other producers, actors, crew members, etc., to get them involved with your project.

For would-be producers and executives, in addition to the above development-related skills, you'll also be interested in the materials related to understanding and supporting a film's release to various marketplaces, including:

- Developing various kinds of synopses, descriptions, and log lines to help pitch and sell your project in a variety of traditional, digital, and social media.
- Creating and presenting yourself as an industry professional through effective written business communication in the form of pitch letters, press relations, cover letters, etc.
- Creating materials such as screening invitations, targeted pitch letters, and behind-the-scenes information that support a film's release, along with the management and marketing strategies to most effectively deliver these materials.

The chapters in this book are arranged in roughly the "chronological" order of events related to the production of a film or television property, with the caveat that many practices overlap in time, and each project has its own unique timeline and history. Because most of my own experience is in feature films, the discussions and examples will largely be geared toward that specific form of work. I will, however, make occasional notes about and include additional perspectives from the world of series programming (television, cable, streaming, etc.) that dominate the current marketplace. You are encouraged to engage with the suggested assignments by using examples from both film and television, or any other media form that might apply (VR/AR projects, interactive entertainment, video games, viral videos, etc.).

I'd also like to suggest some tips for more productive learning as you work with this book. Some of this will be covered in more detail in later chapters, but are listed here so that you can orient yourself toward the material and be ready to engage most effectively.

First, it is essential that you become a master of the very **basics of technical writing**: spelling, grammar, punctuation, capitalization, sentence and paragraph construction, and word choice. The standard I am employing for this book is the general standard for American journalism. Although there are some small differences between various journalistic style guides (when to use the Oxford comma, whether to italicize a film title or set it in quotes), the basic spelling of English words and the standard use of apostrophes and capital letters is by now well established. If you are a college student, it's very likely you are fairly accomplished in this regard, but it's extremely important to know that writing as a professional means you *cannot* be sloppy under any circumstances, particularly as you begin your career, most likely working as an apprentice or assistant to someone else. A boss might forgive the occasional typo or weak word choice; however, if you spell the name of your boss's mother wrong, demonstrate an inability to distinguish between "it's" and "its" (or "then" and "than"), or continually turn in work with confusing sentences, or frequently use "text" language to communicate, then you're going to find yourself doing less desirable tasks around the office and most likely *not* be a serious candidate for promotion unless you are truly exceptional at something else.

Second, you probably would get more out of this book if you can establish a **"working group"** of fellow students or colleagues. Learning how other people write—both their strengths and weaknesses—is a big part of becoming a successful technical writer, as you will frequently be asked to rewrite other people's work. Examining, proofreading, and editing the work of others also reinforces the standard rules of grammar, punctuation, and professional writing that are essential to professional success.

This also allows you to get feedback from multiple perspectives about your own work. Showing your written work to people is something of a vulnerable act. For most of us, our friends don't read anything we write longer than a tweet or a status update; however, we certainly know what it's like when we inadvertently use the "wrong" word via social media and cause a firestorm of reaction from people we did not mean to offend. But in the long run, getting into the habit of receiving simple and honest feedback makes you a better editor and reader of your own work, and will accelerate your learning curve. If you are using this book in conjunction with a class, then the instructor is strongly encouraged to keep people in working groups, with some ideas on how to manage course exercises detailed in the book along with our online supplemental materials.

Third, get in the habit of **writing regularly and setting achievable goals for yourself.** One of the benefits of my being raised by writers trained as journalists was that it demystified the writing process, making it more about "doing the work" than being a "word artist" guided by inspiration. In fact, I'm probably not a very good creative writer, because I like to work on deadline, whether that deadline is a day, a week, or a month or more away. Most of the writing exercises you have here are relatively short—less than 1,000 words (sometimes much less), and easily achievable within a few hours for most competent writers.

Whether you are trying to complete this book in a four-month semester, or just picking it up and using it piecemeal, the exercises and material will work best if you set modest goals to complete the various exercises. In some cases, I will suggest a time frame, but with the strong caveat that every person has a very different writing "speed" and "tempo." If you find yourself easily meeting those goals, repeat the exercises with a shorter time frame; if you need more time, take more time. It's quite likely that the better you get at writing, the less overall effort and time it will take.

At the very least, you will definitely get better at creating strong first drafts, which mean less time needed to edit and proofread. Remember, especially for people who use writing as supplementary or freelance income, writing "rush" jobs usually means a bit more money, and makes you that much more valuable to a prospective employer.

A quick note about the assignments in this book, many of which require you to work from an existing screenplay, teleplay, or other property. I *strongly* discourage you to work from published screenplays of films that have already been released to theaters. Most frequently, these are "transcripts" of what ultimately ended up on the screen, *not* the screenplays that sold. Additionally, the fact the film has already been made robs you of your ability to analyze the screenplay critically before it goes in front of the cameras. It doesn't take much insight or critical thought to read the published script for *Fargo* or *Hidden Figures* or *When Harry Met Sally* and "recommend" the film for production. By the same token, I also discourage you from using your *own* scripts as the basis for samples of your own work. If you have a script you believe is worthy of using, share it with a classmate or colleague in your working group, and let them write coverage and create projects around your script while you base your assignments off of theirs. You need to be completely objective, and to succeed you need to be able to identify the strengths and weaknesses of work by people you don't know. To find scripts for use, there are a number of websites (e.g., simplyscripts.com) that allow you to read or download unproduced scripts. There is also the famous "blacklist" of "the best unproduced scripts" (many of which are readable at blcklst.com), but again, knowing that others have already decided these are "good" removes the potential for some of your own critical judgment.

A FINAL WORD ABOUT THE VALUE OF WRITING

Before we begin, it's worth taking a moment to remind ourselves about the deeper meaning of what "writing" means.

From the perspective of the present day, the ability to write is an almost universal expectation for a citizen of an "advanced" social system. Although many people struggle with advanced writing, and would never choose to write as part of their profession, almost everyone is comfortable writing text messages, putting a personal note on a birthday card, or just scribbling "Have a great day xoxo!" on a note stuck to the bathroom mirror.

In that context, we forget that for the vast majority of human existence, very few people knew how to write even that simple "have a great day," or had any access to written language at all. Just 200 years ago, at the time of the so-called "Great Enlightenment" when universal education, literacy, and access to knowledge was first promoted as a core social value, only 12% of the human population could read and write.[1] Even considering those privileged few who knew how to read and write, we only date written language itself back to about 3000 BCE (5,000 years ago), while our species, *homo sapiens*, has been around for 200,000 years! Do the math: We've had "language" (spoken) of some sort for 200 millennia, but in only *five* of those millennia have there been a written equivalent; and only in the last 200 years—just 1/1000th of our species' existence—has reading and writing been considered something that should be "universal" and a central element of one's historical and social identity.

Think, too, for a moment about what the act of writing "does" in that longer historical context. If there were only a few select people with the ability to write things down, then what was written down must have been very, very important: legal matters, birth and death

---

1   Max Roser and Esteban Ortiz-Ospina (2018). "Literacy." Published online at OurWorldInData.org. Retrieved from https://ourworldindata.org/literacy.

records, reports of important events in history, or informed thoughts about the nature of the gods and the universe. It's no wonder that in many cultures, the oldest written texts are the most sacred—the books of the Old Testament and New Testament, the *Bhagavad Gita*, or the cuneiforms scratched into the walls of the pyramids.

Remember, spoken language—speech—is a "live" and ephemeral thing that has no historical "permanence" except in our flawed memory. So the ability to take an idea that has only been spoken and turn it into an absolute, permanent sign that could, in theory, transcend time and space—to know mastery of the written word—must have seemed an act of divine power. If an illiterate mother or father says "I love you" to their child on a daily basis, those words disappear when the parent is absent or dies. Writing those words down, in their own hand, and presenting it to the child means that those words will exist and retain their power forever.

Even in the modern world, when written words are cheap and plentiful—and we probably cherish hearing our mom or dad say "I love you" a bit more than we might value the "xoxo" at the end of their daily text message—we have retained that notion that the written word has a special power. If you have a friend or relative who constantly promises something with his or her spoken words and doesn't deliver, you might jokingly comment that you want "a written contract" when that person makes yet another pledge, as if the value of the written word is more binding and valid than whatever he or she may say. Legendary film producer Samuel Goldwyn allegedly once said, "An oral contract isn't worth the paper it's printed on." Your vote in an election is not taken with your voice, but with you putting marks on a paper (or a touch screen), turning your intention into a literal, permanent sign. Writing has permanence, authority, and "presence," even long after the person who inscribed the words has left the room.

It is a well-established fact that the film industry is one built on social relations—"It's all about who you know," as the cliché goes. Schmoozing, socializing, collaborating, and compromising are all essential qualities that require show business professionals to interact with one another in real time. In those moments of connection and interpersonal exchange, "writing stuff down" sometimes feels like an extra or unnecessary step.

But if you ask anyone who has been successful in the industry for more than six months, they will tell you how absolutely crucial the written word is. Imagine you are a producer and you meet an up-and-coming filmmaker at a friend's birthday party. That filmmaker tells you her or his idea for a story that is absolutely brilliant, and it's exactly the kind of thing that you know one of your financial backers would be over the moon about financing. The next day, you call your backer—and what do you say? Maybe you've forgotten one small detail about the idea. Maybe you're not as super-smooth a storyteller as the filmmaker. Maybe you can tell that the backer is distracted by a crying baby or driving in traffic, and you lose your confidence in retaining the backer's attention. If you had to recapture that "magic" of the initial pitch every time you wanted to get someone else involved with the project, it would never happen!

Instead, you have writing. You can ask the filmmaker for a synopsis or a treatment (believe me, your backer is going to want to read something short and sweet before diving into a 100-page screenplay). Then you can call you backer and say, "Hey, I'm emailing you a fabulous idea, take a look and let's set up a meeting." The backer can read the synopsis, reflect on it, think about it, read it again, get more excited about the project, and then pass that document on to other potential backers. The authority of the written word—the fact that someone (or more than one someone) has taken the time to turn an ephemeral, singular idea into a permanent, transcendent document—means that the idea has reached the most important phase of understanding and become tangible. The written word makes ideas worth something above and beyond their actual content—indeed, it has creator-like properties that make people feel safer, more secure, and on more stable ground.

So while the act of writing—particularly technical, "noncreative" writing based more on commerce and industry than creativity and inspiration—might seem mundane, unglamorous, or "grunt work" from a filmmaking perspective, I encourage you to engage with the writing process the same way the scribes of ancient times did, as if you are invoking the power of the gods to transcend time and space and turn "ideas" into "things." Although the words you write might only be seen by a few people, and are ultimately in service to a much bigger "thing" that has even greater value (the film, television show, personality, or event on whose behalf you are writing), you are deeply involved and essential to the creative act.

Just as the clothes you wear, the voice you speak with, and the work you do, the words you write represent you and your ability to connect yourself to the world around you. Treat that skill with respect, and unleash the power of its possibilities. You'll find the results can not only be lucrative, supplying you with income to supplement your own creative dreams or giving you skills that make you a more valuable worker, but also quite satisfying. When the words you write result in a project coming to life, the sense of pride is immeasurable, even if what you do is relatively invisible.

EXERCISE 1A: WRITE YOUR OWN BIO

The cliché about beginning a writing career is to "write what you know"—so what (or who) do you know better than yourself?

Providing important biographical information—writing a "bio"—is a special skill that can be part of any one of a number of professional writing projects, particularly when you are trying to pitch/sell a project featuring unknown talent, and definitely in the process of marketing and publicity.

Given enough time, any competent writer would be able to complete this assignment, but this is also a chance for you to develop an instinct toward completing a writing assignment quickly. Thus, I'm encouraging you to try to complete these exercises in the suggested amount of time. If it takes you longer to complete, that's okay, but it will give you a gauge on how quickly you can consider, write, edit, and proofread a simple assignment.

A professional bio is something that highlights professional work, with a minimal amount of "personal" information. It is not "the story of your life"—it's a description of what you have done that is relevant to your audience/reader.

The more words/space you have to work with, the more details you may include. Be sure to review the samples below to see how they each contain additional "layers" of information as they get longer.

For this exercise, you should write *three* bios of yourself, and of these sizes:

- Two sentences (30–50 words) (Recommended time: five minutes)
- One paragraph (100–120 words) (Recommended time: 12 minutes)
- One page (250–300 words) (Recommended time: 20 minutes)

BEFORE YOU WRITE

You might not think of your life so far as being very exciting or interesting, and that's okay. But there are basic facts about you that you can start building from—where you were born and/or grew up, what schools you attended, what you have studied (or are now studying), and probably some kind of work history.

For the purposes of this assignment, don't feel like you need to "hype" or "sell" yourself; this is just a description of some basic info.

You'll see from my samples that I have focused bios on my life and work experience connected to the information in this book. I have not, for example, cited anything about my many years as a theater director or acting teacher, or mentioned how important my mother is to my educational development and identity as a professional writer (she was, for the record, very important, but she never worked in the entertainment industry. Hi, mom!). I suggest that if you have had "many" careers or experiences, you try to pick one "focus"—perhaps a career in show business—to help you decide what to include and what to leave out.

SELF-ASSESSMENT

- Which of these bios was most difficult for you to do in the allotted time?
- Is each sentence clear, focused, and offering new information?
- Have you avoided using specific nouns, verbs, and adjectives more than once in every sentence? More than once in every paragraph? More than once in the entire bio?
- Are your verbs and adjectives appropriately chosen?
- For your longest bio, are the paragraphs organized and focused? Are your transitions clear and effective?

GROUP ACTIVITY

If you are in a class or working with a group, share and exchange your various bios with names redacted or replaced by pseudonyms. See if you can guess the identity of the author based on their bio. This also gives you a chance to offer and receive feedback from your peers about which of the bios they found easiest or most interesting to read.

EXERCISE 1A: SAMPLES

Short

Jason Davids Scott has been a freelance public relations consultant and professional writer for more than 30 years. A graduate of New York University and UC Santa Barbara, Scott currently teaches in the School of Film, Dance and Theatre at Arizona State University. (Word count: 43)

Medium

A graduate of New York University and UC Santa Barbara, Jason Davids Scott's professional career began as a teenager working for father Richard, a veteran studio publicist. For the last 30 years, Scott has created marketing materials for more than 200 projects, and served as the unit publicist on the films Dazed and Confused and The Crow. Clients include New York and Los Angeles-based publicity firms, production companies, celebrities, restaurants, musicians, comedy troupes, and international charity organizations. Currently, Scott is an assistant professor at Arizona State University, whose publicatons include essays on the history of film acting, and the career of actor Robert Downey Jr. and directors Wes Anderson and Hal Hartley. (Word Count: 119)

Long

Jason Davids Scott grew up in Southern California, and learned about writing for the entertainment industry from father Richard, a longtime film publicist and studio executive. After earning his degree in cinema studies at New York University, Scott joined the boutique PR firm of Clein + White as an assistant publicist and staff writer. Assigned as unit publicist for Richard Linklater's classic *Dazed and Confused*, Scott later held the same position on Miramax's *The Crow* and the indie hit *Party Girl* starring Parker Posey.

After relocating to Los Angeles, Scott served as a staff reader and later assistant to the story editor at Castle Rock Entertainment, before becoming a creative executive for Hunt/Tavel Productions. Returning to graduate school at UC Santa Barbara, Scott earned his MA and PhD in theater, specializing in the history of film acting.

Scott began teaching at Arizona State University in 2009, and is currently an assistant professor and assistant director for film at the School of Film, Dance and Theatre. Courses include the required Sex and Violence in Film and Television and the History of Independent Film and Professional and Technical Writing for Film. Scott has published chapters on the history of acting in early sound cinema, the career of Robert Downey Jr., and the work of independent directors Wes Anderson and Hal Hartley. With the company writawayink. com, Scott continues to serve as a consultant and writer for companies on both coasts, with recent clients including HBO Documentaries, Amazon Films, Netflix, Lionsgate/STARZ, and the Discovery Channel.

Scott lives in Mesa, Arizona, with three cats, and tries to attend as many baseball games as possible. (Word count: 278)

A note to the reader: because I prefer to be identified as gender neutral, I tend to use my last name more than might be customary. You will notice that none of the words I use to describe myself connote either male or female gender, and I have avoided the use of possessive pronouns where they are not necessary (e.g., "learned about writing from father Richard" rather than "his/her/their father Richard.") It is exceptionally important when working for a client to ask about pronoun preference.

CHAPTER 2

Reading and Writing About Entertainment Media

To introduce you to some of the basics of technical writing for film, we're actually going to start at the "end" of the process, since that's the type of writing most of you will be familiar with as moviegoers and consumers of popular culture. This chapter considers more general "professional" writing conventions by looking at traditions, rules, and standards of film journalism.

When you read a film review, or a news item about a shakeup at a television network, or an interview with a star, you are seeing the same kinds of journalistic techniques, skills, and practices that need to be mastered by professional writers in the industry. The audience is different, and the reason "why" the writing exists is a bit different, but in many cases the same words, phrases, and writing strategies are involved throughout all of these processes.

IDENTIFYING PUBLISHED WRITING STYLES AND TYPES: MEET THE TRADES

The entertainment industry's "insider" publications are referred to collectively as **the trades**. This comes from the term "trade publication," a periodical devoted more or less exclusively to reporting on one specific industry or profession, and often meant to be read only by people within that profession. There are trade publications for the airline industry, educators, medical professionals, contractors, engineers, and accountants. There are also trade magazines for doll collectors, crane operators, parking garage owners, and people who make pizza (*Pizza Today*).

For show business, there are a handful of significant trade publications. Most movie fans have heard of *Variety* (which began a weekly publication in 1905, published a daily print version from 1933–2013, and now runs online) and *The Hollywood Reporter* (started as a daily publication in 1930, and converted to a weekly publication and online portal in 2010). Several other online outlets have emerged as solid sources of trade information, including *deadline .com*, *thewrap.com*, and *indiewire.com*. A trade publication geared toward actors and the theater is *Backstage*, while the music industry is covered by *Billboard*. There are also a number of even more specific trades for editors, cinematographers, animators, visual effects professionals, etc. Some of these are published by unions or professional organizations, and many are supported by advertising from companies that are heavily invested in the craft (i.e., lighting equipment for cinematographers, new software design platforms for animators, repair/resale providers, etc.).

One of the best pieces of advice I ever received is one I heard from three bosses on three occasions—and from my father when I grew up: "Read the trades every day." Once upon a time, that meant getting hold of my office's shared copy of *Variety* or *The Hollywood Reporter*, and glancing through it at lunch sitting at my desk, or yanking my boss's copy off of her desk when I knew she had already left for the day. With the Internet, of course, access is a bit easier. You can access most trade articles online, and while information between the trades is often redundant, there are still unique features to each trade outlet.

"SLANGUAGE"

When *Variety* began publication in 1905, it was in the middle of a period in American culture when "new" words were all the rage. This was in the wake of the industrial revolution, the turn of the recent century making people think more about progress and the future. Just as America had "conquered a new frontier" and established itself as an important global power, so too did Americans seem to embrace new inventions, technologies, and practices that made the world a truly marvelous place. According to Jeremy Butterfield, a noted lexicographer and expert on the history of written language, the vast majority of "new" words in the Oxford English Dictionary during this era were American in origin, and it's where we first find use of such now-common words as "dorm," "eatery," "trivia," "fandom," and "hip," all of which date to between 1900 and 1904.[1]

Variety focused on the very modern entertainment industry—mostly vaudeville, variety, and Broadway, but soon to include the business of motion pictures (the term "movies" dates from 1909) and radio (a term first used in 1903, but not really a "business" until the early 1920s). While *Variety* may have been unique as an entertainment trade magazine, it was hardly unique as a publication: indeed, in New York City alone, there were 53 daily publications and another nearly 1,000 publications that were weekly, biweekly, or monthly.[2] This was also the era of sensational "yellow journalism," when well-told stories and grabbing the reader's attention were more important than "facts" and "truth."

Add to this the fact that publications were laid out essentially by hand and required a very efficient use of space in headlines (minimal letters whenever possible). As such, you

---

1 https://jeremybutterfield.wordpress.com/2017/03/23/where-does-the-word-television-come-from-twentieth-century-words/; https://jeremybutterfield.wordpress.com/tag/20th-century-words-year-by-year/
2 *Rowell's American Newspaper Directory of 1905,* accessible at https://archive.org/details/americannewspape1905newy

had a perfect storm to produce new words. It's no wonder then that the publishers and editors of *Variety* encouraged their writers to come up with what is now informally called **slanguage**, the "lingo" of show business. Those who read the articles in *Variety* and understood the clever use of new words and language felt like "insiders" with special information, reinforcing the way in which written language helps to demonstrate a certain kind of "in the know" power. Over the last century-plus, many of these terms and new words have become part of standard industry language, while others remain delightfully obscure or specific.

It's also meant some very clever headlines over the years. One of the best known is from 1935, when one article proclaimed "Sticks Nix Hick Pix." The moment is recreated in the 1942 film *Yankee Doodle Dandy* when an elderly George M. Cohan (played by James Cagney), retired on his farm, shows the headline to a group of college students who are confused. He translates word by word: "Sticks" (rural audiences) "Nix" (reject) "Hick" (rural-themed) "Pix" (movies).

You can search for "*Variety* slanguage" and find a link to the publication's long list of several unique terms and phrases it has used over the years—some of which *Variety* invented, others of which it simply made regular use of. Here are some of my favorites:

Ankle—a verb meaning to quit or be dismissed from a job

Biopic—a film that is a biography (by the way, it is pronounced BUY-oh-pick, not bi-OPP-ic)

Cleffer—a songwriter (a "clef" is a written musical symbol)

Exex—multiple executives

FYC—"for your consideration," a marketing campaign to be discussed later

Hype—manufactured "buzz," short for "hyperbole"; either a noun or a verb

Ink—a verb meaning to sign a contract

Kidvid—children's television or media

The Lion or **Leo**—a reference to the studio MGM

The Mouse House or **The Mouse**—a reference to Walt Disney Studios or the Disney Corporation

Oater—a western

Ozoner—a drive-in movie theater

Peacock—a reference to NBC

Praisery—a PR firm

Scribbler or **Scripter**—a screenwriter

Sitcom—situation comedy (a term invented by *Variety*)

Socko—a film that is a hit at the box office (also, "boffo")

Tyro—a "first timer" or new writer/director/filmmaker

Wrap—to finish a production

Many elements of the trades should be essential reading for everyone in the industry, such as the weekly box-office or television ratings reports, job/position ads, or special issues devoted to covering major trends, new technologies, or important events. But for our purposes, we're going to be focused on the various elements—we'll call them "articles" as a catch-all term—that most directly correlate with other professional and technical writing practices. Reading these various articles—understanding how they were written and what they are trying to communicate, and "tuning" your reading eye to the various word choices, grammatical tendencies, and formatting standards—will give you the "muscle memory" needed to become a solid first-draft writer and a crack copy editor and proofreader.

Let's also add that you'll see this type of writing in almost all major outlets or **periodicals** (that's what we used to call newspapers and magazines when all were in print, because they were released to the public "periodically"). Thus, in addition to the trades, people in the industry should regularly check the "Arts" or "Entertainment" sections of major newspapers, particularly *The New York Times* and the *Los Angeles Times*, or magazines such as *The New Yorker, Rolling Stone, The Atlantic,* or *Time*. While those are not "entertainment only" outlets, they often feature extensive coverage of issues related to the industry, along with interviews, criticism, and other articles. There are also outlets such as *People, Time Out,* or *In Touch* that focus on entertainment news and celebrity culture, and that may also include gossip or reviews, along with numerous online outlets that serve a similar "lighter" market.

We will divide these "articles" into four types, each with its own function and standards: **news**, **features**, **editorial**, and **social media**. (Social media is obviously a much broader entity, but we'll briefly discuss it here in the context of industry journalism.)

NEWS—REPORTING AND NEWS ANALYSIS

News is pretty much what it sounds like—things have "happened" and what happened needs to be recorded and disseminated. Journalism is, for the most part, news-driven (though, as we will see, not everything that is presented as "news" is actually "newsworthy"). We can also divide this category into two subcategories for some clarity.

What we might call **reporting** is when an article gives you the facts about an event, with some context and commentary about the event's meaning from various perspectives. Despite what politicians or your crazy Uncle Frank might tell you, most news is not "fake," as most news outlets have very strict standards on how to report "what happened." What the reporter or reporters write as "factual" is often checked by at least one other person for accuracy. People who give information (both on and off the record) are scrutinized to ensure they are credible and reliable sources. If a reporter doesn't actually see/hear/record something on his or her own, then that reporter must have at least two credible sources (sometimes more) to attest to anything that is second-hand information. News reporting attempts to live up to the standard of being factual enough to serve as an objective historical record. Generations from now, someone will read a good news reporter's words and have faith that the words (and what they convey) are accurate because they have been held to the strictest of journalistic standards.

Another kind of news article might be called **news analysis**. These are often articles that ask broader questions or discuss various events and trends "in general" without centering around one specific event or action. Here, a writer or reporter might ask for people's opinions about things, rather than merely getting them to relay "what happened." While news analysis may imply or include some type of explicit editorial commentary or perspective, the goals are still to be factual, rigorous, and objective.

For the entertainment industry, news reporting most often involves business dealings, including hirings and firings, release of corporate financial reports, mergers and acquisitions, and other things you would expect to find covered in most major industry publications. Because these news items are often fairly cut-and-dried, movie studios, producers, and television networks have figured out that they can supply well-written press releases that provide the outlets with all the news they need in prefab form.

For example, let's pretend that you work for a company that has just signed a contract with a major TV star to make her feature film debut. Sure, you could just let people talk about it on the street and hope a reporter from *Variety* hears about it; however, it's so much easier to write a press release and send it directly to an editor at *Variety*. The editor won't doubt that it's big news, and she'll have all the information she needs to run a story. If she wants to hire a reporter to ask more questions or get another quote about the signing, you've provided your contact information on a **press release** (you'll practice many of those in later chapters) so the reporter can reach you on short notice. You'll send the same release to *The Hollywood Reporter*, *The New York Times*, and so forth. Each of those outlets will decide how to "cover" the story, but you've essentially reported the news *to* them.

On the other hand, there are reporters who cover unusual or unexpected events that require investigative work, research, or more perspectives or sources. Let's say that three weeks after that star's contract is signed, the actress and your producer boss decide it isn't working out, and the actress has decided to spend more time with her family and take six months off. That's not the kind of "news" that anyone really needs to know about, since it involves personal relationships that don't really affect the world at large or the direction of the industry. A curious reporter might hear about a "fight" between actress and producer and decide to investigate, in which case your company may or may not choose to engage with the reporter for various reasons. Perhaps the studio will supply a "statement" regarding the matter, or maybe your boss will agree to an on-the-record interview explaining that what happened is disappointing but really no big deal.

In terms of news analysis, a clever producer or publicist will always be looking for a way to provide his or her client or project with any opportunity to sound intelligent, relevant, and important. Being able to anticipate or identify "trends" in the news might help you nudge a reporter or editor into writing a more analytical piece; or, hearing that a specific trade outlet is doing a particular kind of story, you can be prepared to pitch your project or client as a potential subject.

Keeping in touch with general news and cultural trends often helps to provide your projects with some context. In recent years, for example, there has been much discussion about gender imbalance in the workplace in terms of equal representation, fair pay, and harassment and abuse. Thus, any project with interesting female characters who encounter these issues should be on the radar of any news journalist, cultural critic, or public figure who is active in that real-life discussion. Trade journalists might be persuaded to write a special article about "the changing role of women in the industry" or how "women are taking control on screen and off," especially when you can ensure the journalists have access to your female-empowering new TV series or interviews with prominent and progressive company executives. Securing that coverage will require you to write letters and emails that clearly articulate the importance of making these connections between journalist and subject, and to do so in the language and style of the article that will ultimately be written. In other words, the tone needs to be serious, factual, and "objective"—rather than the usual publicity style of exaggeration, hype, and sensation.

FEATURE WRITING

Feature writing is the kind of writing and journalism that allows a bit more hype, and functions in a slightly different manner. As opposed to being about events or incidents that are of historical importance, features tend to be about things that are "interesting" or unusual without necessarily being "essential." Traditionally, newspaper and magazine features were considered supplementary to news and news analysis, but over the years numerous outlets developed that were more or less dedicated to running feature material. Early in Hollywood history, "fan magazines" such as *Photoplay* and *Modern Screen* served this purpose, printing interviews, behind-the-scenes photographs, and gossipy sidebars about the world of celebrity culture; in more recent years, publications such as *People* or *Entertainment Weekly* or programs such as *Entertainment Tonight* and *Access Hollywood* and the E! network provide that kind of feature-level access.

The important thing to know about the placement of feature articles is that it is never "accidental." Almost every feature article will be part of a larger campaign that attempts to engage the reader as a potential customer or action agent of some sort. For example, you might read a cover story in *People* magazine about a celebrity who recently had a personal ordeal and is now "coming back" into the spotlight. It's very likely that celebrity has a specific film or new television show that is about to be made available—even if the article doesn't really mention that project in any great detail.

Beyond that, the content of the feature article has always been carefully designed, proposed, and negotiated between publicists (who used to be called "press agents") and the article's writer or editor. There's a reason the female lead is the subject of a big interview in *Cosmopolitan*, while the male lead is shown waving the flag at a NASCAR event in *Sports*

Illustrated. There are frequent exceptions to these rules, but in almost every case there is some immediate cultural reason related to the entertainment marketplace that makes the feature article viable.

That said, feature articles provide deeper information and have a potentially greater influence on viewers, readers, and consumers. Seeing an advertisement featuring your favorite movie star in a new film might intrigue anyone, but reading or viewing a one-on-one interview with that star makes you feel even closer to their creative process and artistic life. Although stars may do multiple interviews and appearances as they make or promote a film, each of those events is slightly different, as reporters ask different questions and the actor has more time to reflect on the work she or he is promoting.

An **interview** or **profile** is perhaps the most common type of feature, but an outlet also might run a feature article that explains a new use of technology (special effects), an unusual production choice (casting a comedic actor in a straight role), or information about the production of a film (particularly in an unusual location or under unusual circumstances). While most features are initiated by a publicity team, there are also journalists and editors who approach publicists with possible ideas: How do we get an interview with the director of this true-life Olympic story to *Sports Illustrated*? Can we do a photo shoot with some vintage costumes since the series is set in the 1930s? What about an article in a tech magazine about the film's unusual combination of practical effects and CGI?

Feature writing can also offer varying degrees of *importance* and *quality*. The previous examples reflect feature ideas that will help enrich the viewer's experience of watching the film or series: it's not *essential* to the viewing, but it is effectively supplemental. **Gossip**, on the other hand, is perhaps a bit further removed, and ultimately very likely satisfies a different element of a viewer's curiosity. For example, if the star of the movie eloped in Vegas in recent months, that's "interesting" to some, but really has no direct influence on how people read the movie (unless, perhaps, the movie is about someone eloping in Vegas). There are also different types of gossip: whispers about who might be cast as the next superhero, or which studio executive might be forming his or her own company, or a retired actor who is thinking about running for political office. But stories about who is dating whom, which celebrity is covering up a nasty gambling habit, or the subject of some salacious hacked emails are really just about people's personal lives and would most likely have little effect on individual projects or the industry as a whole.

Gossip is not ineffective in promoting a film's visibility, but generally speaking it is of slightly less value. Fans of the subject of the gossip would probably see the film anyway; people who don't care for celebrity gossip are perhaps more likely to be put off. Likewise, most creative artists, producers, and companies like to stay away from gossip-centered marketing. There certainly may be a time when an agent, manager, or publicist circulates a "gossipy" rumor to keep his or her client visible in the public eye, but for the most part those items tend to be separate from major project marketing campaigns.

That certainly wasn't the case in the heyday of the studio system, when gossip columnists such as Hedda Hopper and Louella Parsons were key partners with the studios in helping craft the off-screen images of the stars and using "fake" gossip stories to cover up real-life scandal and behavior. For example, the actress Loretta Young had crafted an image as a "good girl," and was known for her conservative Catholic faith. But at the age of 22, she became pregnant by her costar, Clark Gable (who was married to someone else). Rather than tarnish her image, she was kept out of the limelight for a few months with an "illness" that required her to seek treatment away from Hollywood. She secretly gave birth and turned over her daughter to an orphanage. Then, 19 months later, she announced to gossip columnist Louella Parsons that she was "adopting" a beautiful, 19-month-old girl—in fact her biological daughter. It's unclear how many people knew about the young girl's parentage at the time and were in on the ruse, but it's one of many examples of how gossip played an important role in maintaining the public image of a Hollywood celebrity.

Such gossip today, of course, is usually relegated to supermarket tabloids and similar websites. Because we live in an era when more stars are encouraged to live "authentically" and can be more candid about their personal lives, gossip about the "secret lives" of stars doesn't have the same cultural value as it once did. But while such things as unmarried parents, divorce, and sexual preference are far more acceptable in most social circles, any kind of personal gossip, even if somewhat "innocent," can be damaging. For example, when the science fiction film *Passengers* came out, the marketing often played up the "chemistry" on screen between stars Chris Pratt and Jennifer Lawrence. The two did interviews together in which they joked as if they were close friends, talked about their more intimate scenes in the film, and generally looked "flirtatious" in a way that suggested their roles in the film were enhanced by their personal relationship. Although there was no direct suggestion of a real-life romantic affair, it gave coverage on the film some extra "heat." Several months after the film was released, however, when it was announced that Pratt and his wife Anna Faris were divorcing, "evidence" of trouble was cited as fans and gossip mavens speculated as to whether the "affair" with Lawrence was a catalyst. (All of the parties involved vehemently deny that Pratt and Lawrence had an affair.) While the marketing of *Passengers* probably had very little to do with the real-life relationship issues of these actors, in the public eye they are inevitably and inextricably linked. Ultimately, using gossip to promote a project or career is something that should only be done with great care and the consent of the subjects involved, and with a specific strategic purpose in mind.

OPINION, EDITORIAL, REVIEWS, AND CRITICISM

The third type of article is called **editorial** or **opinion** (you often hear the term "op/ed" to describe this category). There are times where news analysis comes close to editorial or offers an editorial perspective, and op/ed pieces frequently use news and news analysis as frameworks for discussions. But the essential element of op/ed is that what is being expressed is the opinion of an individual (or perhaps a number of individuals representing an organization or entity). While they might cite facts, their conclusions, recommendations, and observations are understood to be personal, not universal.

While entertainment figures might certainly find themselves in mainstream op/ed pieces for whatever reason, most industry opinion is reflected in the form of **reviews** of projects by critics or other professionals. Indeed, this is the form of film journalism that you are probably most familiar with: the "yes/no," "thumbs up/thumbs down," "three out of four stars" perspectives of critics who write for newspapers, magazines, established Internet outlets, or on TV. In academic circles, reviews are usually referred to as **film criticism**, and are usually understood to be written and published *simultaneous with the release of the film to the public.* Traditionally, this means when the film comes out in theaters, but in recent years criticism has also been published when films are released on DVD or given another high-profile level of exposure (anniversary screenings, etc.).

Film scholarship, on the other hand, is critical perspective and opinion that is broader, and might consider films that were released long ago or are not immediately available to the public. For example, you may have taken a film appreciation class and had to write a "review" of a film such as *Citizen Kane* or *Casablanca*. Your review is obviously going to be informed by 70 years of opinion on the film and knowledge that you have that was unavailable to critics at the time. With *Casablanca*, for example, you know that ultimately the Allies were on the winning side of World War II; with *Citizen Kane*, you probably know that Orson Welles never made a film that came close to *Citizen Kane* in its ambitious scope and cultural standing, although his career lasted another 40 years.

For the purposes of the entertainment industry professional, it is the daily/weekly critic who is the most important figure in terms of circulating opinion about the film. Often, these critics are also staff writers or editors who make other decisions or suggestions on article placement, feature assignments, etc. If you know a critic likes a film, then it's easy to pitch that critic (or his or her editor) on running an interview with the star on Thursday, followed by the 3-and-a-half-star review on Friday. In a later chapter, we'll address the crafting of **screening invitations** that will get critics to advance screenings of your films, and providing them with production information (a press kit) that effectively suggests the film's value and meaning. We'll also briefly look at how to ethically and effectively read reviews for culling forceful quotes.

SOCIAL MEDIA—CONVERGING, CONNECTING, AND COMMUNICATING EVERYTHING

Finally, a few words about the evolving role of **social media** as a component of film journalism. Social media, as you probably know, performs many functions. For example, there is direct communication between individuals and the public—a star, for instance, may use social media to announce she or he has agreed to star in a new project, as Reese Witherspoon did when she posted a video of herself in a pink outfit on Twitter to announce she was going to play Elle Woods again in *Legally Blonde 3*. A "rumor" had circulated for a few days, confirmed by this "drop" by the star herself, an effective coordination between studio, producer, star, and publicist to maximize the effect of that announcement.

Social media is also obviously used to share and disseminate other forms of coverage or information—a catchy headline and link that guides you to an online interview with the film's director, an image that is hyperlinked to the film's official website, etc. It can be used to engage fans in promotional practices or interactive experiences (meme contests, selfies in costume or in line, "share this with 100 friends," etc.). Far out of control of the studios, social media is also a platform for fans to exchange information and opinions on their own, often fostered by "official" hashtags suggested by the studio/network. Again, we have numerous examples of social media working for "good" on behalf of a film, and also negatively (such as the backlash regarding "reboots" of films such as *Ghostbusters*).

No current marketing campaign can be successful without both the strategic use *and* focused awareness of social media. A studio can't just invent a hashtag and let it go at that; someone needs to be monitoring that tag, seeing how it is used by people who support the film, and subsequently direct/execute additional efforts. It is far beyond the scope of this book to explain or instruct on the most effective uses of social media marketing; however, the important element is that, just as the other forms of entertainment publicity and journalism, successful social media campaigns ultimately involve the use of written language. Even if the social media element is a gif, meme, or three-second video, the right tagline, hashtag, description, or caption give those visual elements context and impact. If a particular social media campaign happens to be "hot" and noteworthy, then a staff publicist very likely would want to draft a pitch letter suggesting that a journalist write an article about the trending new hashtag.

It's at this point that some might find marketing efforts bordering on the absurd—how do we generate a hashtag to go viral in support of a selfie that promotes the star at a charity event where the film is screening? As "down the rabbit hole" that might be for some casual consumers of pop culture, those are now the kinds of discussions and ideas that occupy a large number of film industry professionals determined to maximize their project's visibility.

STANDARDS AND STYLE GUIDES FOR FILM JOURNALISM

As a discipline, journalism uses several codified systems and practices, some drawn from proscribed uses of written grammar, others specific to a certain trade or industry. You are probably familiar with the general application of the **Five W's** to news-oriented journalism: Who, What, When, Where, and Why. A "good" piece of news writing will convey answers to those five questions (and usually in that order): WHO did something, WHAT did they do, WHEN did it happen, WHERE did it happen, and WHY did it happen. Certainly, a news article may cover a lot more information: What are people saying about the event? What is expected to happen next? Has this ever happened before? But those essential five elements will most likely be established within the first few sentences of the news story. (In fact, one of the ways to distinguish between "news" and "feature" writing is that the Five W's are a lot less important or prominent in feature writing; the Five W's are essential for "reporting" events, but not as essential in "describing" something interesting.)

A film professional might keep this in mind when crafting a press release—something designed, for the most part, to look like news. A strong lead paragraph that covers the Five W's will appear to a news outlet to be "ready for publication." You'll get some practice with this when you create a **start-of-production release**. The Five W's are also helpful in highlighting key event information such as on a screening invitation or invitation to an awards ceremony or premiere—you want the reader to clearly see when and where they are expected to be.

There are other standard journalism practices and terms that inform professional writing for the entertainment industry, most of which are governed by what are called **style guides**. Style guides are created or adopted/adapted by individual outlets and publishers, and they determine the "rules" of written publication that must be followed. Other disciplines beyond journalism also use style guides. You've probably heard of such style guides as APA (American Psychological Association, for use in the social sciences); MLA (Modern Language Association, for the humanities); Chicago (general publication); or AP (Associated Press, for mass-media journals and periodicals). But individual outlets such as *The New York Times* and *The New Yorker* have their own style guides.

Style guides regulate and proscribe more "flexible" grammatical and publication questions such as use of the terminal ("Oxford") comma; how many spaces to use after a period; standard font style, size, and spacing; how to properly cite a source (footnote, endnote, inline citation, etc.); how to refer to a subject (*The New York Times* always refers to individuals as "Mr." or "Ms." or official title, while other outlets may only use a last name); and how to format the title of a film, program, book, etc. (italicize, underline, in quotes).

It would be maddening for any individual to try to remember all the nuances and differences between style guides unless you are immersed in academia. For the professional writer in the entertainment industry, it's more important to know that the guides exist, and to keep that in mind as you read various pieces of film criticism or coverage.

What is going to be most important is *your* style guide—or the guide suggested or employed by the people you work with and the companies you work for. Larger studios and networks will have well-established style guides that dictate their preferred practices. Sometimes, that kind of consistency and detail is not specifically mandated in a smaller company, as use of the Oxford comma in business communication is usually not at the top of the list of concerns for most studio executives. But at the very least, should you be employed by a company as a writer, you should ask about a few standard and recurring formatting issues you will encounter most:

- Formatting of project or titles. Be sure to ask whether there is a formatting difference between films, television shows, episode titles, plays, novels, articles, songs, albums, etc. Options include italicization, underlining, bold, use of quotes, or use of capital letters:

- ○ *The Treasure of the Sierra Madre*
- ○ <u>The Treasure of the Sierra Madre</u>
- ○ **The Treasure of the Sierra Madre**
- ○ "The Treasure of the Sierra Madre"
- ○ THE TREASURE OF THE SIERRA MADRE

While you may come across requests for the use of more than one formatting choice (i.e., all caps and bold with quotes, **"THE TREASURE OF THE SIERRA MADRE"**), this is usually considered excessive and unnecessary.[1]

- Use of the terminal/Oxford comma
- Number of spaces expected after a full stop (period, colon, question mark, exclamation point)
- Proper reference to real-life people (producers, stars, etc.). Almost always, it is the use of a person's surname (last name), with some style guides amending with *Mr*, *Ms*, etc. In more personal communications, the use of a real person's first name may be more acceptable; your boss will let you know whether "Dear Linda" or "Dear Ms. Molina" is suitable for a specific piece of correspondence.
- Fictional characters may be referred to by first name.
- Preference of punctuation within or without quotation marks at end of a sentence. Most style guides dictate that commas and periods go *within* the quotation marks.
- Preferences for font and font size
- Preferences for use of bold letters
- Preferences for headers/footers and formatting of page numbers (What location on the page? Do they expect "Page 2 of 4" or is "2" sufficient?)
- Formatting of dates (mm/dd/yyyy? dd/mm/yy?)
- Preferred style of business letter format
- Preferences for spacing (single, 1.5, double, etc.) and margins
- Preferred formatting of hyperlinks
- Preferred standards and procedures for use of digital images or files, including company logos, branding, images, graphs, charts, embedded video, etc.
- Preferred naming format for digital files

Throughout the book, I will describe even more specific formatting variations for various writing practices (for example, what should be on a cover sheet for a story report, or what information to include in a press release).

---

1 Except for the use of all caps, all formatting choices have the same rules for use of capital letters. I recommend the website grammarly.com for thorough review of how to use capital letters, basic punctuation, use of quotation marks and apostrophes, and other ground-level writing/formatting skills and proficiencies.

And it's very likely that if you are at a company with less than 30 employees, when you ask these questions your boss will look at you with a blank stare and probably say, "Whatever." That doesn't necessarily mean the company thinks such details don't matter: hopefully it would agree that the writing material that represents the company would always look professional and be easy to read. But company officials probably haven't thought much about the details. In that case, develop your own consistent style. Do all of your work in a font that is more or less "universal" to most word-processing platforms; minimize excessive formatting so that any file transfer or conversion will meet with a minimum of technical resistance.

In addition, even if the company doesn't have a standard way of naming document files, you should develop your own consistent, easily searchable way of locating files. Ask if your company has a policy of tracking changes or preserving multiple versions or drafts of company documents. I suggest that any time *you* make a substantial change to a document—including substantial copy editing, proofreading—you save your file with a new name. Names that contain the subject and date (or draft number) of your document make these files easy to find if someone else needs to find them.

A note about .PDFs: If you are get clever with fonts, images, formatting or margins, you may find occasions when the PDF file that you convert from your preferred software does not look right. Always take a look at each page of your PDF to see that it is readable; and always give your shared PDF files the same name as the origin file.

Even if you are a freelance writer or someone who will be doing most of the writing for your own company, getting into the habit of treating every document you create as a "professional" document will help you better organize your various projects. That means making sure that whatever style and formatting choices you use, they are applied *consistently* and that every written project goes beyond "jotting down a few ideas for yourself."

It's also important to note that for some writers—good, bad, experienced, "amateur"— thinking too much about the rules of writing and typing while you are actually engaged with the process is difficult and intrusive. That's okay; in fact, I would say it is far more important to feel comfortable while you are writing than it is to get everything absolutely perfect on an early draft. If that is the case, then the style guide is your best friend in the process of proofreading and editing. Go ahead and write in a blaze of glory without worrying about italicizing every title, whether or not "winter" is capitalized, or how to spell that German producer's last name. Then take the extra time and deliberation when you go back for corrections. Remember, when you have finished a first draft of a piece of writing, you are no more than half done. But the more you practice writing and proofreading, the more you will begin to "internalize" your most common errors, making fewer mistakes in your first draft. Trusting the process of learning and developing your "writing muscles" will pay off if you have a consistent set of rules and guidelines to work by.

CHAPTER TAKEAWAYS

- Most professional film writing is created according to the general conventional standards of American journalism.
- The "trades" (notably *Variety* and *The Hollywood Reporter*) are primary outlets for most entertainment industry news, information, and analysis.
- Feature writing is more common in mainstream publications and outlets, weekly/monthly magazines, major portal websites, etc.
- Critical reviews from daily/weekly outlets are most important to industry professionals because of their potential immediate effect on the film's release.
- Style guides help focus, organize, archive, and "brand" the writing of an individual, a company, or an outlet.

EXERCISE 2A: WRITE A REVIEW ON DEADLINE (GROUP OR SOLO)

- Identify an outlet that publishes film reviews or criticism. If you can, determine its style guide and write this exercise according to its publication standards.
- Have everyone in your group watch a film you have never seen. If possible, try to watch it together.
- Watch the movie *only once*, and complete a 600–700 word review within 24 hours.
- Share and discuss your reviews, focusing on how effectively you and your peers maintained professional standards and expressed a critical opinion.

SELF-ASSESSMENT

- Is everything formatted, punctuated, and spelled properly?
- Did I tell the story of the film in the present tense?
- Did I identify key actors and other creatives?
- Have I properly and consistently distinguished between character and actor?
- Have I been judicious with spoilers and avoided them as much as possible?
- Are my strongest opinions backed up with specific examples?

EXERCISE 2B: FILM JOURNALISM SCAVENGER HUNT (SOLO)

- Identify a film project that was recently released (within the last two weeks) or is about to be released (within the next two weeks).
- For one week (Monday-Friday), you are going to consult *two* outlets every day:
  - One should be a "trade" outlet such as *Variety*, *The Hollywood Reporter*, *thewrap.com*, etc.

- The other should be a broader "general" outlet such as *Huffington Post*, *Buzzfeed*, *Vox*, or any major newspaper or news organization that provides content on a daily basis.
- You may read the same two outlets every day, or you may vary outlets from day to day, as long as you have one trade and one general readership outlet.

- Identify *all* of the articles or items that substantively mention that film and make a virtual "clippings file" by collecting the weblinks.
- When the week is done, use your clippings file to find examples of each type of film journalism article:

  - One news item
  - One published review
  - One feature
  - One mention of a social media campaign or digital marketing strategy

- You should also identify articles or elements that don't exactly correspond with one category or seem unique. If that is the case, talk about it with your instructor or study group. Why has this element been published? What writing practice or journalistic form does it most resemble, and in what key ways is it different?
- **Bonus Exercise**, particularly for those interested in film marketing: These questions can help you start evaluating how marketing campaigns can be assessed by evaluating published articles that were generated during the campaign. A more in-depth course in marketing will provide more rigorous qualitative and quantitative measures for assessment but, as a writer, you may be able to identify the more effective words, phrases, or perspectives that support a successful release.

  - Looking at your clippings file as a whole. Can you identify the elements and themes of the films that the producer/studio would be most eager to be part of the public discussion? What are the positive values associated with the film, according to the published articles?
  - Can you identify opinions, interpretations, or other subjective elements that a studio/producer would not expect and/or agree with? Are these opinions anomalous (i.e., just one "hater"), or do they extend to more than one outlet and more than one type of coverage?
  - Specifically, what are the words that convey "positive" and "negative" attitudes toward the film? Are there also "neutral" words or ways that language is being used more "objectively?"

CHAPTER 3

After the Screenplay Is Done

The Flow of Words and How to Write 'for' a Project

Throughout this book, you'll be asked to imagine yourself as an industry professional responsible for creating various written elements that support the acquisition, development, production, and distribution of a creative work (film or television show). This chapter will serve as a general overview of how these various writing practices work in conjunction with the filmmaking process. A **practice** in this case is a "type" or "format" of writing, which you will get to do on your own in specific exercises later.

It's here that we will establish and define important terms, briefly introduce and describe different written elements, and give you a general framework and philosophy to best appreciate and take advantage of your own ability to write productively and effectively. This is the "road map" for the rest of the book, roughly corresponding with the phases of filmmaking ("preproduction," "production," and "postproduction").

CRITICAL POINTS BEFORE WE BEGIN

Before we look at our map, it would be helpful to discuss and emphasize a few critical points that will allow you to navigate your way through the various exercises and suggestions throughout this chapter and the rest of the book. To that end, I'd like to make four related points.

POINT ONE: THE IMPORTANCE OF THE SYNOPSIS

Throughout this book, you most likely will notice that by far the most common and specific skill that applies to almost every exercise is the ability to synopsize. The word *synopsis* is derived from Greek origin, with "syn" being the Greek sign for "together" and "opsis" meaning "seeing." Thus, this act of "seeing together"—being able to put a series of events "together" through the act of witnessing and testifying—is at the root of what a film professional must do on a nearly constant basis.

Synopses take many forms; they can be verbal (the "elevator pitch"), written (a "log line"), or even visual (a collage of images, a storyboard, etc.). Even a bio, such as the one you did in the last chapter, is a "synopsis" of a life. What each form has in common is that they are representations of a larger work—a novel, a screenplay, a performance, an episode, or a feature film—distilled into a shorter form.

Creating a synopsis might seem like a somewhat objective or scientific exercise. In fact, the way in which someone creates and presents a synopsis says a great deal about one's perspective, opinion, and creative sensibilities. As an example, you might want to try **EXERCISE 3A: THE SYNOPSIS**, which is illustrative not only as a solo exercise, but also in pairs or groups.

Because what you decide to include, and how you decide to "frame" the story in your own words, has a profound influence on how the person reading the synopsis will approach and understand the work. As an example, consider the following three "log line" (one sentence) descriptions of a well-known film:

> Desperate to escape a drab existence with her elderly caretakers, a young girl imagines a journey to a colorful land of magical characters and dangerous adventure.

> A young girl is whisked away to a strange land, and finds herself on a quest to return home by banding together with an odd group of characters and defeating an evil witch.

> A quartet of unlikely characters must set aside their individual desires and work together in order to defeat an evil witch and expose a charlatan wizard.

Each of these is accurate description of *The Wizard of Oz*, but which one you prefer says a lot about how you interpret the film. Is it a story of magical wonderment and the power of the imagination to liberate us? The first one offers that reading. A morality tale about the importance of "home" and the preservation of established social values? The second one works. An ensemble-driven quest that emphasizes the importance of friendship, loyalty, and community in the face of despots gone mad with power? Maybe you like the last one. Figuring out which approach to take and what kind of synopsis to create and use depends on a variety of factors, which are related to the points that follow.

POINT TWO: THE IMPORTANCE OF COLLABORATION, CONSENSUS, AND COLLATION

It certainly might be the case that the only person who "cares" about a synopsis or other written materials at any one point is the filmmaker/creator. If you are a screenwriter sending your work to an agent, you can probably come up with a short log line or paragraph-long synopsis for the cover letter that will whet your reader's appetite and get them to dive into the full script. At the other end of the process, if you've finished your independent film and are submitting it to film festivals, then you are probably the best person to create the catalog description.

But most of the time, particularly when you work for producers, studios, and networks making more than one project at a time, these materials are generated as a result of group discussions. Thus, it's important to remember these "Three C's" as you walk through the various exercises: **collaboration**, **consensus**, and **collation.**

Collaboration can happen at an in-person staff meeting, or virtually in digital discussion boards, email chains, etc. Anytime there is a "boss" who is going to make a decision and an "employee" who has to provide options, the process of collaboration will be engaged—and oftentimes, of course, there are multiple bosses and multiple employees. We'll investigate some standard workflow procedures and institutional hierarchies in later chapters, but for now it's important to understand that if you are writing for a company, it is most important that your writing reflects the "company" line, not your individual interpretation or perspective. (It's entirely possible that your perspective might be identical to the company's—and if that's the case, congrats, you have a great job! But it's not always the case that you will value and/or understand the project the same way your superiors and colleagues do.)

When engaged in collaboration, it's important to be able to recognize that you are only one voice in the room and, as the designated "writer," part of your job is to listen to and appreciate all voices. In that sense, you have to be particularly sensitive to the idea of **consensus**. Others in the room or those involved in the collaborative process might not have the same investment as you in the conversation: perhaps the boss wants someone's opinion, even when they don't expect that person to do any further work on the project.

Think about a possible development meeting for *The Wizard of Oz* project. Vice-President of Such-and-Such Joey thinks the synopsis should emphasize Dorothy's miserable existence and how amazing Oz is; Executive in Charge of Such-and-Such Maria thinks the story should be framed from the Wicked Witch's perspective. They haven't listened to each other or paid attention to each other's comments, and they're not going to be producers or creative contributors on the project down the line; they're just important executives who have earned a seat at this table and been asked to express an opinion. You, however, are responsible for getting everyone's feedback and incorporating it into action. Can you find common ground between Joey and Maria's comments? Are their ideas mutually exclusive, and will require someone else to make a decision about which way to go? Or can you come up with the perfect log line that makes everyone happy?

That action the assistant takes is the last "C," **collation**. After establishing some idea of consensus, getting a collective "read" on whatever it is that needs to be done, someone is responsible for articulating that consensus through gathering, cataloging, and sharing (in written form). Collating—"assembling" the ideas into a document that reflects consensus and moves the process forward—is a kind of "second-order" writing skill, more akin to editing, less akin to personal expression. Indeed, sometimes collating means copying and pasting and editing the notes of others from emails and discussion boards, and presenting them as a unified whole.

Ultimately, those Three C's are a part of the writing process that might be unfamiliar to a writer used to working alone and engaging with writing as a solitary process. Embracing the idea of writing for a collective can make you a stronger writer because it increases your ability to hone in on key words and concepts that represent specific ideas, and your understanding of filmmaking as a collaborative effort that requires a lot of discussion, revision, and process-oriented work. To that end, you'll want to complete **EXERCISE 3B: ESTABLISHING YOUR GROUP**. It's a group exercise that asks you to begin the process of collaborative/consensus-based writing as part of starting your own creative business entity.

POINT THREE: WRITING IS SELLING

"Process-oriented" practices are key because you need to understand that your writing functions as part a larger system of creative processes. For many of the practices in this book, writing is not intended to be "finished" writing in the same way a novel, article, or poem is: much as a film screenplay, whatever you write is more of a "blueprint" or description of the "actual" project. Yes, the writing might be technically excellent—even beautiful and worthy of praise—but the point is, your writing has to DO something. *It has to engage your readers and give them the confidence to take a specific action that will move the project forward.* In that sense, it's similar to a television commercial: the commercial might be brilliantly entertaining, but if it doesn't get you to immediately purchase the advertised product, it will be considered a failure.

That's something we'll emphasize throughout this book: almost all of these written materials that you will learn about and, ultimately, practice must generate "action." While it might not involve literal currency, your writing is always "selling" something and asking the reader to "buy" in the form of positive feedback, financial or industrial support, or spreading positive word-of-mouth.

Just to briefly provide some examples (each of which requires a different kind of synopsis, for the record):

- An agent has to write a **cover letter** (or email) to a studio executive to get the studio executive to read a screenplay.
- The studio executive reads the screenplay and loves it; the executive has to generate a positive piece of **script coverage** that is fair and objective to persuade the studio head to buy the script.
- The studio head buys the script, then has to write **a letter** to a major director to get them to read the script.
- The director has to send **emails** to possible editors, line producers, or cinematographers, describing the project in an exciting way to get them involved.
- The producer and casting director have to create **plot and character descriptions** for agents and managers to supply actors who audition (often referred to as **breakdowns**).
- Publicists must encourage journalists to visit the set or invite the stars to a talk show; they have to **pitch** the film and the part and emphasize why the project is exceptional and interesting.

- Publicists create **screening invitations** that must persuade film reviewers to attend advance screenings and/or watch a digital download so they can publish a review of the film the day or week the film is released.
- Producers must present **synopses** and other marketing materials to film festivals or potential distributors; those festivals and distributors, in turn, need to persuade festival audiences and exhibitors (theater owners) to support the release of the film.
- Social media and promotions must use language to **hype** the film (in 280 characters or less!) and generate excitement so that fans and the general public are encouraged to share/like/retweet and increase the film's digital/viral footprint.

You can see how all of these acts of writing, each of which you will practice, are part of the "flow" of the overall process. It's important this this writing is not only "accurate" and descriptive, but enticing, engaging, and eliciting a specific action or response. Ultimately, that brings us to our final point.

POINT FOUR: KNOW WHO IS READING WHAT YOU WRITE

"Knowing your audience" is often something that we encourage filmmakers and other creative types to consider. Sometimes this is a simple matter of logic: If you are pitching a film idea to a family-oriented entertainment company, you would probably want to pitch your charming coming-of-age story about a girl and her beloved puppy, not your high-minded erotic period drama about a teenaged refugee in 18th-century Paris who falls in love with a transgender alchemist.

In the industrial process of technical writing, sometimes defining your "audience" isn't quite as easy, but hopefully you will be well prepared to understand what your writing is supposed to DO, and you can then tailor to your audience accordingly. Consider the previous sequence of events and recognize that in each case you are asking for a different kind of action, and that means you are asking a different type of person (in different occupations and with varying obligations and responsibilities).

For example, let's imagine the process of **script coverage** (discussed in detail in the next few chapters) in which a relatively anonymous story analyst ("reader"), often freelance, has to write a long synopsis and extended comments on a script's strengths, weaknesses, and potential. If you are that reader, you have to keep in mind the kind of company you work for and the sensibilities of the executive who will be reading your coverage, and you need to understand why the coverage is needed. Perhaps you really, really hate the script—it's offensive, poorly written, and something that no decent human being would ever want to see get made. Well, you have to generate comments that specifically describe why the script is weak without getting nasty or snarky (saying, for instance, that "no decent human being would ever want to see this get made.")

Because that executive is going to read your coverage and have to call the script's agent and tell him or her why you are passing (saying "no") on the property. If that executive tells the agent, "No decent human being would ever make this script, Dan," then Dan the agent is going to feel insulted (because Dan the agent wants the film to get made) and will not want to work with your company or send you any more scripts. That coverage needs to have a sentence such as "the plot is a bit too simplistic to generate much interest, and it's unlikely that audiences will be sympathetic to the film's main character." With such language in the coverage, the executive can then tell Dan the agent, "Sorry, but I just couldn't get into the story and the character."

You'll start to realize as you practice your writing that even if you don't know exactly who is going to read your work, the words that you choose will give that person a "language of action" to take. Most of the time, the writing will encourage a positive response: "Like this!" "Share it!" "Pass it on!" "Give us money!" (Coverage is the one notable exception to this rule, as will be discussed.) You'll expand your vocabulary beyond words such as "great" and "good" and "nice" because you will become increasingly sensitive to engaging with that reader and appreciating what she or he requires from the writing: specific words, phrases, and ideas, that "excite" others about the film.

You can see from these four points that we are starting to get a better sense of the kind of writing abilities that one must develop to be successful. Again, I think the analogy of the television commercial or the movie trailer is most apt here, since this is something we encounter so often. The commercial or trailer introduces you to "something" and creates a space in your mind where that new something might live, should you choose to purchase that product or spend money and time to see that movie. Almost no one buys anything "blind" with absolutely no knowledge of what they is getting into: Commercials, trailers, packaging, and other marketing tools are essential in getting you to want something. And how disappointing it is when the thing you buy or the film you watch does not "match" what has been promised in the commercial or trailer! Oftentimes, you regard that product or movie as a "failure" simply because it didn't match the expectation, and didn't fit into that space in your head that was defined by the initial advertisement.

Technical writing is much the same: it creates a space in the mind of the reader, a space that something else (the script, the movie, the event) will later occupy. The executive likes the script because that great log line in the email from the agent had just the right words and framework to get the executive engaged; the talk-show producer wants to book the project's star because, yes, this is indeed a landmark role that elevates the actor into Oscar contention, just as the pitch letter indicated.

In that sense, the words you create have that almost divine power of saying "what is" before "what is" can actually be experienced. The more you are in tune with that part of the process and that deeper power of what you are doing, the more care you could be expected to take with each and every word, each and every idea, and find yourself fully engaged with the material just as intensely as the writers, directors, actors, designers, and other creative artists who put so much work into the film itself.

OVERVIEW OF PRACTICES, TERMS, AND CONCEPTS

These are some terms and concepts that will be used throughout the book: most should be familiar to you if you have studied film and media production, but I encourage you to refresh your memory and develop an understanding of how this book will specifically define these terms.

PHASE ONE: FROM SCREENPLAY TO GREEN LIGHT

This phase roughly corresponds to the practices of acquisition, development, and preproduction. The writing materials generated here tend to focus on "selling" the project to an entity (person, company, studio, network, etc.), and are rarely seen or known to the general public.

Screenplay/Teleplay/Script

This is the document that contains all of the action, dialogue, and description of the proposed film or television project. Although "screenplay" specifically refers to a feature film and "teleplay" to a television broadcast, both are more referred to generically as "scripts" or "screenplays." A general rule of thumb is that each page equals about one minute of screen time for a feature film screenplay; teleplays may differ depending on how they are formatted.

Most screenplays are written in a specific format, with dialogue centered on the page and description/direction in single-spaced, block paragraphs, and composed on an industry standard software such as Final Draft, Celtx, Adobe Story, or Fade In. While "paper" scripts are still used by many studio executives, most scripts are now shared via a digital format (such as a PDF file), and often carry a digital watermark for security purposes. *Any unproduced script you read should be considered "for your eyes only": be sure to take extra care that you do not share or expose any hard copy or digital files.*

Treatment

A treatment also might be called a "very long synopsis." Treatments are often extended, scene-by-scene descriptions of the screenplay—almost as if the movie is being told in "short story" format. It is often used more as a "step" for screenwriters in their creative process, and not very often shared with anyone besides the writer's immediate creative and professional circle. On occasion, an agent, manager, or producer might submit a treatment for consideration to a studio or network, with the expectation or promise that a full screenplay is in the works; however, this tends to only occur with already established talent or a very high-profile property that could be expected to generate great interest or demand.

A treatment can be anywhere from four or five pages to more than 30 for a feature film, depending on how detailed the writer gets in that part of their writing process. A treatment may also include a *dramatis personae*, a term borrowed from theater, which is a list of all of the important characters and a brief description of each, including age, identity markers (ethnicity, gender, etc.), occupation, relation to other characters, and personality traits. (Note: While standard in many playscript and theatrical formats, a *dramatis personae* is not generally considered standard or necessary for a feature film script, though it may be considered helpful for a television pilot script.)

Property (Or Submission)

A property is the "thing" that gets submitted to a studio, network, producer, or other production entity for consideration. Most of the time, the property is a finished script; however, a property can also be something that could be adapted into a script. This includes treatments; short stories, novellas, or novels; nonfiction works such as biographies or histories; newspaper/Internet/magazine articles; theatrical plays; or previously produced properties such as old movies or television shows that might be suitable for a remake, reboot, sequel, prequel, etc.

Agent's Submission Letter

It is exceptionally rare, for legal reasons, for an individual screenwriter to submit a property directly to a producer or studio for consideration. Instead, an agent, manager, or lawyer who legally represents the writer and/or the property are the ones to officially submit. While the agent's submission letter is more of a formality—it's very likely that the agent has spoken to the studio executive about the project, or the executive has asked for the submission—it's still a small piece of writing that usually has a log line description of the property and other "pitch"-style information that emphasize the project's potential value. The submission letter is also the place to include information about attached **elements** (defined later in this book) or other technical or legal information about source material, availability of the writer for further assignments, etc.

Log Line

A log line is a brief description of the *story* of the property. The standard length for a log line is typically 25–30 words, but most industry professionals agree that the exact word count is less important than the ability to contain the story within a single sentence (or possibly two short sentences). Note the emphasis on the word *story*: a log line is *not* a description of the property (i.e., "This is a science-fiction story about ..." "This will star Idris Alba and Judi Dench ..."). A log line should emphasize situation, plot, and character. A log line might be considered the written version of the **elevator pitch**, a short, verbal description of the project that could theoretically be delivered in as much time as it takes to ride in an elevator.

It's important to recognize immediately that log lines, in some form or another, are employed almost continuously throughout the filmmaking and distribution process, and even long after a film has been released. As such, although the story, screenplay, and film remain the same, the log line might change depending on the phase of production or the intended audience. A log line from an agent to a studio executive might be "pitchy"—designed to make the script sound as desirable as possible. A log line on a piece of coverage would very likely be more objective. Finally, the log line that one sees on a DVD box cover or on the film's Netflix page are likely to more comprehensively include non-story elements (such as the film's stars or critical acclaim) in order to attract a potential buyer/viewer. Regardless of how it is used, the log line is one of the most crucial elements in a film's production life cycle, and any creative professional (writer, director, producer, actor) should be well-practiced in developing, revising, and presenting log lines.

Coverage/Story Report

Coverage is the written document generated by a **story analyst** or **reader** that objectively evaluates a property/submission, offering a **recommendation** (*Pass* or *Consider*) regarding further review. Larger studios and networks retain in-house analysts who work full time, but most production companies, agencies, and other entities use freelance analysts who work on a per-project basis. A company may also assign coverage to employees with other duties or responsibilities within the organization (such as interns, assistants, or junior executives).

Every network, studio, and production company most likely has their own unique format and standards for coverage: most companies now process coverage through a digital platform of some sort, with readers inputting or uploading their work directly to the studio via the Internet. It is still useful, however, for would-be analysts to generate their own formats when creating sample coverage in the process of seeking employment: if your sample coverage impresses, a potential employer would very likely ask you to read a submission the employer is familiar with so that you can write an additional sample in the studio's preferred format.

Talent Coverage/Writing Or Directing Sample

Frequently, a story analyst will be asked to read a script and/or watch a film or television show to evaluate the talents of the writer and/or director, or perhaps even an actor, director of photography, or editor. In some of these cases, an agent has very likely suggested a client as a possible hire for a project currently in development, and has submitted samples of relevant work to demonstrate the client's abilities. In other cases, a studio executive might hear about a "hot" screenplay that has already been sold, but want to set up a meeting with the writer for a potential future project. For the most part, coverage regulations and standards are similar to typical submissions. What is obviously different are the final comments, which are now focused more on execution by the individuals being examined rather than on the potential of the property for development and production. Thus, the comments will focus much more on specific creative technique rather than answer the question: "Will this script/property make a good movie/TV show?"

Second Read

If the first story analyst recommends a project—or, perhaps, if he or she passes on a property that is very high profile or important—then the property will typically go for a **second read** where one or more additional analysts will weigh in. Sometimes, the second reader only needs to provide comments, since a synopsis has already been written; often, the second reader is someone within the company (a full-time analyst or executive) who is even more familiar with the company's standards and expectations. A reader should *never* consider a second read to be a challenge to his or her opinion or a comment on the quality of the reader's coverage—it's just part of the process of getting consensus and perspective from multiple readers.

Story Notes/Development Notes

Once a property is purchased, it's very likely there will be a meeting with many executives talking about the property and what the next steps will be to get it ready for production. If the property is not yet a screenplay, then a list of potential screenwriters will be put together; if there is already a completed screenplay, discussions will occur on how to improve it in a new draft, which also may involve hiring a new writer. Regardless of the situation, it is very likely that a set of **story notes** will be generated. These are notes that will be given to the "next" writer on the project, with the company's collective ideas about what it expects to see in a subsequent draft.

Producer's Pitch Letter

With a property in hand, the company will want to get other people involved, from potential financiers to behind-the-scenes creative artists such as writers and directors to on-screen talent. Just as an agent had to compose a letter to a studio executive, now that executive (or a producer on the project) has to include a cover letter that introduces the property to a new set of readers. While this is, again, mostly a formality, a producer's pitch letter might include new details such as anticipated dates of production, a listing of potential creative or financial partners, or brief ideas about how a subsequent draft will be improved. Again, a log line or paragraph-length synopsis are essential in framing the key elements, tone, and potential value of the story.

Talent Lists

While relatively easy as a writing exercise (it is, after all, a list), a talent list is the company's "wish list" of potential writers, directors, and actors in major roles who might be approached. With some talent lists, companies will include descriptions of the "type" of person/talent they will want to pursue, which requires more nuanced writing from someone who has a strong understanding of both the script and the company's vision for the project. While talent lists may or may not be generated at some point in the development stage, they become more critical as the property moves closer to preproduction.

Draft Comments

As subsequent drafts of the property are submitted for review, studio executives and producers will very likely produce a new round of written comments, which evaluate the ways in which the new draft addressed the previous round of story notes. These comments might themselves be turned into an additional round of story notes for a subsequent draft, or may contain language or recommendations about moving the property forward for preproduction. While draft comments may be shared in a staff meeting or via other informal channels, written evaluations are often expected, as they may be used to evaluate whether to retain the current writer if a new draft is required.

Start of Production Release

While producers and agents frequently issue press releases announcing a property's acquisition (particularly for high-profile projects involving major talent), the **start of production release** is often the first indication to the general public that the property is actually being made and going before the cameras. This is typically generated by the film's **unit publicist** or a studio/network publicist, and circulated to the trade magazines and major entertainment news outlets.

Rolling Press Releases

"Rolling" releases refers to issuing a series of press releases, and is also often employed upon a project's release. In preproduction and production, a rolling release strategy often involves the process of signing talent (on- and off-screen). For example, the initial start of production release might indicate the director and the film's two major leads; a week later, an additional release might announce a high-profile performer being cast in a supporting role. While framed as "news," these rolling releases don't necessarily correspond with the actual details of when a particular person was cast or signed. For example, it may have been known for months to the studio that John Lithgow was going to play the part of Sandra Bullock's dad, but they hold off on "officially" announcing it until a week into production just to maximize his participation and keep the film in the headlines.

PHASE TWO: FROM 'ACTION' TO 'FINAL CUT'

This phase corresponds with the production sequence of preproduction, principal photography (production), and postproduction, when the movie or program is being physically produced with film, media, and audio technology. Most of these practices are in anticipation of the product's release and distribution to the public; it may also include a continuation of rolling press releases or producer pitch letters that were part of the development process. The vast majority of these writing practices are the responsibility of a unit publicist and/or a company publicity staff or contracted publicity firm that report to the film's producers and other executive interests. Key elements and terms from this phase are:

Unit Publicist

The unit publicist is an individual who is assigned to manage all publicity-related events and materials during production, particularly during preproduction and principal photography.

In some cases, unit publicity is managed by a studio or network publicity staff, or contracted to an outside firm, rather than assigned to one specific individual. You'll read more about the roles and duties of a unit publicist in chapters seven and eight.

Outlet

Any place where a publicist might want to place a story, interview, or news item ultimately destined for public consumption. Outlets include magazines, newspapers, television news programs, websites, podcasts or radio, or any other publicly available forum. (Note: there are also advertising outlets such as billboards, television commercials, newspaper ads, and so forth; those are not determined or managed by a publicist, but rather by someone who works in marketing and advertising. We'll investigate these differences in more detail in a later chapter.)

Feature Pitch Letters

An inquiry from a publicist to an outlet, suggesting a possible feature story regarding the project. This might include a **set visit** from a journalist, access to stars and creatives for interviews, behind-the-scenes information about the production process, or other interesting facts that increase the project's cultural profile and define its value.

Publicity Status Report

A live document or spreadsheet that catalogs and details all of the publicity efforts being made on behalf of the project, including current status of feature pitches, status of production of the EPK or production notes (see next section), screenings for and reactions from critics and relevant outlets, status of interviews and personal appearances, etc.

Electronic Press Kit (EPK)

The "behind the scenes" material that features interviews with key cast and crew members, "B-roll" footage of the production process, etc. Frequently included in home video/DVD releases or made available via project websites.

Press Kit/Production Notes/'Press Book'

Technically, a **press kit** has traditionally involved multiple elements including production notes, production stills, and other general production information. Informally, many in the industry now conflate the terms press kit and **production notes,** and are ultimately referring mostly to production notes. Production notes are the written materials supplied to critics, editors, and outlets that offer important information about the project's conception and creation and frame the project's cultural value, along with providing biographical profiles (**bios**) of key cast and crew members.

PHASE THREE: PREVIEWS, THE RED CARPET, AND BEYOND

Some films are finished with principal photography and fully assembled ("in the can") before this phase of technical writing is engaged; other films are still working through the last phases of postproduction when these strategies start to engage. Regardless of exactly when during the production process these materials come into being, they are intended to serve the project in anticipation of the film's initial release and distribution, and to supplement subsequent distribution to additional platforms or new media outlets.

While a unit publicist may continue to serve in some capacity as marketing materials for the project are completed, most of these duties are ultimately taken over by a studio or network publicity and marketing team, or contracted to an independent publicity firm that specializes in release-oriented campaigns. Film producers and studio executives are also deeply involved with conceiving, creating, and approving these materials in the context of broader marketing strategies that include **advertising** and **promotion**. (Chapter 8 goes into great detail about the differences between publicity, advertising, and promotion.)

Tag Line/Slug Line

More abstract and less specific than a log line, the tag line or slug line is often the brief, compelling text that is featured in a film's trailer, commercials, or posters. Classic tag lines include "In space, no one can hear you scream" (*Alien*), "Just when you thought it was safe to go back in the water" (*Jaws 2*), and "You'll believe a man can fly" (the 1978 version of *Superman*). Staff members and executives who work in any arena of marketing—advertising, publicity, or promotion—are often involved in the conception and creation of tag lines, with filmmakers, producers, and other studio executives also generating ideas and holding final approval. Oftentimes, multiple tag lines are developed, catering specifically to different regional or international audiences to maximize a project's appeal in a certain market.

Screening Invitation

Sent from a publicity department to critics, editors, content producers, or other tastemakers, the screening invitation usually offers a brief log line or description of the film's story, identifies principal talent involved in the production, and information about attending a private screening or gaining exclusive digital access to the film for review. Now often done via email, design elements, interactive RSVP responses, and other digital technologies require that the text of the invitation helps frame and present the film in a consistent and compelling manner.

Release Pitch Letter

Similar to the feature pitch letter, this inquiry from publicist to outlet suggests ideas for stories, items, or press coverage to be coordinated with the project's release. Because the project is finished, most pitches are centered around personal appearances and interviews by the creative talent for magazine interviews and photo shoots, television talk-show appearances, or other public events such as premieres, charity benefits, etc. Pitches are also made to specialty outlets that reach specific audiences, and to regional outlets in markets where the project is expected to generate a positive reception.

Awards Campaign

Depending on when in the calendar year the project becomes available to the public, there may be an awards campaign conducted simultaneously with a release campaign—or the awards pitch might occur months later, during awards season (late spring/early summer for the Emmy awards, late fall/early winter for film awards such as the SAG or Oscars). While some awards campaigns might take the form of talk-show appearances or other high-profile interviews, they also involve special screenings, events, promotions, or other points of contact with specific voting bodies such as critics' organizations or TV or film academy members. These campaigns are often more evident in the industry trade outlets (*Variety, The Hollywood Reporter, Deadline.com, Indiwire.com, thewrap.com, IMDB.com, etc.*) than in more publicly visible spaces.

CHAPTER TAKEAWAYS

- Four points to remember:

  ○ The Synopsis
  ○ Collaboration, Consensus, Collation
  ○ Writing Is Selling
  ○ Know Your Reader

- Technical writing occurs throughout the production process, with different practices being employed at different points in time.
- Development and publicity/marketing executives and professionals are expected to generate much of the technical writing on behalf of producers, projects, and studios.

EXERCISE 3A: WRITING A SYNOPSIS

From memory, write a 750–800-word synopsis of your favorite film or a film you think you "know." Allow yourself no more than 45 minutes to complete this exercise.

Then, watch the film again, and write another synopsis from scratch of the same length, in the same time frame.

SELF-ASSESSMENT

Compare and contrast the two efforts. Which version was "easier" to write? Which version seems more accurate?

If you have a colleague or writing partner, ask that person to read each synopsis (without watching the film) and then to offer his or her thoughts on which version seemed more effectively written.

Here are some general points to consider about your writing process after this exercise:

- Look at your use of verb tense: get used to writing in the present tense unless necessary (i.e., referring to past events).
- Look at your use of "framing" or "process" language (i.e., "The film begins with ..." "The scene cuts to ..." "There is a long montage ..."). Ultimately, you will want to eliminate this type of language to conserve word count and to focus on the story, *not* the storytelling.
- Look at how you introduce and refer to characters: be sure you consistently use names, that pronoun references are clear.
- Look at how you construct sentences and paragraphs. Are all of your sentences complete? If one runs longer than four lines of text on the page, would it be better to split it into two sentences? Are your paragraphs organized by "sequence" or "beats" in the story?

Don't worry for now if some of your writing is clunky, or if you aren't quite sure how to sequence information or handle storytelling techniques such as flashbacks, multiple timelines, visual technique, or comedic timing that are often hard to describe in writing.

EXERCISE 3B: FORM A PRODUCTION GROUP

If you are in a literal or virtual class, the instructor should assign the class into groups of four to six people to remain together throughout the course or semester. Future assignments will refer to the production groups for various collective and collaborative exercises, and the instructor is also encouraged to use these groups to do in-class or virtual presentations.

- With your working group, have a discussion about your fantasy production company, and have each member then write **a description of the company** and a **mission statement** articulating the values and goals of the company. Share and discuss your various written statements, and collectively **determine a final written mission statement along with a company name and logo**.
- Develop a **leadership/operational "rotation"** for your group, so that at various parts of the semester, every student has the opportunity to function in a different role. You can divide groups into three roles: **executives, management,** and **assistant**. This is especially effective for holding "company meetings."

  ○ Executives should lead conversations, solicit opinions, and make final decisions.
  ○ Management should offer ideas and show expertise on specific projects.
  ○ Assistants should organize paperwork, take notes, schedule meetings, etc.

(Students are also encouraged to function in less traditional operational structures, so long as they are given appropriate mechanisms by which to evaluate and reflect upon their experience "working" in, with, and for their group.)

CHAPTER 4

'So, Tell Me About Your Movie'

Mastering the Art of the Synopsis

As foregrounded in the last chapter, mastering the art of constructing a synopsis is very likely one of the most useful, general, and valuable skills for any film industry professional in a nontechnical capacity (and not a bad thing for the editors, camera ops, and sound engineers to know either).

But that's not to say it is exceptionally difficult. I liken writing a synopsis to building a set of bookshelves. Someone gives you some raw material, and you use your own tools and skills to turn that material into something functional. It doesn't have to be "spectacular" or "genius" or "beautiful," it just has to be solid, efficiently produced, and ready to do its job.

And, much as building bookshelves, the first few times you do it are going to be sloppy, clunky, and wobbly. Your tools may still do the job, but the more you practice—and the more you use advanced tools of the trade instead of just pounding away with a hammer, hand-saw, and nails—the easier your work will become, and the more solid, sturdy, reliable, and impressive your product will be.

This chapter is going to introduce the production practices of acquisition and development from your point of view, as a young professional writer just starting out as an assistant, intern, or employee of a working studio, agency, or production company. We'll go through some of the key terms and elements of these processes, and how various levels of professionals, from executives to management to assistants to "others," are involved in the decisions and activities related to these phases of the business.

Throughout the chapter, we'll focus on the importance and many functions of the professionally written synopsis. We'll work through various examples of both verbal and also written summaries of a property that occur across multiple professional situations, giving you the opportunity to not only practice the creation of various kinds of synopses, but also to understand how they perform in different industry work environments. By the end of the chapter, you'll be ready to learn the basics of script coverage and story analysis that are the life blood of a property coming to life as a produced project. And you'll also have the core skill necessary to begin learning how to do great story analysis and script coverage.

A PROJECT IS BORN

A standard Hollywood cliché tells us "it all begins with a blank page," and a "movie is born" when creative writers start filling that blank page with ink (or whatever the digital equivalent is). Indeed, nothing can happen without some action being taken to write down an idea, a story, dialogue, characters, and other elements that ultimately might get told on a screen.

But to say that a project is "born" with the writer is somewhat similar to saying you were born when your parents first gazed into each other's eyes. Certainly, that gazing was a notable step toward your arrival into this world, but your actual birth required a lot of effort (some of it fun, some of it not) for quite some time after that first loving look. In this clumsy metaphor, a writer finishing a screenplay is more akin to a successful conception, with the live birth still a challenge to accomplish somewhere down the road.

Bringing a script project to "life," then, in the form of getting a green light and seeing the project shown to an audience, must begin with an institutional entity such as a producer, network, studio, or production company deciding to "gestate" the project. The process of deciding which properties to bring into the company is called **acquisitions**; the acquired projects are then allowed to "mature" through the process of **development**.

In larger studios and production entities, acquisitions and development might be two departments with different executive staff members; it's very likely that the two departments work closely and in alignment with each other, but also entirely possible there are some people who *only* deal with "buying" material and others who *only* deal with "developing" material. But in some companies, particularly smaller companies where there are fewer people to do discreet, specific jobs, the two processes overlap quite frequently. In my experience, I have worked with acquisitions people who contributed fundamentally in the development of projects, and also with development executives who served as "buyers" of scripts. This book is going to address these processes in a very general sense, with the caveat that companies may organize these duties and practices in different ways.

So let's imagine you've gotten your first job in the industry, and working for someone whose full-time job is engaging in the process of acquisitions and development. It might be any of the people cited in the following section, for whom you will be required to produce various forms of synopses in support of your project.

For example, you might work for an **agent** or **manager** or other legal representative (a lawyer or producer) of the submitted property (which we will call "the script," with the understanding that a property can also be a play, short story, book, article, etc.). It is the role of the representative to engage in a legal agreement with the author to represent the property, and then to submit the property to producers and studios.

A quick note about screenplay writers or authors who submit their own work. Just about every legitimate studio or producer will not read or consider something submitted by an author (unless the author's agent or manager is aware of the submission). There are myriad legal reasons for this; most obviously, studios receive hundreds of unsolicited submissions per year, and if one of them vaguely resembles a film the studio makes, a would-be screenwriter might try to file a lawsuit claiming that the studio "stole" the idea. In rare cases where a producer will read a screenplay from an unrepresented writer, that writer will almost assuredly need to sign a legal release.

But legality isn't the only reason suggesting the need for a representative. When something is submitted by an agent or manager, at least one other person besides the author has read the script. A good agent or manager will probably have worked with the writer on several drafts of the script, ensuring that some development, editing, and "work" has gone into it. Obviously, this can vary from agent to agent and project to project—but it's an extra "quality control" step already built into the process.

Like acting, screenwriting is a "career choice" that some outsiders think must be "easy" or all about luck, salesmanship, or connections, and less about hard work or technical know-how. Of course, the good writers, the serious actors, and the real artists all know their craft will take hard work, refinement, and the ability to develop ideas through collaboration and feedback. But there's also a lot of people out there who are so convinced of the value of their brilliant ideas or stellar personality that they feel entitled to "break the rules" by "being my own manager" or "representing myself in all negotiations." Most industry professionals shy away from such people, as most industry practices require that talent be represented: just as an actor usually requires representation to have an audition, so too do writers require representation as they enter the marketplace.

Back to your new job! You might be working for an **executive** at a studio or production company who works in acquisitions and/or development. For example, you might work for a **story editor**, the junior-most executive whose job it is to administrate the company's development processes and staff. (Note: On television series, there is also a title called "story editor," which is a similarly "organizational" position but one with very different duties and responsibilities.) A story editor is usually the person who helps coordinate readers and coverage, keeps track of submissions going in and out of the company, circulates drafts, revisions, and story notes, and generally helps to keep the work flowing. As with any position, story editors in some companies are also relied upon for their creative ideas, or expected to develop and maintain relationships outside the company with key players such as agents, managers, and producers.

A step above the story editor is the **creative executive** or **production executive**. Essentially, these are the "project managers" who are key points of contact for agents, managers, and others who want to submit properties for consideration. Small companies might have one or two people at this level who also have other duties; large studios will have several people at multiple levels of "management" whose job it is to solely find and/or develop creative material.

Above the management level are the high-level, titled **executives**. These are people who have titles of "director" or above (vice-president, senior director, senior VP, etc.). These executives often have some measure of yes/no power in terms of negotiating contracts, hiring and firing, making decisions about which properties to pursue, or even "green-light" power. Their time is often very precious, and even if they are voracious readers and deeply committed to the development process and making great projects, they need everything they read to be organized and efficient and clear.

Whichever person you might be working for, it's very likely you're working to help with that person's reading and processing of materials. As an assistant, you'll probably be the first to see anything that is said or written about a property, whether it's the cover letter with a log line from the agent, the synopsis from a freelance reader, or notes from your boss delivered on the phone while driving back from lunch through traffic.

This discourse about the script is focused on two main questions: 1) What is it about? and 2) Is it any good? Answering the first question involves the rest of this chapter. We'll get to the second question in a later chapter.

PITCHING 101

It's important to know there are two ways to answer the question "What is it about?" and which method you choose depends on who you are working for, and to whom you are speaking—because you might be "pitching," or you might be "describing."

A couple of things to say about the terminology and definition of these two approaches. First, while *pitch* is an industry standard term, *describing* is used in a very general sense. Your boss might say, "Tell me the story," or simply "What's the plot?" rather than saying, "Describe the script." Second, and of more importance, a pitch often includes a substantive description—but a description can be done without a pitch.

So, if your boss says, "Pitch me the story," it means that he or she expects you to "sell" the idea. A **pitch** is a way of telling the story that is designed to present the story in the best possible light. It is an attempt to make the property most attractive to someone else, someone who will be more encouraged to read it, recommend it, or even ultimately buy it.

There are many workshops, tutorials, books, and other resources available that *teach* the details of pitching a project. Some writers and producers get a lot out those resources, while others find that they learn more through experience and practice. What's important to know is that a pitch cannot function alone as an agent of action: the best pitch needs to be delivered at the right time and place, and whatever follows the pitch must continue to meet the expectations and standards suggested in that initial pitch. In other words, a good verbal pitch can help, but the art of pitching goes beyond just knowing how to encapsulate your film in a single sentence or high-concept idea.

And, as an entertainment industry professional, you're going to have to develop the ability to synopsize, describe, and analyze things quickly *without* pitching or "taking a side" on the value of a property—what I have called *describing*. (Look for a moment at the derivation of that word: you are "de-writing" what has been written, "undoing" the work of the scribe.)

You're also going to have to learn how to listen to and read pitches delivered by others and assess them both before and also after you encounter the actual submission. Thus, you will have to "describe" pitches: you say to your boss, "The cover letter pitches this as a completely original romantic comedy, but it's ultimately a very generic premise." The baseline measure for all of this is your ability to understand, read, write, and evaluate various forms of synopses.

So, what makes for a "good"—or even "great"—synopsis? Any good screenwriting instructor or industry guru is probably going to say that when someone asks you what your film is about, you need to give that person an idea of the *story* of the film. Maybe the tone is important, maybe the characters are important, but ultimately the project is going to be sold on the strength of the story.

In this case, the conventional wisdom is correct. When someone says, "What is your movie about?" you can't simply say, "It's about a very lonely man who lives near an abandoned gas station" or "It's about how we're all isolated from one another but don't realize it until it's too late." You have to say, "It's about a reclusive artist living in the desert who embarks on a road trip to the big city when he is diagnosed with a life-threatening disease." Listeners are interested in the character and the "theme" of the film because they understands there is a story that makes good, active use of them.

Therefore, any synopsis, usually first and foremost, attempts to **tell the story** of the film: the shorter the form of the synopsis, the more all other descriptive elements get stripped away, until only the basic "action" is left. Do not be fooled into thinking that every project can ultimately be reduced to a simple sentence, specific number of words, or a perfectly comprehensible high-concept. Sometimes the story is complicated enough that you need two sentences, or it simply can't be "reduced" any further without becoming meaningless. What is important to remember is that with any synopsis, you have to start with the *essential* beats of the story, and then work *outward* from there.

Another way to think about this question of *pitch* versus *description* has to do with whether your synopsis is intended to be a **teaser** or a **spoiler**. Again, these are not industry-specific terms—I'm borrowing them from their more colloquial use to describe another part of the synopsis-building process. To explain, a teaser synopsis is going to be something that lures your readers in so that they want to know more about what might happen. It's going to emphasize the setup of the story and describe the essential conflict and situation, ideally suggesting that such a scenario might result in who-knows-what kind of conclusion. A movie trailer is a form of this teaser you encounter all the time, and the people who make trailers are always in danger of revealing "too much" that might give away some of the more surprising or impactful moments of the film.

A spoiler, however, doesn't care about engaging the interest of the reader in the same way. For the purposes of script coverage, as you will see in the next chapter, a "no-spoiler" synopsis is essential because the reader of the story report has to know the entirety of the plot. If there's a mid-story twist ("the doctor is really an alien!") that is particularly unbelievable, then the story analyst needs to both describe that moment accurately and also make a substantive critical observation as to whether it's effective.

Most general movie audiences are more used to teaser information and language. Even objective critical reviews are often spoiler-free, or carry warnings so as not to ruin the film for those who haven't seen it, effectively deferring to "no spoiler" as the default mode, even if the synopsis is more of a description than a pitch. There are more plentiful examples of spoiler synopses within the industry or different forms of film criticism, less visible to the public; thus, mastering the ability to synopsize in all modes—pitch vs. description, teaser vs. spoiler—is a valued writing skill.

HORRIBLE LOG LINES QUIZ

Just for fun, I've created "vague" log lines for some films that going back to 1968 won the "Best Picture" Academy Award. Each log line might, in fact, represent *more* than one film. Can you see how many films you can name that fit each description?

1. An ambitious grifter and a streetwise con man form an unlikely friendship on the gritty streets of a big city.
2. A brilliant but mentally unstable person and ends up wreaking havoc in the lives of those around him.
3. A lowly and unlikely hero undertakes a journey where he must prove himself to earn fame and glory.
4. A developmentally challenged man overcomes seemingly impossible obstacles to become a famous and important person.
5. A famous person has to take stock of his career when personal and professional changes all seem to happen at the same time.
6. The true story about a determined group of professionals who must work together against great odds to reveal the truth about something those in power would want to keep secret.
7. An intimate exploration of personal relationships that may or may not survive life's unpredictable turns.

ANSWERS:
1. *Midnight Cowboy, The Sting, Chicago*
2. *One Flew Over the Cuckoo's Nest, Rain Man, The Silence of the Lambs*
3. *Oliver!, Rocky, Gandhi, The Lord of the Rings: Return of the King, Slumdog Millionaire, Gladiator*
4. *Forrest Gump, A Beautiful Mind*
5. *Annie Hall, Amadeus, The Artist, Birdman*
6. *Argo, Spotlight, The Hurt Locker*
7. *Annie Hall, Kramer vs. Kramer, Ordinary People, Terms of Endearment, Out of Africa, The English Patient, American Beauty, The Shape of Water*

For fun, see if you (and/or your group) can create log lines that suggest more than one famous film.

STEP ONE TO BEING A 'PROFESSIONAL READER'—BE A GREAT READER

It's very likely that if you are reading this book, you have some experience reading screenplays, and it's hoped you've had the chance to read a screenplay that has not been produced. (As mentioned in an earlier chapter, published "screenplays" of released feature films are often more accurately described as "transcripts" based on the final version of the film, not the screenplay that was sold to the studio.) You probably already have an instinct about what works and what doesn't for you in terms of story elements, characterization, action, and dialogue: maybe you've already noticed that it's easier for you to visualize what a film might look like based on the genre of the screenplay, or that you are more likely to identify with a certain type of leading character.

Whatever your experience reading screenplays, as a professional reader you build upon those initial instincts and develop new critical reading skills with each new coverage assignment. As described previously, you're going to need to mesh your own instincts and taste with the requirements and expectations of your employer. If your employer is interested in projects with "believable, three-dimensional characters," then you're going to want to read each script focusing on the elements of characterization that are effective or ineffective—even if you are more of an action-oriented person.

But the most important thing you will need to focus on in your reading is the plot—because the bulk of your coverage is going to be the synopsis and an analysis of the script's core story points. As a reader, there are a few key things you will want to "check" off your list as you are reading: it might be helpful to take some notes as you read each script so you can later refer specifically to relevant points in your coverage.

Note that for many professionals, the words *plot* and *story* are used interchangeably, but it's worthwhile to make a distinction here. The story is everything that happens within the fictional universe of the film—and can refer to things that may or may not be seen on screen. Plot refers to the arrangement of the events in the story, including various narrative techniques such as flashbacks and flashforwards, foreshadowing, elisions of time, etc. Your coverage is going to want to err on the side of reflecting the plot, while including all of the "important" stuff from the story. (In a way, you can think about your own synopsis as being yet another plot of the story—a rearrangement of the events in a specific kind of storytelling format.)[1]

---

1   Film theorists and film studies students might know these terms borrowed from Russian formalist literary theory: *fabula* (story) and *syuzhet* (plot). Film historian David Bordwell explains these terms, and writes about various ways in which cinematic narrative might be constructed in his essay "Three Dimensions of Film Narrative," found at his website, http://www.davidbordwell.net/books/poetics_03narrative.pdf. Although a bit academic, I highly recommend the work of Bordwell to give you multiple analytical tools to consider. Remember that as a reader, you need to imagine the *film*, not just evaluate the *screenplay*. One mistake new readers make is believing that a screenplay must conform to a "formula" (i.e., Robert McKee, Syd Field, *Save the Cat*). These formulae may indeed aid writers as they create their work, but a good reader should employ critical frameworks that go beyond "does the action begin by page 10?"

Let's take, as an obvious example, the movie *The Hangover*. The **story** of that film is about friends who go to Vegas for a bachelor weekend and get involved in a number of crazy shenanigans, wherein one of them goes missing. The other friends scramble to find him, which they eventually do, and they return to their previous lives having shared this weird and funny ordeal together. The **plot** of the film initially skips the "crazy shenanigans" part, instead only revealing the chaos of the night's adventures through memories and flashbacks suggested by the characters as they look for their missing friend "the morning after." Coverage for a script such as *The Hangover* would want to preserve that plot structure. By the same token, in a murder mystery, you most likely would arrange the "plot" so that the murderer is not revealed until the end—although the "story" has the murderer established from the beginning.

Here are some of the key elements to look for when you are preparing to write coverage. Pay attention to these as you read—if you are someone who remembers details and processes better by taking notes, then by all means do so.

- Leading and supporting character names, identities, and relationships
- Locations and settings (broadly speaking)—"an urban housing project," "1950s Los Angeles," the small town of Goshen, Indiana
- Temporality: watch for nonlinear elements such as flashbacks, flashforwards, etc.
- Inciting incident: the moment when the "action" begins.
- Decisions and revelations: most important plot points involve a main character making a decision or realizing/discovering an important piece of information.
- Relevant "B" stories: many screenplays will flesh out the main action with secondary storylines involving minor characters. If these storylines ultimately affect the main storyline in a significant way, you will want to describe them properly and effectively. If these storylines are less relevant (i.e., simply a "comic relief" bit involving a recurring conflict with a minor character), they may or may not be necessary for your synopsis.
- Climax/conclusion and resolution: your coverage must include the entirety of the film's story. There is no reason to obscure or hide anything or to avoid "spoilers."
- Perspective of the protagonist: oftentimes, it is good to "anchor" your synopsis from the perspective of the protagonist and his or her "journey" or experience of the events in the script. Of course, in many scripts the reader/audience will know things that the character does not know—and your coverage should reflect that. But the protagonist is the character (or characters) with which the audience must identify the most: highlighting that character's emotions, actions, and reactions often helps "connect the dots" with other story elements. Your comments would very likely focus on whether characters are believable and "relatable," and you will want to read the script looking for the evidence with which you can make your argument.

By the same token, here are a few things that are perhaps less relevant to read and describe in detail:

- Movement of characters and the "ordinary" passage of time: how characters travel from one place to another, or how long the time between scenes, should only be mentioned when relevant to the plot.
- Extended action sequences
- Montages
- Dance sequences or musical numbers (except in a musical)
- *Meta*-narrative elements such as news broadcasts, newspaper headlines, "mockumentary" interviews

You'll find that for most of these examples, you can reduce these elements to just a few words (I will provide some examples in a following section). What you will most likely find is, as in the previous cases, you are often more describing "the film" rather than the story or the plot. I want to caution you not to *ignore* these elements as you read—oftentimes, these are the more refined cinematic and narrative techniques that make for great filmmaking. You should definitely mention and describe them more in your comments, particularly if they determine your recommendation: but taking too much space in the synopsis will only slow that reading. Distill each scene and sequence down to their most important actions and consequences—usually as illustrated through the characters—for the synopsis, rather than describe the cinematic or literary techniques used to do so.

In previous generations, when scripts were circulated on paper, a reader may have been able to make small notes on the page or dog-ear or bookmark a specific page. If you don't have a digital bookmarking option, I'd suggest taking handwritten notes that include a relevant page number, in case you want to refer to the script later as you write your synopsis. (Page numbers are just for your own reference: you'll never say, in your comments, "On page 38, James Bond meets …")

EFFECTIVE SYNOPSIZING

The exercises in this chapter will walk you through the "life cycle" of a particular project, and allow you to practice the various forms of synopsizing that follow. But before we start, let's consider a point of focus that professional writers develop an instinct for as they practice it over time. If there is a distinct philosophy I subscribe to, as both a writer and also as someone who teaches writing, it is this: *Effective professional writing is about **minimizing word count** and **maximizing word value**.*

One of the things I sometimes hear from people who teach writing is that effective writing is "personal" and "conversational." I agree that these are interesting and valuable qualities to aspire to in any form of communication. But the way we "conversate"—the way we speak to and hear each other—is not the same way that we read and write. Our everyday spoken language is filled with excessive pauses and stops, undiagrammable grammar, vocal inflection, personal speech patterns, and dozens of other elements of communication that are not present in the written word.

Oftentimes, when people struggle with writing, they try to "write like they talk." This isn't necessarily an issue with basic language skills such as grammar and spelling, but is definitely present in the way people organize and communicate their ideas. As such, people often write "excessively," including information that is either extraneous or repetitive. They also fall into the easy trap of using language that, when spoken, might convey something very specific, but when written, feels impossibly vague (e.g., you can probably read the statement "Yeah, that film was pretty good" and imagine it being said in five divergent ways that range anywhere from disgust to rapture).

Thus, my primary point of focus: *minimize word count* by knowing what is essential to communicate, and *maximize word value* by focusing on the most precise and evocative descriptive words—usually adjectives and verbs—to convey the action. If you are someone who prefers to write "free" and just ramble on in your first draft, then engage with that process; but be prepared to bring the minimize/maximize tool with you as soon as you start to edit and revise.

I'll be pointing out some of the common mistakes that new professional writers make along the way, and you will see how, in almost every case, it's a matter of not respecting this axiom. And remember, the goal isn't to necessarily write in as few words as possible, nor is it to create something that must be recognized as a masterful expression of the language arts. It's about honing your language skills to a fine point so that key words can be attended to with precise focus and detail. Great cooks and chefs, regardless of whether they are working in a taco truck, a pancake franchise, or an exclusive French bistro, will seek out quality ingredients and make sure that every plate looks and tastes amazing. Likewise, the professional writer will bring that same sense of efficiency, focus, and precision to the ingredients and presentation of their own work.

CHAPTER TAKEAWAYS

- The ability to create, evaluate, and discuss synopses of various lengths and types is a central professional skill.
- The "essence" of the synopsis is the story action that is central and unique to the property.
- A synopsis is often framed as a "pitch" or a "description," and has to be sensitive as to whether it is a "teaser" or a "spoiler."
- Minimal word count and maximum word value are the keys to effective professional writing and strong synopses.

EXERCISE 4A: COVER LETTER/HIGH CONCEPT/SHORT LOG LINE

SITUATION: Your screenwriter friend has finished a script, and last night at a party met a legitimate agent. The agent seemed interested in the subject matter and said to your friend, "Send your script to my junior associate, and be sure to put on the cover letter that I said to send it along." So now, the writer has to come up with a very short cover letter, explaining the meeting and "pitching" the project a bit.

Your friend decides the letter should include either a "high-concept" pitch and/or a very short (one sentence) log line, and wants the cover letter in the email to be just a couple of short, simple paragraphs. The problem is that your friend is about to get on a plane, and won't be near a computer for hours. He'll pay you $150 and buy you a nice dinner if you could read the script and come up with a draft of a letter by the following day.

- Create a cover letter/email for your friend's project. Using a script from a script data-base as the friend's example, read the script and come up with a short "high-concept" pitch and/or a one-sentence log line.

EXERCISE 4A: SAMPLE

October 14, 20xx

Roger Silvera
Broadchurch and Rivkin Literary Agency
5000 New York Street, Suite 500
Beverly Hills, CA 90212
Via email: rsilvera@brlitagency.com

Hello Mr. Silvera:

Last week at the benefit for homeless children, I met Dan Rivkin, and he urged me to send you my screenplay, "Hail to the Chump," which I have enclosed.

"Hail to the Chump" is the story of Mitch Mickins, an out-of-work circus clown who becomes a national sensation when he is mistakenly put forward as a Supreme Court nominee.

It's "Mr. Smith Goes to Washington" meets "Judge Judy," and I hope you enjoy reading it. I'm currently unrepresented but excited about the possibility of working with you and Mr. Rivkin.

Thank you for your time, I look forward to hearing from you.

Regards,

EXERCISE 4B: AGENT'S LETTER

SITUATION: You're working as an assistant to an agent at a literary agency. ("Literary" in the film industry refers to working with writers in general, not only in "literature" or publishing.) Your boss sends you an email with an attachment (or, if your boss is old-fashioned, puts a hard copy of a script on your desk with a note attached):

> Got this from a writer that our boss met at a party last week ... it's actually kind of a cool idea and I want to send it out as soon as I can sign a contract with the writer. Can you give it a read and see if we can come up w/ a longer/better log line and an angle to pitch this? Thanks!

- Write a pitch letter to a generic producer that includes a revised **log line** (up to two sentences) and a short **comment paragraph**.

EXERCISE 4B: SAMPLE

October 28, 20xx

Beata Chase
Straight Chaser Films
551 South Plum Canyon, 2nd Floor
Los Angeles, CA 90064
Via email: bc@straightchaser.com

Dear Beata:

Thanks for taking a look at this new script, which is from an up-and-coming writer that Dan Rivkin just signed as a client.

"Hail to the Chump" tells the story of Mitch Mickins, a recently unemployed circus clown and one-time law school dropout. Through a series of misunderstandings, his name is put forward by a feeble-minded senator as a possible Supreme Court candidate. What starts as a minor media frenzy blows up into a national crisis as Mitch gets closer to donning judicial robes and becoming the first "regular guy" on the nation's highest court.

It's a high-concept comedy—think "Mr. Smith" meets "Judge Judy"—but Dan and I are also impressed by the film's positive message about the importance of "the little guy" in politics. Given your strong record with smart material, we think this might be a great fit to partner up on and bring to a studio.

Hope you enjoy the read, and let's chat about it soon.

Sincerely,

WRITING TIPS FOR EXERCISES 4A AND 4B

- *For **high concept:*** not all scripts lend themselves to an easy "high concept." The goal with this letter is to convey "just the basics" of the script idea in an accurate and efficient manner. If you can't nail a high concept, focus on the short log line and try a high concept with a future script.
- For ***log line:*** you might want to start by describing what happens as a result of the story's **inciting incident**. The most effective log lines are often constructed as "When something happens, it causes a character to do something interesting."
- It's also effective for some scripts to suggest a log line based on the perspective of a character (or group of characters for an ensemble-driven story). Remember, though, that you want to convey "what happens," not just describe a situation. "A character (or group) takes action when ..."
- In a situation such as this, it might be appropriate to include a simple reference to a genre or tone within the log line, but only if it is otherwise unclear.
- One form of descriptive word you probably want to avoid is a word that implies "hype" or "judgment." Words such as "hilarious" to describe a comedy, "soul-shattering" to define a romantic drama, "brilliant" to describe anything, might sound like "too much" selling. Instead of words that only convey a subjective opinion, choose words that describe *why* the opinion is justified. *Why* is the comedy "hilarious"? Is it fast-paced? Spot-on cultural satire? Unpredictable? Raunchy? Deadpan? *Why* is the drama soul-shattering? Because it has an unexpected twist/surprise? Because it's a "universal" story? What makes the script "brilliant"? Because it's original? Well-crafted? Heartwarming? The point is to use the best words to describe the unique elements of the story as precisely as possible, rather than making boasts about the quality of the work.
- For **comment paragraph:** your boss asked for "an angle" to pitch the script. After you've settled on your log line, see if you can describe the potential "value" of the script to a potential buyer. Again, be cautious not to "overhype": what are the strong descriptive words that help convey the "tone" of the film? Is there an effective high-concept description or appropriate comparison to a more familiar film ("It's *Ghostbusters* meets *Zootopia*.")?

SELF-ASSESSMENT

- Am I writing, whenever possible, in active voice and present tense? (Keywords to look out for: "is," "has," "have been," etc.)
- Are my verbs and adjectives specific and accurate?

FOR EXTRA CREDIT

To challenge yourself, see if you can come up with a series of log lines: one in which the genre or tone is self-evident; one in which those elements are deliberately overhyped and exaggerated; and one in which the tone is completely vague.

Extra Credit: Example 1

Self-evident: An unemployed circus clown becomes a media sensation when he is mistakenly nominated to be a Supreme Court justice. (Notice how you don't need to say that "this is a comedy.")

Overhyped: A hilarious satire about a former clown who comically stumbles into the national spotlight.

Vague: An unemployed actor accidentally winds up being nominated for a big job.

Extra Credit: Example 2

Self-evident: A woman recovering from a mysterious car accident falls into a dangerous obsession with the occult and a decades-old murder.

Overhyped: A suspenseful horror thriller in which a disturbed woman with a violent past becomes obsessed with the ghost of an executed cannibal serial killer.
Vague: An odyssey of trauma and recovery intertwined with a historical legend and a touch of the supernatural.

EXERCISE 4C: FULL SYNOPSIS

SITUATION: You're working for a producer. An agent your office has worked with before sends over a script with a short, pitchy cover letter promising a good read. Your boss is out of town at a film festival, but when the boss calls in, you're given the instruction to just read the script over the weekend and to "email me a full synopsis by Monday."

- Read a *new* script from a script library, and write a full synopsis. For now, don't worry about the length; this exercise is purely a "warm-up" exercise for the work to follow in Chapter 5.

If you are working in a group or classroom situation, I recommend that you read the same script as other students, and compare your results. Can you identify the elements of someone else's writing that you find distracting, unnecessary, or confusing? Are there portions of the story or script mentioned in one synopsis but not another?

SELF-ASSESSMENT

- What part of the assignment did I find most difficult?
- Am I writing in the present tense and active voice?
- Are the characters and their actions clear? (Be particularly attuned to the use of pronouns—when you say "he" or "she" or "they," is it clear which characters you are referring to?)
- Have I divided the synopsis into paragraphs that resemble "beats" of the film?

CHAPTER 5

'Is It Any Good?'

Story Analysis, Script Coverage, Evaluation, and Recommendation

A t this point in our project life cycle and in your imagined show business career, we encounter one of the most important, most coveted, and most "invisible" skills in the film industry: the ability to engage in strong, productive story analysis, which includes close readings of a property; creating a no-spoiler synopsis of a specified length; critically assessing a submission's potential according to specific criteria; writing a brief, but detailed and focused evaluation; and, ultimately, issuing a recommendation as to whether the project should receive any further consideration or support.

The short-hand term for all of this is **coverage**, which we can think of as both a *process* (all of the above actions, and more) and also as a *product* (the written report that is circulated: "Do you have coverage on that script?" or "This is a great piece of coverage!"). This chapter is about the ins-and-outs of creating coverage, and how coverage functions within the processes of acquisition and development. We'll be building upon the synopsis writing skills introduced in the previous chapter, introducing you to some critical thinking and writing tools specific to coverage, and giving you a sense of the importance and value of your opinion and perspective.

It's a bit odd when you think about it. The people who write coverage—often called **readers** but more officially referred to as **story analysts**—are, by some measures, the "lowest" figures on the industrial totem pole. Many work freelance, generating supplementary income while they pursue careers as a screenwriters or independent producers; the few who are employed by studios or production companies on a full-time basis are not part of the executive chain of command, and their salary is often more akin to that of a staff person (an assistant, office manager, etc.) than that of an executive.

And yet, these readers are really the "gatekeepers" of the industry. At some point, every project has to be presented to someone who is completely objective about the work—the first person to look at it in great detail and decide whether anyone else in the company should look at it. Certainly there are instances of that first reader being an executive or VIP: If you've won two Academy Awards for screenwriting and you have a three-series deal with Netflix, then your next feature film script has a chance of getting directly onto Mr. Spielberg's desk, and not be left to the fate of a recent college grad who just started interning in the DreamWorks story department. But more often than not, those recent college grads, undiscovered screenwriters, journalists, and other anonymous professionals who work as readers end up yielding a great deal of power. One of my former colleagues once referred to himself as a "creative bouncer," standing at the doorway of the "green light party" and making sure none of the riffraff are allowed in. I suppose if one has an elevated opinion of themselves, a reader also might imagine themselves as Saint Peter at the pearly gates.

On a more familiar level, you might equate readers to casting directors, who sift through hundreds and hundreds of actors to recommend a mere dozen or so for callbacks: because the system is always flooded with talent, there needs to be people who can effectively process the sheer amount of material moving through the system. Certainly, an individual studio or company or agency can limit the amount of material it considers; however, the more it limits, the more it will require strong coverage processes to winnow the "input" down to the desired level. Also similar to casting directors, readers typically make informed recommendations, but not final decisions.

As such, reading and coverage is a "bulk" business. Even in the last decade, when the "spec" script market has all but vanished and series television has come to dominate both industrial production and cultural reception, there are still hundreds of new scripts and other properties sent out by major agents and managers every month. Professional courtesy and obligation usually means those scripts have to be read, covered, and recommended within a reasonable period of time.

That makes the story analyst's job that much more challenging: in addition to being a company's gatekeeper, you will probably be charged with multiple and simultaneous assignments, to be completed in a relatively short time frame. Again, this is a writing practice where speed and efficiency are rewarded: as you might imagine, readers who are trained as journalists or specialists in technical or short-form writing have an advantage over "creative" writers who might not typically write on deadline.

So let's put all of this together and imagine what you might be facing as a professional reader and story analyst. Obviously, there will be some variation if you are a freelance analyst, an assistant to a development executive, an intern in a story department, or anyone else who might be asked to produce coverage. For example, let's pretend it's a typical Monday, and you receive in your email box three screenplays, all between 100–120 pages. If you are a freelance reader, you'll probably be expected to have completed and submitted your coverage on all three by Wednesday or Thursday; if you work in the office and have other responsibilities, you might get until Friday or even a week.

It's very important to know that everyone reads, processes language, and writes at a different speed: the way we read, write, and speak is as unique to us as our taste for food. It might look like we all do it the same way, but the experience of doing so is something that is different from person to person. As a professional story analyst, you need to learn how to manage and supervise yourself and your own process. If you have three days to do three scripts, do you do one per day? Do you read all three scripts in a row curled up in your bed at night, and then write the coverage the next day after you've had some time to "sleep on it"?

Do you want to absolutely complete one piece of coverage and get it out of your brain before moving to the next one? These are just some of the ways in which an individual's writing process can vary: what's important is that you know your own process and understand how long it will take you to get your work done.

When I was reading full time, I would often receive 10 to 12 scripts or properties of one kind or another per week. This was in the day of hard-copy scripts and coverage reports, when the spec market was much more active and feature films dominated the creative imagination. Since I had been trained more as a "journalist" than as a "creative writer," and had done a lot of synopsis work because of my time in public relations, I started out with some advantages that other new readers might not have. But even then, when I first started as a story analyst, it took me about three or four hours to complete a single piece of coverage, with about half the time spent reading the script, and half the time writing the coverage report. Within a couple of months of steady practice, I began to be able to turn around a piece of coverage between two and three hours. My most in-demand colleagues were the ones who were not only strong writers, but who could also be relied on to produce something *today* if need be, so there is incentive in being able to do this job quickly. But I also had many reader colleagues who were up front about their inability to do a "rush" job—sometimes for reasons related to other obligations (career, family), sometimes because they didn't like working under unnecessary pressure. They wouldn't do an overnight job, but were perfectly capable of working on a slightly slower schedule and covering lower-priority submissions.

Before we continue, a quick word to the screenwriters, directors, and producers who don't see themselves as interested in acquisition and development or very likely to ever pursue a career or a job that requires writing coverage. Let's think for a moment about the term "story analyst," one of the more formal alternatives to the generic and slightly passive term "reader." Although the exercise of writing coverage might seem menial or exhausting or even depressing—after all, you are probably going to "pass" on nine out of 10 things you read—that exercise is perhaps one of the most effective ways to improve your own film literacy and competency. If you are attracted to a career in which you get to tell great stories, then breaking down and analyzing a script before almost anyone else has seen it is a unique learning opportunity every time you do it. It's like being handed a new "movie puzzle" with every assignment, and your job is to explain in detail how the various pieces fit together.

Furthermore, though the ultimate purpose for coverage might be to provide a "yes" or "no," your explanation for that decision has to be detailed, comprehensive, logically presented, and entirely clear. You would want to bring that clarity and attention to detail to your own work: coverage is a way to practice those essential filmmaking, storytelling, and producing skills, and you can bring your own perspective to that as a way to engage with the material. If you're a director, what might excite you about working on this project? If you are a producer, what interesting talent might be available or what interesting marketing possibilities might the property have? If you are a screenwriter, what techniques can you learn from the script—what to do, what not to do—that can make your own writing more accessible and exciting?

That having been said, let's walk through the assignments for this chapter with the goal of establishing basic expectations and standards, and highlighting the ways in which you might improve your efficiency and speed, either immediately (if you are comfortable doing so) or eventually.

REMEMBER: KNOW YOUR READER

Just as every story analyst has a slightly different process to produce the same outcome, so does every company vary in the way it standardizes and processes coverage to achieve the same goals. Before we dive into the how-tos, let's look at the "bigger picture" for coverage and exactly what your writing needs to accomplish.

If you are doing coverage, it means, essentially, that you are reading something that someone superior to you in the company (your boss) may or may not want to read. That person (or persons) has decided that *you* have the knowledge and ability to read something and report on it *as if they themselves were doing the reading.* That doesn't necessarily mean you have to like exactly the same things, or be attracted to the same styles or genres, but it means that you agree on a basic framework and perspective in terms of how to analyze and understand a script's strengths or weaknesses.

Most studio development executives would probably be embarrassed to confess to an agent that they did not actually read the script. Some of them might be honest about relying on coverage ("We didn't get good coverage on this"), while others might use the coverage as a "cheat sheet" to pretend or imply that they actually did read the entire script cover to cover. As a story analyst, *your primary job is to provide a report that offers enough detail so that anyone who reads the coverage will effectively be able to discuss the property as if they have read it themselves.*

When you consider the fact that you will probably pass on nine out of 10 scripts, you can see that the main function of coverage from the perspective of your employer is to answer the questions: "Why am I saying 'no' to this script, and how can I say it as quickly and efficiently as possible?" Some professionals might also consider coverage as a way to offer constructive criticism or point out positives even when a script is a pass, so your employer may specifically ask for comments that highlight such matters.

It's also common for executives to share coverage with one another (the term often used is to "slip" coverage—often meaning it is unofficial and "off the books," since coverage is usually considered corporate property). It might be the case that a producer at a big studio has ties to a number of independent producers who might be right for a certain project, and slips positive coverage to an outside entity that might be a good strategic partner. Or perhaps an executive is good friends with the agent or screenwriter, and feels comfortable sharing the official story report as a form of critical feedback. As such, it's important to consider that while you very likely are writing primarily for a very limited audience—the executives in your company, at least one of whom will read your coverage all the way through—there's also a secondary audience, one that may be someone working very closely with the script, or even the screenwriter(s) themselves. As such, most companies frown on coverage that is written with sarcasm or a lack of respect for the work—coverage can be negative, but it can't be mean-spirited or insulting.

On a more technical level, each company will also very likely have different requirements in terms of the length of the report or level or kinds of detail it wants included. Some might ask you to fill out a digital form; others might ask you to upload a well-formatted PDF to a shared drive; it's even possible that others might want a hard copy delivered or mailed to them. I'll cover some of the more salient differences in the descriptions and exercises that follow, with the caveat that most college graduates of this generation should be ready and able to adapt any of the broad guidelines I've cited into any present-day workflow or administrative operations and practices.

For the purposes of this book, I'm using as my primary example the feature film screenplay to demonstrate basics for creating script coverage. It's important to note that series television, short-form content, potential adaptations of novels and plays, and other forms of produced entertainment all may have equivalent processes with different concerns and requirements (some of this will be discussed in more detail in the next chapter). If you are presented with an unusual property, be sure to ask your employer to clarify any details or instructions in terms of what is expected from your report in terms of length, structure, detail, etc.

COVERAGE BASICS

We've already covered some strategies for reading a script, which is the first step in creating coverage. We'll divide the rest of the coverage process into four additional steps: creating a cover sheet, writing the synopsis, writing comments, and completing your report. Although specifics may vary from company to company, most coverage includes and requires those four elements.

'COVER SHEET'/SUBMISSION INFORMATION

In previous generations, readers generated their own cover sheet to serve as documentation: today, some of this information is collected via digital forms, databases, etc. This information usually includes:

- The TITLE of the property
- The AUTHOR(S) of the submission
- The FORMAT of the property (screenplay, novel, etc.) including total number of pages

- The DATE of the property, if available (the date this particular draft was "finished" or when the book/article was published, etc.)
- The DATE of the coverage and identity of the story analyst
- The GENRE of the property; companies may differ on how specific they get in describing a genre (i.e., do they distinguish between "comedy" and "romantic comedy"?).
- SUBMISSION INFORMATION including where the submission came from, who it is being submitted to, dates of submission, etc.
- ELEMENTS that are attached or linked to the property; "elements" are usually other people or companies that have expressed some degree of interest in getting the film made (i.e., "Jon Hamm attached to play Dr. Kildare"; "A24 interested in domestic distribution"); it might also include other relevant information about the property ("Based on the novel by John LeCarre"). Elements do *not* typically describe the content of the story ("Lots of visual effects" or "Set in the U.K." is not an "element" in this sense). Most often, a reader will be informed of what the elements are (if any), and if that information is to be included in the official coverage. Standard practice is that the reader not comment on the elements within his or her report (e.g., "This is a perfect movie for Jon Hamm!"), but some companies may have differing policies in that regard.
- LOG LINE: The coverage log line can be slightly longer than a "pitch," and should be more objective and without any evaluative comments. It is not necessary that they are spoiler-free, although typically they describe the main characters and "set-up" rather than reveal details about the ending.
- BRIEF COMMENTS: One to two sentences that encapsulate the extended comments.
- RUBRIC or EVALUATION CHART: This is where companies differ greatly, as specific aspects of the property are evaluated and compared. For example, a studio might ask a reader to assign a rating of one to 10 to characters, plot, and production value; it might ask for a "poor" to "excellent" rating on the concept/premise, dialogue, and "franchise potential." When generating sample coverage, it's good to include your own rubric (see the sample cover page), and you should be able to easily adjust to whatever rubric the studio uses.
- RECOMMENDATION: Again, companies will differ on what they want in terms of an ultimate recommendation, which usually determines whether the script will be read by someone else in a higher position of authority, or whether the person to whom the property was submitted should pass. *Pass* and *recommend* are usually standard for "no" and "yes," respectively. Some companies, however, have designations of *qualified recommend* or *qualified pass* or *maybe* for properties that are not easy to evaluate. For example, a script might have an amazing idea but be hampered by poor dialogue; another property might be brilliantly written, but too close in subject matter to a film already in theaters, or too controversial, etc. It is best when developing sample coverage to have clear and decisive pass or recommend evaluations, and adjust as need be if you are assigned to evaluate something that requires a more

nuanced judgment. (And be sure to ask any employer how the company feels about *maybe*-level evaluations: for many executives, a *maybe* doesn't do what coverage is supposed to do, which is "give me a reason to say no.")

WRITING THE SYNOPSIS

You've had some practice writing synopses: unless you are asked to write a treatment, the coverage synopsis is probably the longest-form synopsis you will encounter. This is a good time to review the exercise from the previous chapter, and take a few moments to consider the ways in which you need to adapt your process to produce a three-page, double-spaced synopsis (800–1000 words).

If you've read your script carefully, you'll have some of the basic building blocks of the synopsis: you'll know which characters to focus on, which events are key, what moments of action and decision matter most, and how they influence the characters' emotions and subsequent actions. You also may be familiar with narrative theories such as three-act or five-act structure, or dramatic theory concepts such as "willing suspension of disbelief" or "the well-made play" that are often used to evaluate a story's dramatic value and effectiveness.

What's important to remember is that the synopsis needs to be as objective as possible. Whatever feelings you might have about the quality of the project, or whatever critical approach you might be applying as you evaluate its worth and potential, you need to be sure those don't influence your ability to communicate the essential elements of the screenplay in a concise and accurate manner via the synopsis. (Your comments can and should reflect your opinion, and will be discussed later.)

As such, I have a few general guidelines that I think make for solid synopsis coverage. You'll notice that I've asked you about some of these things in previous exercise assessments and reflections: if you've noticed some of these habits before, now is the time to understand why you might want to address them early in your writing process, so that you don't make these mistakes as a professional.

- **Length and scope:** While companies may vary in what they expect in terms of the length of a synopsis, industry standard is typically about 900–1,200 words (three to four pages double-spaced) for a standard-length screenplay (90–120 pages). This synopsis should be comprehensive: while it might elide or condense some of the action—it is *not* a "scene by scene" description, the way a treatment might be—this synopsis has to include the most relevant details regarding main characters and the central plot(s), including beginning, middle, and end. It includes spoilers and revelations and all relevant details about the ending.
- **Write in the present tense:** The present tense should always be your "default" for telling a story. In some cases—for example, a flashback—it may make grammatical sense to switch to the past tense. (Example: "Harry remembers that long ago, before he came to Hogwarts, he and his uncle went to the London Zoo, where Harry had a psychic encounter with a snake.")

- **Eliminate any words or phrases that have to do with "narrating" or "framing" the action:** These are "process" words that don't have to do with the story. Examples:

Poor: "We open with a shot of a beautiful Tuscan landscape, and we cut to a shot of Madame Rossini on her balcony."
Better: "In beautiful Tuscany, we find Madam Rossini on her balcony …"

Poor: "In the next scene, Polly walks down Fifth Avenue …"
Better: "Walking down Fifth Avenue, Polly meets up with …"

Poor: "As the second act opens, Jafar is attempting to win Jasmine's heart …"
Better: "In his lair, Jafar woos a reluctant Jasmine …"

Poor: "In a flashback, Harvey Dent remembers the first time he saw Batman."
Better: "Harvey recognizes Batman from a previous encounter."

Poor: "There is a montage sequence showing Rocky getting healthier."
Better: "Training on his own for weeks, Rocky slowly regains his health."

If you aren't sure whether something you are using is "process" language or not, eliminate it and see whether there is any difference in meaning or understanding the plot. Most of the time, it is an informal and casual way of transitioning from one plot point or one scene to another. It's not that writing this way is "incorrect," just that it is usually extra words that are not relevant to the description of the plot or important elements of the story (i.e., the main character isn't aware of being in a montage sequence, or that their decision is the turning point).

- **Clearly identifying characters**
  - The **first time**[1] you identify a major character, you should provide any relevant "establishing" information, including:
    - Full name (with nickname if necessary)
    - Age or age range
    - Relevant and necessary identity markers, including ethnicity, if necessary
  - In subsequent references, refer to the character by the name the screenplay writer uses for dialogue (e.g., if the script refers to "Bond" as the character, then describe him as "Bond," not "James").
  - Examples:
    - Harry Potter (13)
    - Detective Harry "Dirty Harry" Callahan (50s)
    - Tituba (40s, a slave from Barbados)
    - Dr. Nguyen (30s, female)
    - Data (a robot that resembles a professional man in his 30s)

---

1   I have worked for companies that like to see character names in ALL CAPS or **bold letters** the first time they are introduced.

- **Pronouns:** Be sure your use of pronouns is proper, consistent, and clear. This is something that you *must* pay attention to in proofreading. The "he" or "him" you reference in your long sentence might be clear to *you*, but will it be clear to the reader that you are referring to Mr. G and not Mr. K, both of whom are in this scene?

  ○ A good rule is to refer to the character by name the first time he or she is mentioned in every new paragraph, at which point you can then use a pronoun (he/she/they) as relevant.

- **Verbs:** Eliminate excessive verbs and verb phrases and try to keep all verbs "active" and direct. If necessary, turn redundant verb phrases into adverbs. (This is particularly relevant for eliminating unnecessary "travel" descriptions—"X decides to go to a bar, gets in a car and drives to the bar, and meets up with Y." All we really need to know, most likely, is "X meets up with Y in a bar.")

Poor: "Alex decides to take a drive to Canada to meet cousin Ike …"
Better: "Alex meets Cousin Ike in Canada …"

Poor: "Maggie thinks about it, and after having weighed the pros and cons, agrees that she doesn't want to run away with Robert."
Better: "Maggie rejects Robert's offer to run away."

Poor: "Dr. Bohz acts like a jerk, and rudely throws a shocked and dismayed Regina out of his office after threatening to call the police."
Better: "Dr. Bohz rudely throws Regina out of his office."

Poor: "Hamlet has figured out that his father was poisoned in the ear, and has made the decision to confront Gertrude, when he finds her in her bedroom."
Better: "After deducing that his father was poisoned in the ear, Hamlet confronts Gertrude in her bedroom."

- **Use paragraphs as "beats" and minimize transitional language:** Simple descriptive transitions ("Later," "Back at headquarters," "In London," "At Suzie's birthday party") can help save a lot of words *and* indicate new action if they are at the beginning of a paragraph, where a "shift" in narrative focus is implied. Scripts will vary, but you might try to aim for about three paragraphs per page.

  ○ It's very likely that your first paragraph will need to introduce the major character(s) and establish the "stasis" or beginning condition of the character's world. By the second paragraph, the inciting incident should be clear and the "action" begun. Thus, the first 20–25% of any script is likely to be condensed into these two initial paragraphs. (A common error for new story analysts is providing too much information about the "first act": in most well-written scripts, this "back-story" information should be fairly easy to communicate efficiently and quickly.)

○ For subsequent paragraphs, use major shifts in time and location to help you move from paragraph to paragraph. It is okay to condense or slightly rearrange some elements, particularly with scripts that have multiple relevant storylines. For example, let's say you have two protagonists who split up for several scenes, with both characters only connecting again for the final action. A script may go back and forth between the two of them dozens of times: you may choose to only go back and forth two or three times, condensing all of character A's relevant scenes into one paragraph, then covering what happens to character B in the next.

- **Reduce montage and action sequences to their results:**

  ○ Example: "After a thrilling chase through the streets of the city at 3 a.m., Big Tony eludes Detective Sanchez by driving his Harley down an abandoned subway tunnel and into the East River." That might be a 10-minute sequence on screen or cover five pages of a script, but you've described it briefly and whittled the words down to a workable length without describing every single crash, near-miss, and sound of screeching brakes. Of course, you could also simply say "Sanchez chases Big Tony, but Big Tony gets away," but adding a bit more detail to an *action*-oriented script helps reflect the tone and scope of the story elements, and gives you something a bit more substantive to build on in your comments. ("The script really offers some impressive action sequences, such as the chase into the East River.")

  ○ Example: "Sam interviews several people who saw Wanda on the day of the murder, and learns that at some point in the afternoon she had changed from a yellow dress into a red one." It may have taken Sam four or five scenes to get this information out of various minor characters such as "Shopkeeper" and "Waiter" and "Traffic Cop," but you've given us the gist in just a couple of lines. Again, you could also say "Sam uncovers evidence that Wanda was lying about her alibi," but at that point you aren't providing your reader with some of the color and insight into Sam's process as a detective.

CONSTRUCTING COMMENTS

For many years, the standard length of comments for most of the studios I worked for was two-thirds to one full page of single-spaced text, or about 500–600 words (between four and six paragraphs). One executive once told me that this was a preferred length because it probably took you about just as long to process the comments as it did the synopsis. Although the synopsis is a bit longer (1,000 words), it should "flow" like a story, while comments should be a bit more dense and intellectually complex, and thus require a slightly slower rate of reading. Comments also need to be specific and comprehensive: a reader can't just say "some of the characters aren't believable," and should include a "for example" or two.

In the digital era, I often see coverage assignments or guidelines that suggest coverage comments should themselves be more than 900 words, and should break down in great detail the strengths and weaknesses of the script. Particularly with properties that have already been purchased and are going into development, extended notes and comments are essential, and indeed some companies may want their story analysts to generate coverage that could be useful in the development process. For the purposes of this chapter and this "sample" coverage, I'm going to ask you to stick with the traditional 500-plus word analysis, and we will discuss how to create more elaborate and effective story notes for development in the next chapter. Should you come across a coverage assignment that asks for more than 600 words of comments, you can use the strategies and structures in the next chapter to do so.

I have a standard "structure" for coverage that I found most effective for myself, and most often suggested to the many story analysts I worked with and supervised. There is some room for personal variation, approach, and style, but for the most part the comments have a "five-paragraph" structure (though the "middle three" of these paragraphs could in fact be more than three).

PARAGRAPH ONE of the comments should include a brief description of the plot. It can be similar to the log line you created for the cover sheet, though it probably should be more substantial and precise. This paragraph should also briefly describe any strengths of the script, and introduce the weaknesses that will be discussed in more detail later. The final sentence should "sum up" and include a clear recommendation.

The example here is just to give you a sense of how this paragraph might be structured:

> "Trial by Fire" is a briskly told murder mystery, framed as a courtroom drama, with the events of the past coming to life via witness testimony. The author manages the elements of the genre very effectively, and there are some genuine surprises as each witness takes the stand. The characters, however, are familiar, and the stakes feel low as the murder victim and his family all come across as unsympathetic. The result is a script that reads more like a 1980s TV movie than a truly gripping feature. It's unlikely to attract major talent, and thus is not suitable for further consideration at this time.

At just over 100 words, I've given my reader an overview of the plot, the plusses, the minuses, and the decision.

PARAGRAPHS TWO THROUGH FOUR (and more if you need them) need to describe in even more detail the strengths and weaknesses you alluded to in the first paragraph. This is where your own perspective and analytical process can come in. For some analysts, they like to move "chronologically" through the script: thus, their middle paragraphs might be about the *beginning*, *middle*, and *end* specifically. This method prioritizes analysis of the plot and story, and offers a solid framework that the reader is already familiar with, since it mirrors the information found in the synopsis.

Another method might be to break down the middle paragraphs according to the rubric or chart in your cover sheet—detailing one by one the elements of the script that the company has asked you to evaluate. Thus, you may spend one paragraph on the premise, one paragraph on the plot structure, one on the characters, and one on the dialogue, etc. This kind of approach requires more than just simple plot analysis, and asks you to see how all of the various elements fit together (successfully or not).

My own advice—and my own approach—was to be flexible, because different scripts might ask for different approaches. In character-driven period dramas, connecting to the emotions of the characters and understanding their perspective on the world means that you will probably need to spend more time talking about whether the characters are believable and relatable. For an action film, you are more likely to be analyzing the "pieces of the puzzle" and ensuring that the story makes sense and is well-paced, rather than exploring character motivations.

The truth is that most professional scripts usually do "okay" in terms of plot mechanics: most of these writers are professional and have an understanding of how basic story structure works. You're more likely to read scripts—many of them—that make you think, "I've seen worse things made than this" or "I see this kind of stuff all the time." Your point of departure for your coverage should not just be "is this technically good enough": it needs to be "why is this script different, special, or so much better than just 'good enough'?" *That* is a much higher standard, and it's where most scripts will probably fail. So while you want your comments to be positive and objective, ultimately you are mostly going to be making comments about what the script lacks. And most scripts tend to lack such things as truly original or compelling characters, genuinely "sparkling" dialogue, unique and interesting situations, demonstrable cultural relevance, or consistently delightful and unpredictable imagination—the elements that make for great movies and television shows.

For my students, writing comments is their most difficult exercise. I think this is because they are sometimes reluctant to have to "break down" a script that might be "okay," or might have a really great premise. As young people entering the industry, I think we want the industry to say "yes" to us, so we feel we have to say "yes" to the industry whenever we can. If we are good collaborators and storytellers, we're more likely to give creative people the benefit of the doubt when we can. But a reader has to be much more selective and impersonal, and you have to do it in some detail.

As you construct your middle paragraphs—however you choose to do so—each observation you make should be supported by at least one example from the script. If you write "the characters aren't very interesting," then give specific detail: the protagonist doesn't have a backstory, his connection to the love interest seems convenient and unemotional, and the villain's motivations for his actions are unexplained. If you write "the story doesn't always make sense," give examples: the details of the bank heist are too complex to comprehend, the multiple flashbacks are confusing and repetitive, it's obvious who the murderer is from the beginning, etc. And know that you can always use the same detail when describing positives: "the dialogue is great" could include a strong point of comparison ("fast-paced like *30 Rock*") or even a line directly quoted from the script that reads as funny or profound.

FINAL PARAGRAPH: This paragraph is a summation of your perspective and judgment, with a clear final sentence that again expresses your ultimate recommendation. It's easy to see this as a "mirror image" of your opening paragraph—and I admit that at times, in my own coverage, those two paragraphs were pretty similar. But remember that your reader now has a deeper understanding of the material—the deepest they are likely to have unless they read it themselves. This final paragraph is how you can now talk to them as "equals" and put all of your thoughts into that new context.

For example, in this paragraph you might offer points of criticism to suggest improvement or include another perspective on the property's value. You can rely on precise detail (such as a character name) to make your "lasting impression" on your reader. You might indicate that while it might be a strong submission for another company, it just doesn't meet the needs of the company you are working for (this is essential to point out whenever it is true). Consider this sample (for the same project just described):

> The writers certainly demonstrate that they have mastered the craft of the courtroom drama, and there's something very appealing about a compromised attorney prosecuting a mystery involving his ex-wife's family. But the otherwise thin characters and less-than-surprising ending fail to elevate this idea to the point where it could stand out. Since this is a well-worn genre, and one that doesn't exactly meet the company's desire to appeal to urban audiences, then it deserves a pass at this time.

There is another way of approaching comments that will vary greatly from company to company or even reader to reader. If you are employed doing coverage, this is something you will want to clarify with your employer—and that *is how to talk about the submission in comparison with other external things in the industry*. I've been focusing entirely on the question of the quality of the story and the writing—we'll call those the *internal* elements. The *external* elements are things that probably should be considered as a decision is being made about the property. These external considerations are:

- *What other produced films can you compare this script to?* What does it remind you of? Is it a better version? A blatant rip-off? A cool twist? For the most part, companies encourage this in a very limited fashion—if it helps you to make a point to say that something is "like *The Hangover* with teenagers," then doing so allows you to show off your cinematic literacy. But be careful not to simply rely on comparisons or references to other works to populate your comments—they are probably most appropriate in the first and final paragraphs. Keep the focus on what the script *is*, not what it is *not* when compared with other things.
- *What does our company currently have in development and does this project "compete" with other projects we are already working on?* Some studios and producers want a lot of the same types of stories, others want to diversify.
- *What possible talent ("elements") might be interested or attached?* Who are the important actors and directors we know who might be interested in this? Since story analysts are sometimes privy to attachments, it can greatly influence their reading of

the script: if a famous comedian is attached to play a very serious, dramatic leading role, your opinion of the script will be influenced as you imagine them in character while you are reading. As mentioned previously, some studios or producers prefer that the reader does *not* comment on the elements, as they may be more likely to change and will want the coverage to make sense even if a new actor gets involved.

- *Does this story address a current social issue, important personal or political point of view, or provocative and important question in some way?* Does it feature significantly diverse characters? For some companies, this is a major issue—some want to pursue controversy, others want to avoid it. Some praise "personal" filmmaking, others want properties that are "universal."

Some companies will want their readers to remain focused solely on the script itself, and ask these externally driven questions further down the line as properties are more seriously considered. I wrote many pieces of coverage that were positive, only to have my boss say, "Yeah, I thought it was great, too, but we already have a courtroom drama thing." It was more important that I evaluated the script as objectively as possible, while the studio executives were in place to better and more fully consider those external factors.

Some companies, however, might encourage their readers to include comments (when necessary) about external factors. If you think it's really interesting that the usually hilarious Gabriel Iglesias is going to play a sad, divorced immigration attorney who reunites with his long-lost brother, then making a positive comment about that unusual casting might be welcome. If a company is particularly interested in making films with more thoughtfully diverse characters, then a script in line with that mission should be highlighted by the coverage.

For the purposes of creating sample coverage, I strongly suggest that you stick with the *internal* script elements, only referring to *external* elements in the most generic way possible. If your sample script is a provocative script from a political standpoint, for example, then your coverage should note that without saying whether it is a "good" or a "bad" thing.

Finally, a couple of things to be sure you avoid with your comments. First, remember that this is about your professional, objective opinion, but it must be expressed respectfully and responsibly. You might read something that literally offends you, and for very good reason, and it's idiotic to assume that you can simply "put that aside." Your comments are the proper place to note that "some of the representations of the minor characters might be considered offensive by some viewers," or a similarly substantive but non-provocative observation. Additionally, it's not the place to make a joke about poor writing or to see how much you can "tear down" something that isn't very good. Many is the time I wanted to make a comment such as "the writers must have used a whole box of crayons writing this one" or "the dialogue reads as if it were translated from American to Russian to Tahitian and back again." But I didn't: I just observed that the plot was simplistic and the dialogue confusing, with appropriate examples.

Second, avoid being too much of a "fixer." In your final paragraph, it's perfectly appropriate to say something such as "if the events of the third act were more believable, then the ending would be more satisfying"—so suggesting what "doesn't work" is a way of perhaps suggesting that something might be addressed in a new draft. But directly offering too much observation about how to make the script more valuable or interesting is probably not your job (it's the agent's or producer's job). That also means avoiding dream-casting (try not to describe the leading female character as a "Scarlett Johansson type" unless the writer does so; just say it's a leading role that could land an A-list actress), etc. Those particular instincts and skills will be discussed in the next chapter, so you'll get your chance to do that elsewhere, both in this book and in your career.

FINALIZING YOUR REPORT

If you've done your formatting correctly, you should now have a five-page report: a cover sheet on a single page, three pages of synopsis (double-spaced), and one page of comments (single-spaced). Proofread *everything*, checking especially the names on the cover sheet (the names of real people), character names, etc. If you do not have strong proofreading and copy-editing skills, read each sentence aloud word for word, or read each sentence backward. Do not just rely on spell-check, and be sure you have fixed all auto-corrects (such as the annoying auto-correct that turns "improv" into "improve"). Look for common mistakes such as "then" for "than," "it's" for "its," etc.

You will also want to include all of the other formatting elements that might be requested by a company. Ask about headers and footers, formatting page numbers, etc. Again, companies that have converted entirely to digital workflow may not require this from you, but certainly think about it for your sample coverage, and remember that digital-based processes might ask you for specific kinds of file-saving, file-naming, coding, etc.

SOME FINAL THOUGHTS ON COVERAGE

As mentioned, what you are most likely to struggle with at first with comments is figuring out how to connect your critical instincts with specific details from the script. In almost every case, the first set of comments written by my students is about 200 words as they struggle to find enough detail and material to say something besides "the script is funny sometimes but not that good." Don't be discouraged if you take a stab at comments only to discover that you have two short paragraphs that don't say much more than that. Just keep in mind that the level of detail is important. Remember that your coverage has two related functions: 1) give a "yes" or "no" recommendation, and 2) give your readers all of the information necessary so that they can take action on the script without having to actually read it all the way through.

It's most likely that the executive will officially pass on the script with a quick phone call or short email. For many agents and managers, these are expected conversations. "Hey, Jake, thanks for sending over 'Trial by Fire.' It's a good read with a solid idea, but we're not really looking for courtroom dramas at the moment. Good luck with it!" That's a fairly "generic" pass that could apply to almost any film if you replace "courtroom drama" with an appropriate genre. But frequently, an agent will want a bit more substantive reaction: "But didn't you think the third act was amazing? Weren't you intrigued by the twist with the love interest?" Or, "I'm working with the writer on developing a new draft—since you thought this was a good idea, any thoughts on how to make it better if we want to resubmit?" Your executive needs that coverage readily available to be able to go point by point, if necessary.

Finally, it is very likely that if you end up in a position where you are doing coverage regularly, you will probably end up making a "mistake" or being out of synch with your employer's opinion or taste. Most executives expect this to happen every once in a while, and it should not be too much cause for concern. You're bound to love something that someone above you thinks is horrible, and you're definitely bound to pass on something that will end up getting made—perhaps even at your own company. As a reader, and later as an executive, I championed screenplays I still believe would make for amazing films, only to have my bosses look at me as if I were an alien life form. By the same token, I remember both reading and getting a live pitch for the film *My Big Fat Greek Wedding* and thinking it was basically the same romantic comedy I'd read 40 times that week, just with Greeks, and I advised that we pass on it. (I was far from the only person who passed on that project—in retrospect, an obvious mistake, as it ended up being a very unique, wonderful, and successful film!)

CHAPTER TAKEAWAYS

- Coverage needs to be efficient, consistent, and complete.
- Most coverage will be a "pass": exceptional work is rare.
- The coverage must be able to effectively substitute for reading the script.
- Specific companies will advise on whether readers should address external factors in their analysis.
- Readers must express strong, specific opinions without getting personal, dismissive, or disrespectful.

PRE-EXERCISE: READ A NEW SCRIPT

Find a new script from a script database and read it with the intention of completing a full set of coverage, according to the standards set forth in the full exercise that follows.

EXERCISE 5A: CREATE A COVER SHEET

Create a standard coverage "cover sheet" for yourself. Remember that even in the digital age, coverage is often printed out in hard copy for executive use (or at a job interview), so a well-formatted cover page is essential.

You can refer to the included sample or other samples you might find online (do a search for "coverage cover sheet" or "coverage format")—but do *not* simply download a predetermined template. **Make your own**—it's a good way of working with your preferred word processing program and learning how to use margins, tables, sections, etc. Think carefully about font selection and size, or how using bold letters or all caps might affect the delivery of information. Remember: simple and clear is more important than "unique" or stylish.

EXERCISE 5B: WRITE AN 800–900-WORD SYNOPSIS

You're off! Remember that some of my suggestions or guidelines I've just cited might not apply to your particular script for whatever reason: it's important that you connect your own critical instincts to a process and use the tools and skills you are comfortable with, especially on a first draft. If your first try ends up being too long, then looking at some of the suggestions might help you trim a few words here and there. As with all professional writing, shorter and more specific is always better than longer or more general.

By the same token, you are given three double-spaced pages: you've got more than enough room to describe the events and the characters effectively and objectively. Remember, the synopsis is not the place for critical judgment or commenting on the strengths or weaknesses of the script. Focusing on "just the facts" usually results in an initial draft of reasonable size.

EXERCISE 5C: WRITE A 500-WORD EVALUATION (COMMENTS)

Remember to use paragraphs effectively, and remember that your recommendation must be clearly stated in both the opening and closing paragraphs. You also might want to be sure that your comments are generally aligning with your cover sheet rubric.

POST-EXERCISE: SUBMIT/SHARE/ASSESS YOUR COVERAGE

If you are working in a classroom or virtual group, I suggest doing the coverage exercise *twice*. The first time, everyone in the group should read the same script, then share and compare coverage. The second time, they should each read different scripts, then share and compare coverage.

If you are working on your own, I suggest that you read two scripts and do two sets of coverage—without taking time to reflect on them until both are completed.

ASSESSING COVERAGE

Throughout this exercise, continue to reflect on the relationship between the coverage you read and the scripts they represent, particularly with coverage that someone else wrote. What did their coverage and comments get "right"? Where do you disagree, and to what degree does that affect your evaluation of the script? How might your company evaluate external elements in a way that isn't indicated in this more neutral coverage?

Whether you are assessing someone else's or your own coverage, you also should examine:

- Is the synopsis clear? If you are writing in a group, note how others chose to include or not include certain events, characters, or descriptions. How do those choices differ from yours? How does it affect your understanding of the story?
- Do the comments "line up" with both the events in the synopsis and also with the cover sheet rubric?
- How "balanced" are the comments? Particularly if you are reading coverage of a script you have not read, do you feel that you "know" the script and have a sense of its strengths and weaknesses?
- Does the writing overall focus on specific, important, and relevant details and observations?
- Does it "read easy," and where are the places where you had to "slow down" or "go back" to figure out what was going on?

FOR CLASSES: EXTENDED GROUP EXERCISE

With the production group you formed earlier, I suggest you build in the following exercise, which can continue in later chapters as you take these virtual projects through the production process. Depending on skill set and group size, you can take on more than one "sample" project, combine with other groups as coproducers, etc.

- If you completed the coverage exercise in this chapter, then everyone in your group should have generated a piece of coverage on a unique script. Share and trade that coverage with other groups in the course so that you have a substantial "coverage library."
- Among your group, assign equal amounts of coverage to each member. Read the coverage (do not read the scripts yet).
- In an initial "staff meeting" of no more than 30 minutes, everyone should give a brief report on the coverage they read, and indicate *one or two* scripts they intend to read in full. There may be discussion, as others in the meeting may have read one of the scripts.
- In a second staff meeting of no more than 45 minutes, everyone reports further on their selected reads. Everyone should "pitch" their top choice. The group executives then determine which one or two projects will get a "green light."
- Once a group's projects have been selected, each member should write a one- or two-sentence log line for each project. These may be shared in future group meetings or used in subsequent assignments.

CHAPTER 6

Advanced Coverage and Development
Ideas, Adaptations, Samples, and Solicitations

There are some additional writing practices in the process of development that are, for the most part, extensions or variations of script coverage. It's also at this part of the production phase that studios and producers need to begin to involve other people (directors, coproducers, actors, new writers, etc.) as creative partners, which often requires written materials to sell/pitch the idea. As you will see, the same basic skills you have already learned in the previous chapters will be applied in slightly new ways.

In this first part of this chapter, we'll talk about writing coverage for submissions other than screenplays (novels, plays, etc.), and "samples"—writing, directing, and other samples. The essential elements of this type of evaluation are the same as a traditional story report, but the way you approach your comments is usually very different.

The later part of the chapter will expand your imagination and develop your producer skills as you create "solicitations" of other entities, trying to persuade them to read and become involved with your project: having been constrained from dream-casting in your coverage, you will be encouraged to make lists of appropriate actors, directors, and other key talent.

SPECIAL COVERAGE: NON-SCREENPLAYS, SECOND READS, AND SAMPLES

As you undoubtedly have observed, a substantial number of feature length films and television series were based on something that existed prior to the screenplay. Take a look at the top box-office films or the shows with the highest ratings and most Emmy award nominations, and it's more likely than not they were based on a preexisting property. As a story analyst or someone who works in acquisition and/or development, it's just as likely that you might receive the "original" material as you might the screenplay adaptation to evaluate.

Thus, coverage of anything besides a screenplay requires you to provide a bit more in terms of how you create your synopsis and fashion your comments. Here are some examples of what to look for with these common forms of property submissions.

NOVELS AND MANUSCRIPTS

Most novels (whether published or in manuscript form) submitted for consideration are very likely to be driven by familiar narrative structures and compelling, interesting characters, and it's usually fairly easy to generate a synopsis in a fashion similar to that of a screenplay.

Obviously, there are some critical adjustments you may need to make to your process. First, characterization in a novel is often rendered in an *interior* fashion—we can *read* or understand characters' thoughts or motivations that they keep private or silent. For novels in which that is a substantial element, be sure to reveal all necessary thoughts and feelings in your synopsis, and use your comments to remark upon how easy it may or may not be to turn those thoughts and feelings into "action" or something that can be seen on-screen. There are a number of good online articles and interviews with professionals that offer writers pointers on how best to adapt screenplays from novels: even if you are not a writer, it would be beneficial to read a few of those just to have some idea about the key elements in that process and to distinguish between effective prose and effective screenwriting.

The other major adjustment is simply one of length: if you have a published novel of 500 or 600 pages, it very likely will have multiple plotlines and characters and might extend over a long period, or span the globe in terms of setting. Most companies will understand that you might need to go far beyond the standard 900 to 1,000 words for your synopsis. Condense the action as best as you can, but don't leave out major plotlines or characters.

The other element that is obviously going to be different are the comments. It's entirely possible that parts of the novel seem particularly cinematic while others don't—or perhaps the novel might be better for a series of films (such as a trilogy) or a television series. Your employer might be a company that specializes in adaptations, and should let you know what it considers workable, valuable, or desirable in terms of source material. Try to focus on the elements of the novel that have cinematic equivalencies: Is there dialogue that can be "lifted" from the book effectively? Is the story driven by cause-and-effect action, with characters making strong, active decisions? Is the fictional "universe" potentially engaging on a visual or conceptual level (i.e., an alien planet, a specific historical era)? Do you "like" the characters based on their actions and desires?

PLAYS

Stage plays have the benefit of having characters who typically have to "do something" or "take action," and in almost all cases have been very heavily "developed" in terms of dialogue and character. This has been the case throughout Hollywood history, as the industry has long turned to the stage as a way of finding "quality" material and talent (particularly in the form of writers and actors). Adolph Zukor's first company was called Famous Players because he was one of the first film producers to exploit the fame of actors and properties already well-known stage names. In fact, he founded the company with the Frohman Brothers, two well-known Broadway producers, and their earliest efforts included an adaptation of the popular stage play *The Count of Monte Cristo* starring James O'Neill, the well-known stage actor (and father of Eugene); and *The Loves of Queen Elizabeth* starring the most famous actress in the world, Sarah Bernhardt.

Today, you can watch the 1931 film *Anna Christie* with Greta Garbo, and literally read along with Eugene O'Neill's stage play, which is at moments a word-for-word transcription (although the film is credited to legendary screenwriter Frances Marion). Films based on Shakespeare's plays may heavily edit the texts, but ultimately are "branded" as quality because of their word-for-word use of some of the most revered dramatic writing in cultural history. One hilarious—but very likely apocryphal—exception is the 1929 version of *The Taming of the Shrew* starring Douglas Fairbanks and Mary Pickford, the first sound-era production of that play. Supposedly, the credits of the film stated, "Play by William Shakespeare, with additional dialogue by Sam Taylor." Taylor was the film's director; the "myth" of his "additional dialogue" credit has most recently been debunked, as there is no evidence that such a credit was ever actually screened with the film. But it's still a great story.

Most stage plays are also often written to run at between 90–120 minutes (not counting intermissions), so the "size" and tempo of the story is usually equivalent to cinematic narrative traditions. What often limits the appeal of stage productions is that there is a lot of talking/dialogue, and a limited number of characters, locations, or settings. For example, the play *Steel Magnolias* has six characters who talk about their lives while inside a home garage-turned-beauty salon in Natchitoches, Louisiana, with "real-time" scenes taking place over the course of a couple of years. While it is a perfectly engaging and effective play on stage, writer Robert Harling and the film's producers realized that movie audiences might feel stifled simply watching a few characters on a single set, and "opened up" the setting to include more characters and locations around the town.

Your coverage for a play would probably want to indicate the production's "opening up" possibilities: Are there other characters referred to who aren't seen? Is the world just "outside" the stage play one that is potentially interesting? Might some of the scenes in the play still be effective if they were set in a different character's home, or at the county fair, or outside instead of inside?

It's also helpful, if you get this kind of assignment consistently, to look at previous examples of great plays brought to the screen, including "straight" plays, comedies, and musicals: high-profile adaptations—from *The Odd Couple* to *Steel Magnolias* to *Fences* to *Into the Woods* to *Hedwig and the Angry Inch*—often provide strong examples of what "does" and "does not" work in terms of making the transition from stage to screen.

REMAKES OF PREVIOUS FILMS AND TV SHOWS

In the early 1990s, Hollywood studios started to "reboot" properties that had been popular a generation earlier at an alarming rate. This had always been something of a practice—for example, there are several "official" versions of the film *A Star is Born*, each made about 20 years apart (with the recent fifth one coming after a gap of about 40 years). But the early

'90s success of reboots such as *Freaky Friday*, *The Brady Bunch Movie*, *101 Dalmatians*, *Charlie's Angels*, and *The Addams Family*, among many others, seemed to open the floodgates for remakes and adaptations that continues well into the present day.

Creating coverage about something that was already made is a curious exercise, and often depends greatly on what you are given as a submission. Some producers might send a script that updates or modifies an old movie or TV show, with the idea that the executive or reader will both watch the original *and* read the new script. In other cases, a studio executive might remember a favorite movie from childhood, and submit the film for consideration simply to see if a staff reader agrees that maybe there is something that might have some present-day value.

It's important to remember that a lot of people (both in the industry and regular moviegoers) have very passionate feelings about remakes and reboots. One common saying in Hollywood is "never remake a classic," but so-called "classics" are remade all the time, sometimes "officially," sometimes in slightly modified form. The science fiction film *Outland*, made in 1981, copies the story of *High Noon*; Clint Eastwood's *Pale Rider* has an almost identical structure and subject matter as the western classic *Shane*, replacing a key young male supporting character with a teenage female. Todd Haynes' *Velvet Goldmine* is (formally speaking) a glorious homage to *Citizen Kane*. They even tried to remake one of the most beloved classics of all time, *Casablanca*, for television—twice!

Also, companies will often assume that something has value just because it was made 20 years ago and people remember the name of the property. That's very likely what drove the makers of *S.W.A.T.* in 2003, a film based on a mid-1970s television show that ran for two largely unremarkable seasons. That's not to say the film doesn't have its merits—the duties of special weapons and tactics teams are inherently dramatic and lend itself toward the genre of crime drama. But all that most people remembered from the 1970s TV series is that it had a cool theme song—it wasn't a series that had much cultural presence, was little seen in syndication, and in fact wasn't even available on home video until the 2003 movie came out.

Finally, previously sold properties might have franchise potential (as is the case with novels, comic books, etc.). Some companies might use "franchise value" as a key evaluation point, in which case you might overlook the specifics of the original text and think more broadly about the property's potential appeal across multiple platforms. Regardless of what the characters experience, is their "situation" interesting? Are there compelling, potentially familiar backstories or iconic moments that can be creatively reimagined? Would the presence of new technologies make this something that could be updated in a creative way (*Mission: Impossible*)? Would the storyline be enhanced by a more visibly diverse cast of characters (*Star Trek*)? Can we approach it as a "period piece" that might give us new insight and perspectives into our historical past (*Wonder Woman*)? Can we turn it into a musical told from the perspective of a previously known character (*Wicked*)?

ARTICLES, BIOGRAPHIES, DOCUMENTARIES, AND 'REAL-LIFE' STORIES

One of the best films about both the screenwriting and development process is *Adaptation*, written by Charlie Kaufman and Donald Kaufman (according to the screen credits), and directed by Spike Jonze. Any script by Kaufman (who also wrote *Being John Malkovich*, referenced in *Adaptation*) is almost always a bizarre puzzle that would challenge most script readers, with multiple timelines or versions of reality, meta-narrative techniques such as voice-over and repetition, and a lot of dense, complicated ideas about how human beings struggle to relate to one another.

In *Adaptation*, we see a writer struggling to extract a cinematic story from a very difficult source novel, which was itself based on a magazine article. (This is similar to describing *Citizen Kane* as "about an old guy who dies" or *Jaws* as "about a few dudes who go fishing.") Like the main character, a real-life story analyst often is given material that is not yet a screenplay—and may not even be in narrative form—and asked to evaluate the property's long-term potential in terms of cinema (movie, series, etc.). Again, it is very likely that a company will have specific thoughts about what it is looking for. One company I worked for told me that it was more interested in "situations" and "settings"—is the time period or location interesting, does it seem like a dramatic or potentially interesting milieu? Another company asked for comments on whether there were specific characters or people (often real-life figures) who could be imagined as worthy of movie-star portrayal.

What you as the story analyst has to be prepared for is the tremendous variety that might be coming your way. One week you might get something that may be very limited in scope and barely fleshed out, such as a 1,200-word newspaper article about a dog that found his way home after getting lost on a family vacation. The next week you might have to analyze something with immense depth and detail, such a 10-hour documentary TV series about the history of North American native tribes. I worked for one company in which a long-term development project was trying to develop a project based on the life of a briefly famous American novelist. For research, I read all of the novelist's publications (many of them out of print) and three very different biographies trying to help a colleague figure out a way to set up a biopic project. We didn't have a single property we were looking at—just the general idea there was a good cinematic story in this person's life. (It never got made, but I'm withholding details because I still think it's a great idea. You can find your own great idea from history in the upcoming exercise, if you wish.)

For submissions such as these, your employer would probably allow you to be a bit more imaginative in your comments in terms of making suggestions and offering perspective on how the property might be adapted. Likewise, your synopsis might be more of a description that requires more "framing" language than usual, since the "story" points may be less visible. ("Chapter Two focuses on the era of 1965–1973, looking at how fluctuations in the stock market and a shift toward fiscal conservatism impacted the way in which government funds were allocated, plunging some tribal councils into chaos.")

Finally, it's reasonable to assume that a "pass" or "consider" recommendation is going to come with a lot of qualifiers (this could be said of most non-screenplay submissions). Don't struggle too much with having to split hairs on the "yes" or "no" of these submissions: everyone understands that those decisions are going to be made based on elements that a first-read story analyst most likely does not have any knowledge, such as an actor or filmmaker who may be involved or interested, an established writer who has a pitch based on the general idea, etc.

FINDING TALENT: WRITING AND DIRECTING SAMPLES

Development executives are not only looking to develop properties such as screenplays and novels, but also professional creative talent such as writers and directors: creating a successful project with someone often leads to further successful collaborations. Also, the same agents and agencies that submit screenplays also represent writers who are available for new assignments and directors looking for projects to join. Very few projects are actually originated with the final writer and director involved (such as the most successful film of all time, *Gone with the Wind*). We'll talk some about his process in more detail later in the chapter. But for now, I'll just mention a few things about creating coverage for something in which you are evaluating the creative talent, not the property itself.

To some extent, every screenplay is a **writing sample,** and in the course of doing "normal" coverage, you're very likely to encounter a screenplay that is a "pass" for obvious reasons for your company, but is exceptionally well written. A sample final comment might read: "Since the company is not looking for romantic comedies at the moment, this submission is a pass; but it should be considered a strong writing sample for future assignments."

An "official" writing sample is most likely a project that has already been optioned elsewhere or is unavailable for whatever reason. To familiarize a producer or studio executive with a writer's talent, samples are often submitted and reviewed by a story analyst. It's possible the writer is being considered for a specific project already in development, or that there may be other projects about to become available.

Thus, the coverage on a writing sample engages essentially the same process as regular script coverage: the synopsis should be the same, while the comments ask and answer the questions "Is this person a good screenwriter?" and "Why"? As with regular coverage, you can choose to break down the writer in terms of general creative tools (dialogue, characters, action), or by highlighting stylistic elements that are exceptionally unique (i.e., complex female characters, a strong visual sense, consistently laugh-out-loud jokes, etc.).

Sometimes writing samples are presented in the form of the finished film. If you know anything about the filmmaking process, you probably know that the difference between a film script and the film that ends up getting made is about as different as reading a cake recipe and eating the cake. So it's something of a flawed and imperfect process to watch a movie and effectively evaluate the credited writer, and everyone in the business knows that.

In the case of a finished film or program being submitted as a sample, a synopsis may or may not be necessary, but again, your comments should be as specific to the writing as possible. Focus on the elements that you can be reasonably sure originated with the screenwriter: the words spoken by the characters, the actions the characters take, the setting and premise of the story. Answer the question: What can we identify as the writer's strengths and weaknesses that might help us determine a future writer-for-hire assignment? Why might I be interested in reading a different script by this same writer?

After you have covered that basic information, you should then focus on the *depth* of the creative world being represented. By "depth," I mean the layers of details that the film eventually represents—this is where you can acknowledge the directing, acting, production design, etc. in a more general way: the script obviously inspired some talented people to work together and create something fascinating. That usually doesn't happen with a "bad" script or an incompetent writer. If the final product is better described as generic or underwhelming, then perhaps the core elements of the screenplay aren't as strong.

You'll bring that same basic process to the exercise of covering a **directing sample**. In some cases, the writer and director are the same person, and you might find yourself writing comments that are half focused on the writing skills and half on the directing. While obviously those two things are going to inform each other substantially, you want to be sure you isolate them a bit, not just evaluate the subject as a general "filmmaker."

What differs with talking about the evaluation of a director, obviously, is that you will make reference to a slightly different set of creative tools. Directors are typically expected to supervise a final work in which all of the creative decisions contribute to the telling of the story in a consistent and believable manner. That usually means respecting the traditional conventions of narrative filmmaking—i.e., making sure the editing, sound, cinematography, and performances are properly executed, interesting, and clearly focused. You may be looking at a directing sample of an average script—a typical horror film, or a martial arts-driven action-adventure—so be sure not to fault the director for the characters being poorly drawn or the overall setting and plot for being too generic. Even with a mediocre script, you should be able to tell that a director has been able to master the basics of their craft.

Remember as well that it's not uncommon to get a directing sample from a style or form that is not a feature film: you might be looking at commercials, documentaries, music videos, or episodic television. Your comments should acknowledge that the sample might be limited in scope—you can't really talk about how well the director might handle an action sequence simply by watching a talking-heads documentary—but try to focus on what the director's work shows, rather than what it doesn't.

I have also, on rare occasion, looked at "reels" or samples of works from editors, writers, cinematographers, and filmmakers in general. In fact, I first discovered the television series *The Sopranos* when the agent for cinematographer Alik Sakharov sent our office the first four episodes of the show (on VHS tape) as samples of his work as a DP (and potentially as a director, and he has since become one of the industry's most high-profile series directors). At the time, I didn't subscribe to HBO, and in general wasn't a big fan of "Mafia" films. Additionally, a very funny comedy called *Analyze This* with Robert De Niro and Billy Crystal had just come out, and was very similar in premise to *The Sopranos* (tough mob boss goes to therapy). So while I had heard good things about the show, it was well off my radar and didn't seem "necessary" to watch, at first.

But watching the first four episodes in a row was my first TV "binge," and soon I was an HBO subscriber. I don't know if that would have occurred had I seen the episodes one week at a time—so the "sample" assignment ended up turning my head around completely in terms of what was possible on series television. Meanwhile, I had nothing but good things to say in my coverage about the incredible and versatile cinematography of Sakharov, who established the show's expressive but realistic visual tone right from the first episode.

Particularly if you have training or experience in a technical form, be sure to let your employer know that you can be an effective scout for other forms of production talent. Very high-profile readers (and most story department executives) are often asked to "read" for specific star acting assignments, or to provide input for a possible director during a creative meeting. Understanding how cinematographers, production designers, editors, and other film professionals effectively do their jobs, and what that talent might mean for a project in development, is obviously a skill that can bear fruit for you as a producer or production executive.

TALENT LISTS AND SOLICITATION LETTERS

Think of this next portion of the chapter as the "fantasy baseball" segment: this is more of a chance to "play" at being an executive while learning a few basic skills. Of course, until you are really in the room where these decisions are made, you can't learn much about how the process of contacting, recruiting, and securing talent actually works, since the process varies so much from project to project. Agents, managers, lawyers, and other experts in contract law can provide far more examples of industry standards and practices that most inform the relationship between artists and a production than someone as myself can within the framework of this textbook. While there are exercises here, they are more designed for you to have some fun and practice your letter-writing skills than they are absolutely identical to what might happen in the real world.

Almost anyone who is passionate enough about film and TV storytelling is probably an amateur casting director: actors, directors, writers, producers, and even cinematographers, all have their wish list of favorite performers who they would absolutely love to work with on a project. If we imagine ourselves as part of the entertainment industry, we playfully indulge ourselves thinking that if I write this female lead just the right way, then maybe Amy Adams or Beyoncé or Anne Hathaway will be the star. The grandfather is a Sam Elliot-type! And wouldn't Judi Dench be amazing as Santa Claus? (The answer is yes, Judi Dench is amazing as anything.)

At some point, if indeed a project is looking for actors, directors, or other production talent to be attached, there usually has to be a *pitch* (yet another pitch!), request, or solicitation that is "angled" at the talent. Talent agents and managers will obviously be very involved in what projects they recommend their clients consider, so someone in that agent's office (and the agents themselves) would very likely read the script before it ever gets sent to the performer. As such, you need to be able to craft a letter that reflects this angle and pitch.

You've done this sort of thing before when you created a cover letter for your friend's script in Chapter 4: the overall goal here is roughly the same, a short, direct, and clear description of the project (usually including a short log line), along with something that reminds the reader of the particular angle, concluded with a request for action or response. (See the sample that follows.)

For a talent solicitation pitch letter, you would probably want to know something about that person's career and where they are in terms of taking on new projects. Let's assume you know the person is available for work sometime next year, roughly in line with your production plans for the movie—and that your movie isn't going to require anything unusual (i.e., moving overseas for several months, being available for shooting over an extended period of time, etc.). You simply want this person to read the script and get excited about being part of it: you want her or him to not only like the script, but it's important for you to show the individual that they belongs and feels some kind of "connection" to the script.

That might mean referencing other roles the actor has played that are either: a) similar to the character in this script, or b) completely different than anything the actor has done before. It might mean pointing out to a director that your script has similar properties to previous projects, or some stylistic or artistic connection to another filmmaker or filmmaking tradition. It might mean knowing that the story takes place in rural North Carolina, and the prospective producing partner has roots in the rural South. You don't have enough time or space in this brief form of communication to explore too much nuance or detail, so highlighting the key elements that are most directly related to the person is important.

This is also a moment to perhaps talk about appropriate flattery and praise. I have had to write letters to the agents and managers of some of the most talented people I have ever seen work in the industry—and sometimes directly to those people. I've also had to write letters to well-established professionals whose work I did not like for whatever reason, so this issue of how to contact and communicate with people you "like" or "dislike" often comes up as you work in the industry. And, of course, like or dislike is something you know as a fan from a distance, not from personal experience with that person.

Unless you have an established personal relationship with the individual you are trying to solicit, then it's immensely important that you keep your tone professional. That doesn't mean that you can't be positive about someone's work—but it does means you should avoid being negative at all costs (i.e., don't write, "Hey, sorry that your last film bombed, but here's one that's sure to be a winner.") It's also best if you connect any positive comment or praise with the project that you are pitching: "We're all such big fans of the work you did last year in *Ocean's 8*, and we think that the role of 'Kara' in our script requires your wonderful ability to be both tough and funny at the same time."

THE SCREEN'S MISTAKE IS THE STAGE'S GAIN—
THE CURIOUS CASE OF THE *WICKED* MOVIE THAT WASN'T

One of the most impressive cultural phenomena of the past generation is the beloved Broadway musical *Wicked*. A clever reimagining of the universe of L. Frank Baum's "Oz" from the perspective of one of the most notorious villains in storytelling history has been delighting audiences around the world since 2003. The original production won three Tony and seven Drama Desk awards, and a Grammy for Best Musical Show Album. It is the second-highest-grossing Broadway show ever (trailing only *The Lion King*), and in 2020 will likely pass *Les Miserables* to be the fifth-longest running show in Broadway history.

Many fans of *Wicked* are very likely aware that the original concept and story are based on a novel by a writer named Gregory Maguire, whose novel *Wicked: The Life and Times of the Wicked Witch of the West* was published by HarperCollins in 1995. Maguire had written a number of novels for children, but *Wicked* was his first stab at "adult" work. (He's since written several novels for older readers that take new approaches to classic material, including three other books in the *Wicked* universe, and new takes on Cinderella [*Confessions of an Ugly Stepsister*] and Snow White [*Mirror, Mirror*]).

But what many fans don't know is how *Wicked* as a musical almost never happened—and only because what looked like it might have been a great feature film got lost in the development process. My colleague Stephen Moore has been a literary agent, representing the sales of books for film and television, for more than 20 years. He joined his current firm, the Paul Kohner Agency, in the mid-90s, when Gregory Maguire was one of its top clients. He tells the story of *Wicked* as one where despite some disastrous turns along the way, the right thing still managed to happen.

"The musical is very different from the book," explains Moore. "The book is a lengthy and rather deep treatise on the nature of good and evil," he says, with a complicated plot that is much more akin to the form of the sprawling, episodic structure of the Oz books than reminiscent of the standard three-act "feature film." "My mentor, Gary Salt, tried to get the manuscript sold in 1994, but he didn't get anywhere," remembers Moore. "Then, right around Halloween in 1995, an absolutely glowing review came out in the *Los Angeles Times*, by Robert Rodi. Suddenly, because everyone in L.A. reads the *Times*, we had everyone calling, including people who had passed on it the previous year."

Very quickly, three production companies emerged as the top bidders. Eventually, the rights to make the movie version of *Wicked* were sold to Universal, brought to the company by actress-producer Demi Moore, who was one of the top actresses in Hollywood. The head of production at Universal was Marc Platt, who worked with the producers and screenwriter Linda Woolverton to write a screenplay based on the novel.

"They developed two drafts over three years," said Moore. "After the first draft, some higher-ups at Universal read the script and said, 'Wait a minute—this isn't a kid's movie!'" They asked that a second draft be more kid-friendly, and to play up the story as a romantic adventure between Elphaba and Fiero, getting further and further away from the novel's more subtle and mature "political" elements. By the time the second draft had come in, mixed opinions about how to further develop the screenplay resulted in a stall. With Platt stepping down as head of production, it seemed very likely that the project would be shelved. This isn't an uncommon practice: When a high-profile executive leaves a company, it is often an excuse to end projects that are proving "difficult" to develop.

But about that time, noted composer Stephen Schwartz happened to read the book and saw the possibilities for a Broadway musical. He approached Platt, who informed him that although Universal had bought the *film* rights, the rights to a *stage* adaptation were still available. "Our agency made a second deal for the stage and musical rights, with Universal and Marc Platt producing, but the nonmusical project went dormant," remembers Stephen Moore.

Universal would keep the option on the film version of *Wicked* for a while longer, but eventually the option ran out. By that time, Gregory Maguire's next novel (*Confessions of an Ugly Stepsister*) had been adapted into a well-received TV movie by a well-established Canadian production company, Alliance Atlantis, and broadcast on ABC. "They were workshopping the stage version of *Wicked* when the option came up," Moore explains, "and Alliance Atlantis bought the option. It then sold the film option to ABC, who still controls them to this day. They've tried several times to put together a *Wicked* project for the screen, but at this point nothing has made it."

Meanwhile, of course, those overlooked stage rights lead to the juggernaut of *Wicked* as a Broadway musical, and it's hard to imagine a nonmusical version getting made for screens. As to why the project didn't take as a feature, Moore can only speculate. "It's entirely possible that not all of the executives at Universal had time to read the book when they bought it—they may have only read the review, and also felt comfortable trusting the producers' judgment and track record," he says. Still, Moore agrees with the suggestion that taking the time to at least read the studio's coverage of the book probably would have helped those involved have a better idea about the book's tone, and not expect a first draft that would be "for kids." The impulsive decision to get involved in a "hot property" adaptation—no matter how well intentioned and how solid the material—ended up nearly going awry because the usually careful process of analysis, coverage, and story notes was rushed or compromised.

CHAPTER TAKEAWAYS

- Coverage for submissions other than screenplays may vary in length, detail, or perspective (i.e., coverage of a directing or writing sample); be sure you ask your employer if there are any restrictions or unusual parameters required for these materials.
- Evaluating talent (such as a writer or director) requires the analyst to understand how all filmmaking processes work together. Screenwriting should be considered the framework from which all other creative elements are organized; directing should be seen as the combination of all creative elements. Be sure your comments reflect how all elements work together with the individual's specific role and contribution.
- Soliciting talent requires that you have an understanding of your subject's recent and current career goals and needs, not just your subject's "type" or experience on projects you want them to be involved in. You should entice the person to work with you because it is the right thing to do now (and in the immediate future), not because it's just what they've done before.

EXERCISE 6A: ADAPTATION COVERAGE

Find a property that is *not* a screenplay—check the list just cited—and write coverage for that property. Be sure that you aren't covering an "idea"—you need a primary text (something published or produced) that you are considering specifically.

If you choose, repeat this exercise specifically with a potential submission from the last category listed—documentation or accounting of a real-life event, person, or historical moment that has not yet been converted into "dramatic" form. This is really a chance to practice some advanced development skills: Can you find something that might become the next *Erin Brockovich* or *Masters of Sex* or *Dirty John*? As much as it will stretch your basic coverage skills, it will give you the opportunity to display even more of your creative producing instincts.

If you are working in a group, share your coverage and talk with your group members about the various ideas, and the aspects of the written coverage that most effectively highlight a property's potential and limitations.

EXERCISE 6B: WRITING OR DIRECTING SAMPLE

For this exercise, it is appropriate to work from material that has already been produced (or to work with an available or published screenplay). You also might want to challenge yourself by looking at a sample from media other than feature film (i.e., a specific episode of a television series, a short film, documentary, etc.).

If you are in a working group that has selected "go" projects, you might want to specifically include in your coverage how the writer or director of the sample work might be an appropriate fit for one of the scripts currently in "development."

EXERCISE 6C: SOLICITATION LETTER

Write a solicitation letter to an agent or manager who represents your "dream" performer for a specific role in one of the scripts you read or a practice project. For the purposes of this assignment, assume that the person you are writing to is someone you have communicated with before—there is no reason to "introduce" yourself or explain who you are.

Format your letter in an appropriate business format—do *not* simply compose an informal email. If possible, print the letter out on paper and make sure it looks professional and is free of typos, poor formatting, and grammatical errors. Be sure your letter includes a very short description of both the project and the part available.

ALTERNATE ASSIGNMENT: The agent or manager has asked you to include a cover letter addressed directly to the talent (your dream director, cast member, or other major creative role, such as cinematographer, editor, composer, or production designer). Again, there is no need to introduce yourself—assume the person will be expecting the submission: but remember that you don't have an established personal relationship to the person reading the letter.

EXERCISE 6C: SAMPLE

April 19, 20XX

Phillipa Kane
Markham Kane Winslow Talent 4000
Skyline Drive, Suite 320
Los Angeles, CA 90064
Via email: pkane@mkwtalent.com

Dear Phillipa:

I'm very excited to be sending you a copy of a new comedy, *Hail to the Chump*, which is currently set up at Purview Pictures with Adam McKay and Will Ferrell set to produce—we're out to Jamie Babbitt to direct. We think this is a great role for Jon Hamm and would love to set up a meeting with you and Jon to discuss the project.

Hail to the Chump tells the story of Mitch Mickins, a recently unemployed circus clown and law school dropout. Through a series of misunderstandings, his name is put forward by a feeble-minded senator as a possible Supreme Court candidate. What starts out as a minor media frenzy blows up into a national crisis as Mitch gets closer to the donning judicial robes and becoming the first "regular guy" on the nation's highest court.

The other producers and I agree that Jon's talent for comedy has been underexploited, and that he's capable of giving the role of Mitch a lot of intelligence and heart along with pulling off the slapstick. I've always been impressed by Jon's physicality, and he'd have a real opportunity to show his range in a role that is likely to surprise and delight his fans.

Assuming we have our director signed by the end of the month, we're looking at a five-week shoot, with one week of location in DC and the rest in Atlanta, aiming for a wrap in April and release by the end of the year.

Please feel free to forward this to Jon, and I hope to hear from you soon.

Sincerely,

CHAPTER 7

Welcome to 'Development Hell'

Story Notes

EMBRACE THE DEMON INSIDE YOU: WHY DEVELOPMENT HELL IS NECESSARY

It's common for screenwriters, filmmakers, and producers to complain about the process of development: "I had a brilliant script, and then the studio ruined it!" Of course, the process of development is at times frustrating and laborious (though most of the filmmaking process can be described this way). Bad decisions are undoubtedly made, and projects that a studio put a lot of money into never make it before the cameras. I'd like to say plainly and simply that ultimately it's all worth it and the best films get made, or that everyone in the business is "trying their best," but that would be disingenuous: horrible films get made, great scripts flounder on the shelf, and rivals often compete for power by putting more effort into personal projects and ignoring the work that others are more likely to get credit for.

I will say, however, that if you do pursue a career in development, I hope you are lucky enough to work with the kind of people that I did. It's not that we were all best friends or that any one of us are or were brilliant people, but we tended to have mutual respect and were generally positive about the success of others in or close to the company. We could see that sometimes our more senior colleagues took a chance on something that turned out to be a bad decision (see my sidebar story about the development of *Good Will Hunting*). I also saw people immediately senior to me make excellent decisions and bring their absolute professional best to an amazing array of projects for years, but not actually get any one of them made. I've also seen projects scuttled overnight because someone broke confidence about an actor's involvement, so I have been very close to both success and also disappointment stories. If you are around people who respect you, and who demonstrate a consistently strong, professional work ethic, you're more likely to be able to survive the ups and downs of the development process without condemning it as inherently evil. Being around people you cannot trust, or who consistently behave in a manner you find unprofessional or counterproductive, is much more likely to leave you with the impression that the process is deeply flawed and antithetical to good creative practice.

It should also be pointed out that some screenplays or projects don't require much "development" from a story perspective: usually, if a studio or producer has committed to a screenplay, it is because they believe in the value of the story and the way it is told in its current form. The more changes a producer has to make to get the script "ready," the more likely that producer will pass or ask the writer for another draft before committing time and money to the project.

Instead, the rewrites, new drafts, passes, polishes, and other forms of revision are often required for logistical or practical reasons related to production. The script says it is set on the border in California, but can it be the border in Texas because we can get a deal on a production facility near El Paso? The lead is written as a "Tom Cruise-type," but Denzel Washington might be interested—can we create a character that would be more appealing to him? The script was originally written three years ago—can we update the cultural references?

Since those things need to be done anyway, producers and studios also look for revisions to improve any element of the script that might need some work. A script might have dialogue that is very "on the nose" (obvious) or lack humor that might add some dimension; it might have a confusing series of events, or there might be characters whose narrative function is not clear or underexplored. You might recognize these observations as the kind of thing that might have been noted in the initial coverage comments. If a property has been purchased, the initial coverage—with perhaps a *second read* report (see later)—will follow the script into the first phases of development as a set of guidelines for making the script better. Development takes those initial instincts about what is not working and turns them into specific recommendations or actions designed to address those issues.

The other thing that complicates the process of development is the number of people involved, many of whom may be in different camps (various production companies, studios, the director/creative team, individual producers, actors, agents, and managers, etc.). This is where learning how to create documents that reflect collaboration and consensus becomes very valuable: what is most important is that despite differences of opinion, all parties involved can have an understanding of what is being discussed and what is being suggested. It's very unlikely that everyone who has a legitimate stake and opinion will ever be in the same room at the same time, so the "written record" and consensus recommendations are that much more important to keep the project moving forward. The greater number of people involved, by necessity, the slower the process becomes—something that would obviously be frustrating for a writer or director who is just dying to get the film in the can. Keeping the project "on track" during development is a producer's key job, and the story notes are one of the crucial elements that helps map, measure, and expedite that forward motion.

SECOND READS

As cited earlier, it's not uncommon for a story analyst to be asked to do a second read on a script that another analyst has already covered. Perhaps a development executive knows that the second analyst is very good at breaking down certain genres, or has life experience that might positively inform the reading of a script (someone with a military background to read a script about troops in warfare, for example). Perhaps there is disagreement among executives about the project and they want a fresh opinion or two to get a better consensus.

Typically, a second read is "comments only," and it's very unlikely you'll be given the previous analyst's comments or synopsis. If nothing else, this means that your writing time is reduced, and you can focus your initial read more on your conclusions rather than worrying about which plot details to include in the synopsis. Make no mistake—your comments should still be just as specific, so plot details are still important! You also might want to ask your employer if there is anything you should be looking for or be commenting specifically upon.

I'll digress momentarily and say that I've been in situations where development executives, with the absolute best intentions, have asked readers to supply coverage with a specific recommendation, effectively saying, "I really need positive coverage of this, because it's a project I believe in and I want to get a green light from my boss." While this may seem like "breaking the rules" of coverage being objective, I think it's actually up to the individual reader on how to process that request. In a way, your boss is "pitching" you on his or her take, and asking you to understand that your job is to reflect the best interests of the company, rather than your opinion. Reflecting on my own experience, I never felt I was ever asked to "lie" in my coverage—I just understood that perhaps my critical bar, in some situations, should have been lowered a bit.

One quick example: Early in my career, my immediate boss read a script by an up-and-coming female comedy writer—a script my boss absolutely fell in love with. One of our better readers had written some generally positive coverage, but my boss saw something a little better than that and asked me to read the script. "This is going to be a hit movie," she said. I read the log line—a high school comedy about competitive cheerleading. Now, if there's one thing my friends know about me, it's that I dislike high school social life and high school cheerleaders almost equally, and would have little reason to want to see a movie about that subject. I read the script, however, from my boss's perspective, looking for what she saw in it beyond just the basic elements of the script. What she saw, of course, was a film with multiple female characters of different backgrounds absolutely dedicated to the very difficult art of cheerleading, and the implications of their actions that have nothing to do with stupid boys and getting a date for the prom. The script was *Bring It On*, one of the first films to successfully engage a growing market of young, modern women, and the inspiration for many sequels and copycat franchises that have influenced the lives of female viewers for a generation. Sadly, my boss and I weren't involved, as another company ultimately bought and produced the script. But had she handed me the script with no comment, who knows how I might have viewed it? It was appropriate that she, in this case, had actively "interfered" with my process to shape my opinion. I suppose if I had genuinely hated the script I would have been honest and told her so, but I was predisposed to like it because of her pitch.

If you are ultimately interested in being a producer or executive in development, second read-style comments are an excellent skill to develop. Just as a prospective new story analyst might be asked to read a script and offer comments, so too might someone being interviewed for a staff or executive position be asked to simply "jot a few notes down" about a specific screenplay. If your basic coverage skills are up to snuff, then you should be able to handle that assignment, and being used to writing slightly "advanced" development notes will give you a leg up on those less experienced.

GOOD WILL HUNTING

One of the more interesting "close-up" experiences I had with a now-beloved film was my proximity to the acquisition and development of *Good Will Hunting*. I confess that I can't speak to any particulars about how decisions were made, and the film's creators, Ben Affleck and Matt Damon, have already spoken in very colorful terms about their experiences in getting the film bought, put into turnaround, and finally made in a way that they could be proud of.[1]

This proved an important moment for me, however, because I already had a connection with Affleck, having worked together on the film *Dazed and Confused* in the summer of 1992. Ben was one of many very talented people who was relatively unknown when making *Dazed and Confused* and we were all about the same age and at the same point in our careers. Most of us who lived elsewhere were staying at the same hotel in Austin, and we became close in a summer camp sort of way. Ben was one of the actors who really seemed to enjoy inhabiting his character, an older bully, as did his colleague Cole Hauser, and they would taunt each other mercilessly with playful banter between takes or late night in the hotel lounge.

But when I interviewed Affleck in private to write his bio for the film's press kit, I found him to be a very mature, experienced actor who took his work and his career very seriously. Ben had been acting professionally since he was eight, and was clearly absorbing a lot about the filmmaking process that was inspiring him to think about his talents beyond acting. It was one of the more delightful and surprising conversations I had working on that film, and it revealed a side of him that went far beyond the "bully" acting persona he was cultivating for the film.

Two years later, while working as a freelance story analyst at Castle Rock Entertainment, I was given a script with no title or author information on the cover sheet. It was an "emergency" overnight read, and I was told I was one of a select few readers at the company to be reading what was clearly a "hot" script. It was long—about 130 pages— and it was structurally a bit complicated. It was the story of a young, street-raised Boston

---

1 *Boston Magazine* has a wonderful oral history of the project with Affleck, Damon, and producer Chris Moore, at https://www.bostonmagazine.com/arts-entertainment/2013/01/02/good-will-hunting-oral-history/.

youth who had a gift for mathematics and was being recruited by a secret government organization. But at the same time, it was an examination of a young man growing up, dealing with the demons from his past, falling in love, and moving on from a group of friends who were holding him back. My comments were well over a page long, as I was truly divided on whether the film would succeed as written. Ultimately, I gave it a "Very qualified pass," simply because I felt another draft would be necessary before seeing the film's true value.

But what I made sure to put in the notes was how exceptional was the writing, particularly in regard to the characters. My comments read, in part: "I don't know who these writers are, but they talk the way that young men in their early twenties talk." I was specifically thinking that "these writers must know Ben Affleck and Cole Hauser, because this is exactly like a scene they would act out with each other."

The film, of course, was *Good Will Hunting*, and ultimately Castle Rock bought the script. That decision was far above my head—I was still just a freelance analyst—so I didn't know the fate of that unnamed script until a couple of months later, when Castle Rock released the film *Before Sunrise*, directed by Richard Linklater, who had made *Dazed and Confused*. The Los Angeles premiere for the new movie included a number of *Dazed* cast and crew members who lived in L.A., and it was at a party afterward that I got to catch up with Ben Affleck. He was beaming when he told me, "Matt and I sold a script!" When he learned I worked for Castle Rock, he said, "That's who is buying our script!" The next day I went to my boss, and said, "Hey, I ran into Ben Affleck, and he said we are buying his script. Can I read it?" She looked at me, blinked, and said, "You already have!" At that moment, I remembered the script from two months earlier, and it all made sense—of course that script sounded like Ben Affleck, because it WAS Ben Affleck!

A few weeks later, as I was leaving my office, I ran into Ben in the lobby of the building; he had just parked on the street and was running into a meeting. We didn't have long to chat, but I said, "Oh, hey, I read your script, I was one of the readers who really liked it" (not "exactly" admitting that I had technically passed). He got a huge smile on his face and said, "We just got paid! I just bought that car, because you said yes!" He gestured to a new black SUV outside. Of course, he knew that my decision about the script was far from the most important one—far, far, FAR from it—but it gave us a special connection to be part of that moment when his career went from one gear to another.

Over the next year or so, my run-ins with Ben (usually accompanied by Matt Damon) were not quite as genial. They had initially been very excited to work with Castle Rock, which was known to be artist-friendly, and gave the filmmakers it worked with great leeway. It was one of the reasons it was a nice company to work for, and even when these filmmaker-driven projects weren't successful, we all tended to feel as if the writers, directors, and producers we worked with felt empowered to make the most important creative decisions. But as has been well-documented, the executives at Castle Rock felt that the key obstacle for the script was the tension between the international spy recruitment film and the "coming-of-age" story. To their credit, Matt and Ben understood this was an important creative decision, and agreed that a new draft could be more unified. They met with a number of veteran filmmakers, including Castle Rock founder Rob Reiner and Oscar-winning screenwriter William Goldman, and the decision was made to minimize the spy story and play up the development and growth of Will's character.

As they began to rewrite, other elements of the development process began to frustrate Matt and Ben. I would see them in the lobby of our offices and say hello, and they'd speak openly about how frustrated they were that some of their ideas about the project weren't being heard, and felt as if they were being treated poorly by the people who worked above me. I had not been privy to any of these conversations, obviously, so I had no way to judge exactly what they were reacting to, but it was clear there was significant friction. In later interviews, many of the key figures involved indicated that the impasse came when Ben and Matt insisted that they be allowed to star in (and perhaps direct) the film, and Castle Rock thought the film would only work with established stars and a veteran director. As these conversations went on, Castle Rock attempted to "partner" Matt and Ben with various veteran filmmakers who might be brought aboard as producers and directors, but those meetings seemed pointless to Matt and Ben—too many old men trying to give them "new" ideas that didn't fit their vision of the script.

At the time, this seemed very personal—and, of course, disappointing. Richard Linklater, who made several films for Castle Rock, had apparently encouraged Matt and Ben to sell the script because the studio had been so supportive of Rick as an artist; but the reality for Matt and Ben ended up being more disagreement than agreement. In what everyone now agrees was the "right thing to do," Castle Rock told Matt and Ben that if they wanted to make the film according to their own vision, then the studio would walk away from the project with no hard feelings. But the studio couldn't just give the film back—it needed the $600,000-plus it had paid for the script. Thus, the project was put into *turnaround*, a kind of "used screenplay" status. It was available to anyone who wanted to pay the fee.

What had been a hot commodity a year before was now considered something of a poison: projects in turnaround have the stench of failure, and there aren't many success stories. At the time, many studio executives considered the turnaround market as throwing good money after bad. Thankfully, Ben had formed a relationship with the director Kevin Smith while working on the films *Mallrats* (produced by the same company that coproduced *Dazed and Confused*) and *Chasing Amy*. Smith loved the script and took it to Miramax, which agreed to take a chance on buying the script from Castle Rock. Matt and Ben would get to star—perhaps their acting talent had also become more evident and their value as actors had increased in the year since the project was bought—and they'd find an appropriate director, who turned out to be acclaimed indie auteur Gus van Sant. The project's industry-level notoriety and new studio backing eventually got the attention of Robin Williams, who agreed to co-star in the key (now greatly expanded) part of Will's therapist. That role won Williams his Oscar in 1998, and later that same night, Matt and Ben took the stage when they won the award for Best Original Screenplay.

We could look at the story of *Good Will Hunting* as a "development hell" story, but I actually prefer to see it as an example of how the development process worked and worked effectively. It's entirely possible that the spy-themed story could have been made into a decent movie. But ultimately, the decision to refocus the story gave the main character a more realistic, universal, and human conflict: Should Will stay and go to college where his talents and skills would be valued and exploited, or should he follow his heart and find a different path more personally rewarding? Too, by pairing up the two young screenwriters with a variety of older filmmakers—albeit unsuccessfully—Matt and Ben were able to find increasingly more opportunities to articulate what was important to them about the project, and to discover through trial and error what "works" and what doesn't in terms of collaborating in the development process. After a fresh start at Miramax, they ended up collaborating with a number of well-established, veteran filmmaking talent, just as Castle Rock had intended. That it worked out with the second studio better than it did with the first doesn't mean that the entire process was flawed; it merely demonstrates one of the many ways in which the process can find its way to a happy outcome.

ADVANCED DEVELOPMENT NOTES/DRAFT COMMENTS

The process of taking a screenplay from *purchased* (or optioned) to *made* is obviously one fraught with peril: industry wisdom says that fewer than 10% of the scripts optioned, purchased, or paid for actually get made. (And remember that maybe only one of 100 professional scripts ever get sold in any form, putting a professional's odds of having a screenplay made at about one in 1,000!) Every company will have a different development process, and there are good scriptwriting books and online resources that can help writers navigate the world of rewrites, polishes, punch-ups, and other terms that refer to the process of generating new and improved drafts of scripts.

As mentioned previously, the need for development is not only to make a script "better," but also to make it "workable" as a potential budgeted film or television project. Budget and production concerns come into play, along with potential casting or new talent. Add to that how various companies view the process, and there are a number of factors in this process that need to be taken into consideration when drafting *story notes* or *development notes* or *writer's notes* (terms that are used somewhat interchangeably).

One of the exercises this chapter asks is to create a set of development notes based on one of the scripts you have already read (and ideally the subject of some coverage you've written). In the working world, this is often something that is the product of consensus and collaboration among creatives and executives, so for those working in a classroom or group study situation, this exercise will replicate that experience. If you are working alone, you're going to have to use your imagination to approach this assignment—as in having internal "staff meetings" with yourself and making decisions on what might be important to emphasize in a specific development situation.

As you make development notes, your company (or working group) will very likely provide some general guidelines and expected outcomes. Once those are understood, those involved in the conversations—production executives and producers, stars, and directors, and perhaps even the screenwriter—will begin brainstorming specific ideas that support those outcomes. Because everyone thinks differently, every collection of people is going to engage in this process in a different way.

For example, in one case you might have a highly invested "VIP" on the project—perhaps a producer, a director, or a star—whose ideas will be considered "most important." That person may dominate a story meeting, or have very limited time, or there might be some other external consideration that becomes an important factor—for instance, is there a significant part for the star's brother, who is trying to make it as an actor? Or you might have a project that everyone "loves" but no one is sure what to do with because the executive who brought it in just left the company. You can imagine such situations might produce meetings that aren't efficiently structured or designed to produce specific, measurable outcomes. No wonder creative artists and executives alike get frustrated with the development process: it's hard to feel like progress is being made when the discussion lacks consistent direction, or is being led by someone who has very different interests than everyone else.

That frustration is something most executives and writers can complain about at an expensive corporate lunch, while their assistants and junior executives back at the office are often charged with generating written notes from those frustrating story meetings. Usually, the person designated to record and produce the story notes is not someone who has a "voice" in the room; someone needs to be focused solely on reporting on other people's ideas and the general consensus of the group. (This is often the case in professional staff meetings of all kinds—it's not that no one cares about the opinion of the "secretary," or that such a person's opinion isn't important, it's simply the secretary's job in that moment to be objective and thoughtful in translating what was said into something that is written.)

It's also common that executives or others may jot down their own notes and share them with the person who is assembling the final document. It is up to the notes writer to determine when it is appropriate to edit/modify someone else's writing, when it is appropriate to directly quote, and other issues concerning how the company would like ideas "authored" and attributed. If you are given this assignment in the professional world, and aren't sure how to address these procedural issues, then ask to see a copy of previous story notes, and also ask what made the notes effective (or not) as far as the executives were concerned.

In the end, you will need to produce a document with specific outcomes or goals for the writer to achieve, and presented as clearly as possible. Obviously, this is important for the writer or writers of the next draft (who may or may not have written the current draft). But it's also essential for determining final credit and ensuring the writer is meeting the demands of the contract: development notes are often used in resolving disputes about screenplay credit and payment, because they serve as a de facto "contract" between the writer and the owner of the screenplay.

But your company also will probably want to make specific recommendations that fall on the "creative" side and are perhaps more difficult to quantify or evaluate until they are actually written. A lot of story meeting will feature "what if" suggestions that posit major changes to the story. "What if they *don't* end up together?" "What if there is no mother character and we just give all her dialogue to the father?" Perhaps these "what ifs" are presented in response to a specific problem in the current draft, or perhaps they're just "crazy ideas" to encourage people to think creatively. I'm sure you've seen TV shows such as *30 Rock* or have some understanding of the writer's room dynamic in creating sketch or situation comedy: while a story meeting in feature film might not be as freewheeling or constantly hilarious, there may be a similar dynamic in terms of "tossing out ideas." In writing the notes, you'll need to be clear about when to use really specific suggestions and when to be more general (e.g., people toss around 10 ideas for making the sister character funnier; rather than list all 10 ideas or pick one, you just make the note "the sister character has a lot of comic potential that we think can be foregrounded—we'd like to see more of her and her outrageous humor.")

Here are some general categories of outcomes you are most likely to cover in your development notes.

> **Length or pacing:** If actual potential running time is a concern, and the script that was purchased or optioned is simply "too long" for either budget or story reasons, then it will be obviously noted, and very likely even written into a contract ("the draft delivered will be no less than 90 and no more than 110 pages"). Rather than focus on an exact page number, story meetings will probably generate conversation on how to either cut (or add) pages to improve the pacing of the story. These comments are ideally a combination of outcomes ("The first act runs long; we think that Bart should be on the train by page 20") and specific suggestions ("Shortening the prologue scene and eliminating some of the detail of Bart's backstory will help tighten the first act").
>
> **Casting and cast size:** Every additional speaking role in a film requires not just the expense of paying an actor (often at union minimum), but also the expense of hiring someone to hire the actor (a casting director) and perhaps having to add to the number of crew members (hair, makeup, wardrobe, and assistant directors) who are

responsible for managing the time and effort of the actors on the set. Did you ever wonder why, in one of those Manhattan-based romantic comedies, the hero or heroine always encounters the same doorman, elevator operator, or building handyman no matter what time of day or night they pass through the lobby of their building? It's because hiring a second actor to play a second doorman or room service waiter costs more money. It also makes some sense from a story perspective: it gives the main character another "minor" relationship to develop and "anchors" the script.

Thus, some development notes are often asking the writer to reduce the number of characters or combine characters (does he need four sisters at his birthday party, or can we get it down to two?). Conventional storytelling dictates that the universe of characters is usually best limited and focused so that relationships can run deep. There also might be the suggestion to add characters to make up for other areas of concern in the script. The film *Adaptation* wryly reminds us of Robert McKee's admonition to not use voice-over in a script, and many producers and directors find voice-over something of a copout ("telling" not "showing"). Creating a best friend character or a confidante of some sort is a way that a main character can "talk about" what they did, but in a more organic fashion than a "Dear Diary"-type voice-over. Adding a love interest, a nearby family member, a boss or a secretary, or someone who would obviously be in the main character's life, might help the character become more "relatable."

Finally, as suggested in the previous exercise, there may be a requirement to rewrite a role for a specific actor or a specific type of actor. As with other notes, sometimes these are general ("we'd like to see more diversity in the characters to better reflect the international setting") to specific ("we'd like to see the school guidance counselor as more of a Tiffany Haddish-type"). If a specific actor is already involved in the project (either as a coproducer or attached talent), these notes may be more detailed and based on conversations with the performer who will play the part.

For well-established actors, working with the script material during the development process is a way for them to feel increased ownership and commitment to the role they will play. In the many years I worked for Helen Hunt, I was always impressed at how well she understood not only the character that she was meant to play, but also the other characters in the script, and how intently she worked with writers in between drafts to develop the complexity of each character and their relationships to one another. Changes in the characters often meant changes in the actions the characters took or the decisions they made: thus, our story notes were more focused on how to develop the characters and how to adjust the action "around" them, rather than trying to fix specific plot points. We tended to believe that better characters made a better story, but there are others who would perhaps want to prioritize story mechanics first and keep the characters more simple and generic. In a children's animated movie, or a zombie film, *depth* of character is less important than *type*; plot-driven concerns such as pacing, increasing stakes, and resolving conflict are thus more likely to be emphasized in the development notes.

PRODUCTION VALUE AND BUDGET

You may have a dictate from your company that the film must be budgeted at a certain level, which obviously affects production value. But it's also important to consider budget from the perspectives of location, wardrobe, special effects, and other factors that might cost money. Scenes that take place in crowded places (lots of extras) might be relocated to places that aren't so crowded; flashback scenes that take place more than 10 years ago could take place inside instead of outside so as to make production design that much easier (i.e., not having to have picture cars line the streets). Does your international spy hero really need to jet from Alaska to Rio to Paris to Bangkok in a montage pursuing the bad guy (and never revisit those locations)?

By the same token, the company may have a larger budget than the writer originally intended, and there needs to be ways of elevating the film's overall value. For instance, we move that last-minute chase from an abandoned warehouse into a well-known museum; we give the hero a hobby of collecting classic cars; or we expand the role of the grandfather because we can afford to make an offer to Robert De Niro or Al Pacino.

CHAPTER TAKEAWAYS

- Development notes and advanced coverage are often necessary for guiding the discussion about which talent to approach and how to work with that talent to develop the property and the creative partnership. No matter how good a screenplay, there is always a need for future drafts to adapt to various production needs and demands.
- With advanced forms of coverage, have a conversation with your executive or employer about what might be expected; don't be afraid of letting them influence your reading.
- Learning how to "read" and cover finished work (as samples) or nontraditional submissions expand your abilities as a producer and/or creative artist. Learning how the elements of setting, story, and character translate from one medium to another is an endlessly valuable skill and experience to have.

EXERCISE 7A: SECOND READ

If you are working in a group, read the coverage produced by other members of your group, and choose a screenplay for a "second read." *Do not* read the extended comments (until later). It doesn't have to be something that someone else recommended—just something that sounds interesting to you for whatever reason.

For your second read report, create only a cover sheet (with a rubric and recommendation, your own log line, etc.), and then comments of standard length.

For the purposes of this assignment, do not directly address the other piece of coverage— pretend you've never seen it. Just write your own comments from your perspective.

After you have completed the exercise, look at the earlier coverage and compare/contrast the way you and the other reader broke down or evaluated the property.

It is also productive to repeat this exercise having read the full coverage, including comments (as an executive might). In this instance, you may more directly address issues or perspectives not included in the initial coverage, or perhaps craft comments that are more related to the company's needs and mission, rather than simply the quality of the script or the writing. (These skills will also be used in the next exercise, so it is merely optional here.)

If you are working alone, this is a more difficult exercise to replicate. If you have access to a popular script database in which others may share coverage or there is sample coverage, do your own "second read," particularly of scripts that are highly ranked or rated by others. To get maximum value from the project, I suggest you complete the coverage as suggested in the previous paragraph—tailored for your specific imaginary company's needs.

As always, proofread, edit, and review your notes for basic clarity, paragraph organization, effective/efficient word choice, and citing specific examples.

EXERCISE 7B: DEVELOPMENT NOTES AND STORY MEETING

If you are working alone, consider yourself a *sole producer* who is working one-on-one with the writer of the script so that the next draft can be presented exclusively to a specific studio, coproducer, director, or major performer. It is up to you to imagine what this important reader will want in terms of the content and workability of the new draft, and to communicate that clearly to the writer. (For the purposes of this exercise, assume the writer of the new draft is the same writer of the draft that you have read.)

There is no standard length for development notes, and, in this circumstance, you should feel free to get as detailed as you want, as you are a key collaborator on the project, not just a random studio executive. Assume that your writer will respond positively to new suggestions, ideas, changes, etc., but be sure that you aren't overburdening them. Try to make sure all of your suggested changes and edits are for a specific purpose related to making it a better read for the next VIP reader.

If you are working in a group, it's productive to engage with this exercise in a slightly different manner (though the solo exercise is well worth an attempt if you have the time or something to do for extra credit).

Your group should have a "story meeting" that lasts long enough for each group member to lead a discussion on a specific project for 10–15 minutes. Prior to the meeting, everyone should have read all coverage of the projects that will be discussed in the meeting (and when possible and feasible, have read the scripts as well; if you are in a group of five, try to have read at least two other scripts besides the one you are talking about).

Everyone is an "account executive" who has a project that has been put into development, and each executive is in charge of initiating the discussion about the project. Another person in the group should be designated as that executive's "assistant" on this project, and the assistant is responsible for taking notes in the meeting and ultimately generating a set of production notes. (I suggest that to make it easy, you take notes for the project immediately after the one you presented—see my suggested meeting agenda at the end of the chapter.) Thus, every member of the group will serve as both executive and assistant.

It is up to the executive to ensure that his or her most pressing concerns about the next draft of the script are addressed. If you have specific points you want to discuss or have a perspective on, then be sure to ask them clearly and up front. Starting off your discussion with "what did everybody think" might not be the best use of your time. This is where any second read notes you have done might come in handy: draw your points from there, and open your discussion by pointing out what you think the major two or three elements are that need to be addressed. Be sure to communicate important points to your assistant—things that you want put in the story notes specifically.

The assistant does *not* have to write down every idea or every single comment: it is up to the group (and individual members) as to whether the assistant should also be an active participant in the discussion. But as the assistant, it is exceptionally important that someone is "keeping track" of the better ideas, helping to organize ideas, etc. It's helpful to let each assistant have two or three minutes at the end of each presentation to summarize the key points and ask the group whether there is anything else they want to get into the notes.

The assistant should then assemble notes and "turn them in" to the executive, who will review them and make any necessary edits/changes. Unlike the one-on-one notes, these should probably be less focused on minute detail and more about broader improvements and suggestions. (After all, each executive in the meeting may have disagreed on *how* to make an improvement, but they all agreed that something needed to be improved.) The executive will then submit/share/distribute the final notes to the entire group. (If you are a teacher grading this assignment, I suggest splitting the grade 50/50 between executive and assistant—each student should receive equal credit, regardless of the role they played in the creation of the document.)

As with all exercises, the more you practice this skill with different kinds of material and different aims and objectives, the easier it will be to effectively organize and communicate your ideas in future real-world assignments.

Sample "Story Meeting Agenda":

- Adam—*Made in America* (Elena takes notes)
- Brenna—*The Horseshoe Road Inn* (Adam takes notes)
- Celine—*Mad About the Boy* (Brenna takes notes)
- Duy—*Prince of the Moon* (Celine takes notes)
- Elena—*The Mayor of Heartbreak City* (Duy takes notes)

After all of the notes have been turned in, read them and have another meeting to discuss the process and reflect upon how well the notes reflect what was discussed in the story meeting.

CHAPTER 8

When the Cameras Roll

Unit Publicity

The light is green. The cast and crew have been hired. The studio space and equipment have been secured and insured. The public has been informed, the release date announced, the honeywagons schlepped to location—and a movie is finally being made.

At the beginning of a film's production period—after what has most likely been at least a year of planning, negotiating, budgeting, haggling, financing, refinancing, begging, and pleading on behalf of the producers and filmmakers—"marketing" the finished film probably still feels like a long way off. For most feature films or television shows, getting that green light and going in front of the cameras has been such a huge mountain to climb, that the back end of the process seems like a tiny hill in comparison, and one that is far enough away to not worry about. After all, it's still very likely that at least six months to a year from now the project will make its way to the public. There's so much work to do between here and there—as in actually making a good movie—that many filmmakers might assume that the marketing will eventually "take care of itself," or at the very least be the responsibility of people who work in buildings and offices far from the set.

To some extent, for most people involved in a production, such a perspective makes sense: gaffers, makeup artists, stunt performers, drivers, and assistant camera operators, similar to the dozens of other highly trained and dedicated professionals who populate a working set, have their own job to do. They can't worry too much about how the film might do at the box office, or which awards it might win, or what kinds of critical favor it might receive. Sure, it's nice to work on an "important" film or one that has major talent involved, but most people on the set measure the success or failure of a film in terms of whether they get their pages done and come in on time and on budget. Many of the crew may not even have read the full script, and it's very likely no one ever asks them their opinion about the film's cultural value or box-office potential, except as to engage in friendly conversation between takes.

Producers and directors, of course, along with the principal actors and perhaps the screenwriter, are a bit more invested, and very likely have a longer-term vision for the project. Producers know that getting their film into the theaters and public consciousness is more than just a theoretical obstacle down the line, but something that must be anticipated and prepared for. Directors and actors are usually cognizant of the fact that even if they finish this particular job in six or eight or 10 weeks, they'll need to "return" to the project in the public eye when they are booked for public appearances and interviews several months from now, when the film opens in theaters or the series debuts. While that might not be at the forefront of their minds during production, they can't completely deny the fact there is a long way to go to make the film successful.

From the broadest possible perspective—that of the producer or studio whose finances are on the line—the making of the film during the production process has to work "toward" a marketing strategy. Much of this has probably been discussed, debated, and contracted, from choices made about casting to clauses in the director's contract regarding running time and MPAA rating. But on a more substantive level, savvy producers also know that the "why" of the film's existence—the same kind of "why" that got the film's script read, sold, and greenlit in the first place—is a discussion that needs to continue throughout the production process. Selling the film with writing doesn't stop once the cameras start rolling—in fact, the most important part of that process is just beginning. And much of that process is put in the hands of the unit publicist.

BASIC MARKETING PRACTICES: ADVERTISING, PROMOTION, PUBLICITY

Before we get to the work of unit publicity, a practice defined and driven by intelligent and focused writing, we should take a moment to remind ourselves of various marketing practices that are often conflated or confused in the mind of the typical moviegoer, and often even by industry professionals who work in other areas of production. Even the veteran cinematographer, the most polished assistant director, or an accomplished production accountant might not know the difference between some of these terms, but a smart producer, writer, or director will have a sense of how these practices overlap and influence one another, and offer something completely unique in the film marketing process.

These three practices are **advertising**, **promotion**, and **publicity**. Although they all ideally work in unison to help market a film to the public, they are distinct practices that often involve different professionals and personnel. In many studios and networks, these are "sibling" divisions or units with full staffs of their own: they work together and communicate often, but use varying practices and exercises that require different skills and communicate with different audiences and corporate and industrial partners.

ADVERTISING

Since most people are engaged with them on a daily basis, ads are often mistaken as the primary or "most important" marketing practice: often, publicists are asked questions about TV commercials, trailers, billboards, and other marketing elements that typically are far out of the purview of a publicity team. In the world of entertainment, however, **advertising** is a fairly narrow practice that can be defined as a cultural modality or space that has been purchased (or leased, or otherwise "paid for") by the studio on behalf of the production. By "cultural modality or space," we are referring to all of the places an advertisement might be encountered, including a digital billboard on the side of a busy highway, a television commercial during ESPN's *SportsCenter*, a full-page image in the *New York Times*, a flashing banner on your email homepage, or a trailer or other promotional image seen at your local cinema framed by the enticing promise "coming soon." In each of those cases and many others, the studio/network/producer has purchased and/or negotiated for the rights to show pretty much whatever desired in terms of content (within legal restriction, of course).[1] The movie theater owner can complain that a "coming soon" trailer is boring or confusing but can't make the studio change it; and assuming it conforms to broadcast standards, the television station has no say over the content of the 30-second commercial airing during the local evening news that reminds you of the superhero film opening "this Friday at a theater near you."

What makes advertising distinct from publicity and promotion? Advertising is almost always being directed to the general public (one exception is advertising in support of year-end awards, which is specifically targeted at awards voters). Now, a producer might decide that the "general public" is too wide a target for a particular film, and concentrate only on a certain segment of the population—kids under 15 to see the latest G-rated animation film, adults in big cities for the latest suspense thriller, college kids for the new stoner sex comedy. But regardless of how wide or narrow the target audience, the goal is to inform the potential moviegoer or watcher that the movie is going to be *in the theaters* (or *on demand*) at a certain time and place, with the implication that the viewer will respond by paying money to see the film at that time and place.

So most advertising needs to contain information such as **when** does the film open ("this Friday"), **where** is it playing ("at a theater near you"), and **why** someone should go see it ("critics have said … ," "audiences are howling for … ," "Lada Gaga's sensational debut … ," etc.). If your stars are well known, you'll want to feature them prominently. Further inducement comes from tag lines (developed in a later exercise), which may in some cases be crafted by a publicist or member of a more general marketing team.

PROMOTION

In a general sense, all marketing practices help to generally *promote* the presence, visibility, and availability of a film or program, but the specific practice known as *promotions* has a narrower definition. A **promotion** is something—usually an opportunity, an object, or an experience—that is given *to* the viewer as a result of that viewer making some measurable connection to the film *besides* seeing the film itself. Hollywood has a very long and colorful

---

1 In recent years, studios and producers have found ways to use advertising materials—such as extended trailers and commercials—in digital modalities and spaces that do not cost money in the same way as traditional advertising. Dropping trailers on YouTube, for example, does not require or mandate that a company "purchase" time on YouTube, which is free—but drawing attention to that trailer or ad is another matter, one that requires publicity and the dissemination of information to companion outlets.

tradition of promotions, which can originate at almost any time with any production, including long before the movie is in theaters.

For example, one well-known preproduction promotional activity is the *open casting call* (very rarely done these days, but a more common practice in previous eras). In such a case, to highlight the beginning of production on a major project, a studio would hold open auditions for actors to appear in the film. For example, when MGM remade the classic father-son melodrama *The Champ,* in 1979, it took out advertisements in papers nationwide asking for young boys to audition for the lead role to star opposite Jon Voight. It held "casting sessions" in major cities—I recall the one in Los Angeles, where I was one of dozens of boys to fill out some forms, stand in front of a blank backdrop, have my picture taken, and be dismissed with a polite "thank you." Eventually, young Ricky Schroder got the part after being "discovered" through the open audition process (although he had an established professional career in commercials at that point). For the studio, the casting call was not really designed to discover unknown talent: the point was that I, as hundreds of 8–12-year-old boys all across the country, now had an "experience" with the movie that made us want to see it when it opened. Our friends and family who knew we had "auditioned" for the part would also be aware of it. In fact, these "casting calls" were often just expensive and unnecessary events, producing very little in the way of talent while generating early interest in film projects. (See the sidebar in this chapter for a history of interesting movie promotions.)

Indeed, the casting of films in general is often used for the purposes of publicity as well, as high-profile stars are rumored to be attached to play various roles as a way of keeping a project visible in the public eye—consider all the excitement and chatter that emerges when a studio announces that a reboot of a franchise will feature a new actor as James Bond, or Spider-Man, or Superman.

The bottom line for promotion is that in exchange for attention, information, and the possibility of favorable word of mouth, the studio offers moviegoers something tangible that connects them to the movie. If I pick up a new *Star Wars* character cup from Taco Bell, I have something "about" the film in my home reminding me that the film has a personal value. Now, of course, the movie might stink, and I might use that cup to store old pennies in the garage, but as long as I've paid to see the movie, the studio would consider that a successful promotion.

PUBLICITY

Advertising is paid space; promotion is an exchange. What then, is **publicity**? Publicity is the practice of creating, disseminating, and magnifying positive word-of-mouth about a project that implores the receiving party to respond in a particular way. In other words, it's giving the viewing public the "language" and perspective to best talk about the film in the most positive light, and then encouraging the public to *pass on* that same language and perspective.

There is a saying that "there is no such thing as bad publicity," and you can make a logical argument that it's better for a film to be talked about—even if negatively—than ignored. For the purposes of the next few chapters, we're going to be ignoring that rather cynical gray area and emphasizing the idea that almost all efforts made in the name of publicity are intended to be positive and generate positive **spin**.

In later chapters, we will break down more specifically how professional writing supports more common publicity practices, so we'll just cite a few here to offer you an idea about what we are talking about. When an actor appears on a late-night talk show to show a clip from their latest film and jokes around with the host, that's publicity. When a critic gets access to an early screening and publishes a review of the film the morning it comes out in theaters, that's publicity. When a television show's creator gets a six-page interview in *Rolling Stone* magazine, or a starlet winds up on the cover of *Cosmopolitan*, or the actor who plays a pot-smoking anti-hero hosts a cartoon marathon on *Adult Swim*—that's publicity.

What is the difference between publicity and advertising? Well, you can buy six pages of advertising in *Rolling Stone*, but that doesn't hold the same critical weight as an article written by one of the magazine's contributors. You can buy commercial time during *Adult Swim* (and it's very likely that if your stoner anti-hero is hosting, then there will be plenty of commercials for the film that night as well), but an ad for the film is different than a "personal appearance" or special performance. And it doesn't matter how much money you have, you can't buy your way onto *The Tonight Show* or *The Late Show* or *The Today Show* or *The Morning Clambake with Daddy G, the Walrus and Wanda on 95.3 the Clam*. You have to be booked at the approval of the show's producers. Exercise 8A will give you the opportunity to catalog a publicity campaign, so you'll get to see firsthand just exactly how much goes into the work of release publicity.

Although most of the work of publicity is visible at the point of release, the work, in fact, starts much, much earlier—and is often originated and managed by the unit publicist.

UNIT PUBLICITY

Here's something to contemplate about the role of a unit publicist on a film set: That person is the only person on the set who has absolutely nothing to do with the actual making of creative content for the film. You could ditch the publicist and absolutely nothing about the final product of the film would look any different. Even the stills photographer—whom we will discuss in a few moments, as this person works closely with the publicist—can actually have a function that affects the film by providing images of scenes that can be used for the purposes of continuity. No one else on the set, in a way, matters "less" than the unit publicist.

As someone who has spent much of his professional life living and working as a publicist or directly with publicists, I believe that this simple observation helps explain two things that go a long way toward illuminating how many people view publicity. First, because the publicist's work is not really part of any creative department's "workflow," none of the creative professionals on the set really have an idea about what the publicist does (with the exceptions, as we will see, of a few people connected to production management and on-set coordination). Unless a publicist "has" to be on the set, no one expects one to be there, and that person is not missed in the slightest when away, at least in terms of meeting the demands of the scheduled filming.

Second, and perhaps more significant, this invisibility and the unnecessary aspects of the publicist's work has led to a shift in the way filmmakers utilize publicists during production. A generation ago, every studio film and every major independent film very likely had a full-time unit publicist working on location for the entirety of production, and sometimes through the beginning of postproduction. That meant a full-time salary—very likely more than $1,500 per week—plus possible housing, meals, per diem, and other location-based expenses. When budgets began to get tighter—particularly for more independent films or higher profile films with limited budgets—producers and studios realized they didn't actually need a publicist for the entirety of their schedule. In some cases, they would hire an outside firm, or rely on their studio publicity teams (based in New York or Los Angeles), to do some of the work remotely, and only send an actual human to the set for a couple of weeks when having someone present was an absolute necessity. In some cases, an associate producer or a local professional would be available to "fill in" and perform the duties of a publicist when needed.

To be fair, this kind of adjustment makes sense. After all, if someone doesn't need to be on the ground full time, then why pay for it? For example, let's say your film has one scene with a few stunts. If you aren't going to shoot that stunt scene until day 19 of your schedule, then you probably don't need the stunt coordinator or the stuntmen around for days one through 15; similarly, you don't want to pay a horse wrangler to work on the days when you don't need any horses, or a school teacher to work on days when there are no young actors who require schooling.

But woe to the film that decides a single publicist—even one working far from the set, or only visiting the set for a few days when absolutely necessary—is not a worthwhile expenditure. Too often over the past decade, I have been asked to consult on the release of a film that did not hire a unit publicist or engage in any publicity during production. There are no production stills, no behind-the-scenes interviews, no press coverage from the set (immensely valuable when on location), no information in trade articles, and so forth. At that point it might be months—or even a year—since production ended. Now, the producers are excited that the film has been invited to a prestigious festival or given a release date on Netflix or Hulu or Amazon—only to discover that they have nothing for the festival program, or streaming service, no usable artwork, and nothing to give the critics and tastemakers who are available and ready to talk the film up to anyone who will listen.

So what is this valuable work that the publicist does? A unit publicist's work can be divided into two basic categories. *Above all, the unit publicist or publicity team is there to create materials that will be used in support of the film's release to the public.* This includes: production stills; production notes; cast and crew information and biographies; electronic press kit (EPK) material, including interviews and B-roll; and developing feature article ideas and pitches based on the film's themes, on- and off-screen talent, and production history.

The second category of work is more immediate, and varies in importance from project to project, and *this is the matter of pitching, managing, and supervising set visits from the working press to the set of the film.* This might mean arranging a special interview with the director by a major film critic, inviting a fashion photographer to the set to shoot the leads in their amazing costumes, or allowing a local newspaper reporter a day or two to witness what it's like when a big Hollywood movie studio arrives to do some shooting right in the local community's backyard. Since most sets prefer to remain closed to visitors, or set visits are impractical because of time, access, or available resources, this may or may not be a significant effort on behalf of the publicist.

Certainly, the fewer of these visits there are, the less likely a production will have anyone "on call" and immediately available on an everyday basis. Still, such visits are not always related to basic production needs. For example, you might be working with an actor who receives an award nomination for last year's breakout role. That actor is scheduled to be on set the morning the nominations are announced, and it might be the publicist's job to coordinate the interview requests and find the right time to get the actor on the phone or a video call with *Good Morning America* or another congratulatory outlet.

I learned this very early in my career, when I helped produce a student film at NYU. We were fortunate enough to land a major actor as the lead in our film—the great Sam Waterston, who is well known for his public activism on behalf of the arts. He was asked at the last minute to appear live on the late-night news program *Nightline* with Ted Koppel to discuss government funding for the arts. It forced us to shave several hours off our anticipated shooting schedule, though we managed to have Sam out of makeup and in the limo to the studio promptly at 10 p.m. We took a break from shooting to watch him do the interview on TV an hour later. After the TV show, the limo brought him back to the set and we went back to making our student film. (Sam was an absolute pro: he even agreed to drink the alcohol that his character consumed on camera before his TV appearance, and we all wondered if he might have been a little bit tipsy while being interviewed—he certainly didn't show it!)

Another factor that has changed the ways in which a unit publicist functions involves new technologies and modes of communication. In almost every case, a unit publicist reports to the producers on set, but also to someone "up the ladder" at a studio or production company. For example, while working on *Dazed and Confused*, I was communicating to executives in New York (my company's home office) and Los Angeles (Gramercy Pictures, which distributed the film) along with everyone on the ground in Austin, Texas. Even at that time, generating a report often meant producing and distributing hard copies. Communicating with someone on any sort of matter was done via telephone more often than email, and production materials such as stills, video footage of interviews or B-roll, were produced, duplicated, and distributed via "hard media," requiring packages to be labelled and shipped overnight. Digital media greatly reduced the time required to manage the basic communication of the job, and a publicist or publicity team working remotely for a majority of the production schedule simply became a standard practice.

For the purposes of this chapter, we will consider all the things a unit publicist would do if working on the set, with the caveat that some of the preparation and follow-up for that work could easily have occurred remotely.

PRODUCING PUBLICITY MATERIAL: FINDING 'FEATURES'

Every unit publicist and every production employ best practices by making sure their principal photography schedule includes the following:

- Employing a stills photographer to create images suitable for publicity and marketing purposes.
- If required by contract or otherwise desired, developing a workflow process of photo/video approval by filmmakers, actors, production executives, and talent representatives.
- Employing a video production crew to conceptualize, produce, and edit material for an **electronic press kit** (EPK), including interviews, B-roll, and other "behind the scenes" footage.
- Collecting up-to-date biographical information on principal cast and crew; collating, formatting, and editing all bios.
- Creating no-spoiler log lines, synopses, and plot descriptions of various lengths for immediate distribution to trade outlets, creative teams, and media partners.
- Conceiving, developing, and executing feature-style pitches for either set visits or a release campaign.
- Developing and/or implementing a clear and consistent policy regarding social media (to be observed by cast, crew, and set visitors), and working with social media teams on creating and managing official social media feeds.
- Producing an initial **press kit** that includes basic cast/crew info, synopses "about the production" or other informational text, biographies of principal talent, and other visual and descriptive elements related to the film's release to the public.

THE STILLS PHOTOGRAPHER

On some sets, a still camera photographer is a production requirement. Professional stills photographers are often members of the same union that represents cinematographers and camera operators, and have a deep knowledge and appreciation for the unique ways in which films and television must be lit, designed, and turned into a visual image on traditional film stock and/or digital media. So on most projects produced by major studios and networks, having a qualified stills photographer, one who often comes with highly specialized equipment and is able to deliver images that can serve a number of functions for the film, is literally written into the production contract. Most nonunion and smaller films still try to employ a stills photographer, but current professionals caution filmmakers or producers against hiring someone who has no experience on a film set, or is used to other forms of commercial photography.

For a unit publicist, working with a stills photographer often means helping the photographer ensure that his or her work is getting seen and approved. In the digital age, it is easy to share images, so the workflow on this process has much improved. A generation ago, a photographer would need to get dozens of rolls of film developed and printed every day. In the form of "proofs"—essentially thumbnail-sized images laid out end to end on a large sheet of photo paper—the photographer would first use a colored wax pen to X out any images deemed unusable from a technical perspective. Then, the publicist would take the set of proofs—hundreds of images every day—to the director of the film, or an actor who has photo approval in his or her contract, or to a producer, or to all three—with everyone circling images they liked and X-ing out ones they didn't. Ultimately, the goal was to produce one to two dozen images that could be used to support the release of the film. Over time, these images became somewhat standardized, and remain the *essential* types of images.

These are the types of images that a publicist should ensure a photographer is getting:

- Images of the main characters in the film *in action*—these images should essentially resemble "screen grabs" of what the film camera is recording and producing.
- Images of any large-scale scenes with many extras or high production value.
- At least one image of the director behind, next to, or near the camera.
- Images that feature full-length views of unusual or expressive costumes.
- Images that represent the range of locations, spaces, and other visual markers that are represented in the film (i.e., your photographer should be at every location for at least one day).
- For films with heavy special effects, images of effects creators and designers using models, illustrations, etc. (Avoid pictures of people sitting at computers.)
- A character "head shot" with a neutral background.

A photographer may also do a lot more—candid shots of people working, posed shots of cast and crew standing and smiling together, etc. The photographer might also offer his or her images to a script supervisor for purposes of continuity, and thus have other functions necessary to production workflow. The publicist needs to ensure that the basic publicity needs will be met, and the photographer needs to have a clear understanding of those needs to successfully navigate all the potential demands on his or her time and talent.

Finally, it is usually the publicist's job to produce a caption for the approved stills, though depending on the timing and workflow of the approval process, that duty may fall to a studio/network/producer's office staffer or art department employee if the unit publicist has wrapped his or her production-based duties.

THE PUBLICIST AT WORK

Let's shift to examining the kind of writing that a publicist does and give you some examples to consider and exercises to complete. We'll focus on two areas of practice, each with specific exercises to test your skills.

- Start of Production Materials: New log lines, synopses, announcements, etc.
- Developing Feature Pitch/Set Visit Pitch Ideas

The next chapter will build on these materials and discuss production of the Electronic Press Kit materials and completing the Production Notes.

START OF PRODUCTION MATERIALS

Congratulations! A producer contact of yours has just emailed you to confirm that yes, you'll be hired as the unit publicist on a new film. For the purposes of this chapter, we're going to use a *pretend* film with an absurd premise as our model; for the writing exercises, we encourage you to use one or more of the projects you did extensive coverage and story notes on in earlier chapters, since you will already be familiar with the potential value of those stories.

Our film is a sports comedy called *Soul on Da Ice*, and it's about a former hockey player who gets in a minor scrape with the law and must do community service at an inner city rec center in Detroit. He meets a bunch of misfit kids who aren't the right size or temperament for hockey but hears about a youth curling competition in Toronto, and decides to learn curling and coach this underdog team to victory. It's *The Mighty Ducks*, but with curling. It will star a famous comedian from Canada we'll call "Bruce McFudd." His girlfriend will be played by ingénue Tony-award winner "Caroline Crane," and two key supporting parts will be filled by Samuel L. Jackson as the boss at the Detroit rec center and John Lithgow as the US Olympic Curling Team coach.

So what do you do even before your first day? Well, the first thing you'll have to do is create *three* short, written elements that can be used by the production immediately: the **LOG LINE,** the **SYNOPSIS,** and the **START OF PRODUCTION ANNOUNCEMNENT** (Exercises 8B, 8C, 8D).

FEATURE IDEAS/SET VISIT PITCHES

Our next step is to think of what the main **feature** ideas might be regarding the project. A **feature** is a secondary, more focused *story* or *pitch* that highlights a specific aspect of the production that might be suitable for publicity purposes.

Furthermore, some features lend themselves to set visits, where a journalist, photographer, or other observer comes to the set of the movie during production to get a *firsthand look* at how the film is being made. The article from a set visit might run immediately, but set visits can also be arranged for articles and other forms of coverage that will be employed upon the film's release. For this chapter, we'll try to imagine feature ideas that will lend themselves to set visits, and to features that might be suitable for more activity down the road.

How do you come up with a feature idea? Well, remember that a feature is a story that highlights a specific aspect of the production, rather than "the entire film." One of the most obvious feature ideas for many films is related to the film's **location**. Particularly if shooting away from a sound stage, the idea of a movie being made in a *real-life* neighborhood or natural environment is a built-in angle that, at the very least, local reporters might be interested in covering. Are there scenes where your project has to take over a major public landmark, building, or sports arena? Does your crew travel to an exotic, distant location where cameras have never been? Or try to make the streets of New York today look as they did 40 years ago when the film takes place? Or take over a small town in the Midwest or South for six weeks? There's usually a location angle built in, with producers, directors, and production designers hopefully eager to talk about the challenges that your project's settings brought about.

Another possible feature angle has to do with your **cast**. Now, most people are always interested in what movie stars are doing and, generally speaking, most marketing campaigns will feature the lead actors as a primary selling point for the film. As a publicist, you have the chance to add something *above and beyond* for your cast. For example, did the lead have to gain/lose a lot of weight for the role? Were there other kinds of physical training or body modification necessary for this particular role? Is this the first starring role in a film for someone better known on television? Is this everyone's favorite funny man doing a serious turn in an effort to broaden his career? In other words, is there a way that you can present the work of the cast as something that is new, different, unexpected, or otherwise distinguishable from the usual demands of acting? You also might expand the idea of "cast" to include all talent, such as the writer, director, or producer, who perhaps have an unusual personal investment in the story, are making their debut as a professional, etc.

For many films, one of the primary feature elements has to do with the presence of **special effects** in the film—which doesn't just have to be space vehicles at war, hideous CGI monsters fighting our green-screened heroes, or the latest in zombie head explosion technology. You should really consider special effects an extension of production design, and think about any unusual set construction, costume, makeup, or other craft positions that might be engaged in something a little different than the ordinary, or is exceptionally challenging.

Finally, it's common to develop feature ideas based on a film's **themes**. A film about World War II would very likely employ a consultant who is a legitimate historian and/or witness to the events depicted in the film, and someone who can not only testify to the technical authenticity of the project, but also the cultural and historical meaning of what is being represented. A television series about a detective tracking down a serial killer will obviously reflect complex cultural problems such as the role of the justice system, the medical and mental health professions, and how we understand the nature of "good and evil." A documentary that profiles an amazing trumpet player who is redefining what the instrument means will suggest that a history of that instrument or famous trumpeters from the past would be solid feature idea to pitch to a music-centered outlet. An ensemble comedy about a 40-year high school reunion suggests looking at what was relevant and popular 40 years ago and developing pitches around nostalgia for that era. In some cases, these pitch ideas will suggest a set visit, but will also have resonance in the long term.

As a publicist, you might develop one or two of these feature ideas as short mini-articles to be included in the production notes. Or, you might suggest that they be turned into video segments (*featurettes*) for the EPK (these will be discussed later). For now, let's assume you are developing these feature ideas as potential pitches to outlets you want to publicize your film. How can you get a journalist or editor excited to visit the set and get an "exclusive" look of something specific that will have value to the visitor's audience? We'll try two exercises (8E and 8F), through which we create a *list of pitch ideas* for our producers/studio/network to consider, and two *pitch letters* to specific outlets, introducing them to the film and suggesting an idea for a feature.

A SHORT HISTORY OF FILM PROMOTIONS

Let's face it—not every film is great. Not every film sells itself with the cast, story, or special effects. I've often wondered why, with some exceptions (notably franchise blockbusters, whose "collectible" promotions are almost a given), it's often the lesser-known, lower-budgeted, and "schlockier" efforts that have generated the most unusual and memorable promotions.

Early on in film history, selling tickets to the movies was far more of a "local" concern: the studio system was still forming, and generally speaking, the idea of promoting or advertising a product on a national level was still a very new cultural practice. Prints of films often had to travel from market to market: D. W. Griffith or Lois Weber or Mack Sennett would shoot a two-reel film and prints would be sent to theaters in New York, Chicago, and a few other big cities for a week or two, then those prints would travel to secondary markets (medium-sized towns), then to small towns and second-run theaters. It was up to a distributor to be sure that the Chicago theater had suitable posters and lobby cards in the first week, while then ensuring that similar marketing materials got to the theaters in Milwaukee two weeks later, then to the little cinema in Galena or Waukegan the week after that.

One can imagine that the small town theater owners often got the short end of the stick when it came to cashing in on a film's marketing strategy, so it was those local exhibitors who began creating unique promotions that would attract audiences. That might mean hiring local artists to draw original posters or handbills to hang around town; designing contests, giveaways, and special discounts ("Ladies Day" or special showings for children); or supplementing the cinematic offerings with live music, theatrical acts, or public speakers.

In fact, it was a promotional stunt possibly conceived or initiated by a small town theater owner that may have resulted in one of the most significant developments of the early era of cinema—the establishment of the star system and the birth of the first movie star, Florence Lawrence. Lawrence had made a number of films for Biograph, one of the top studios of the pre-World War I era and early home to D. W. Griffith. An aspiring stage actress who knew how to ride a horse, Lawrence, as almost all of the performers of her era, was unbilled and uncredited; producers didn't want to pay actors much money, so they had a reason for keeping them anonymous, while professional actors mostly believed that film work was "beneath" the dignity of the stage, and did not want a potential employer in the theater to know that they may have had to make a living working for the motion pictures.

But Lawrence was growing popular: fans wrote to Biograph about the "girl" in the movies, and she became known informally as "the Biograph Girl." Sensing a potential for fame and a more lucrative career, Lawrence and her husband (a cameraman at Biograph) decided to hold out for more money, at which point Biograph dropped her contract—it could get any girl who could ride a horse and call her "the Biograph Girl." After all, advertisers and brands replace models all the time ("the Gibson Girl" or "Cover Girl").

Independent film producer Carl Laemmle, eager to establish his new company IMP (Independent Motion Pictures), saw an opportunity. He signed Lawrence to a contract, promising to make her famous, and promptly dubbed her "the IMP Girl." They made a few films, but Lawrence remained essentially anonymous. That is, until early 1910, when, according to legend, a rumor was spread that the beloved "IMP Girl" had died in an accident. IMP took out one of the most famous ads in early Hollywood history—"We Nail a Lie" proclaims the ad, explaining that, in fact, Miss Lawrence (her name now proudly claimed) was alive and well, and would be appearing at the debut of her new film *The Broken Bath* in St. Louis. It was the first time a movie star had been tabbed to make a personal appearance at a film's public opening.

For years, most people believed that Laemmle had spread the rumor himself about Lawrence's death as a publicity stunt to enhance the in-person promotion. But recently, scholars have uncovered evidence that the originator of the death rumor was actually a theater owner in Louisville, Kentucky, named Frank Talbot. Talbot also owned a theater in St. Louis, and apparently wrote a letter to Laemmle in which he either suggested the idea of a rumor or asked about the rumor, and that gave Laemmle an idea. It explains why he chose to have Lawrence's "not dead" reveal in St. Louis, of all places (a great city—my mom's home town—but not exactly a site of show business legend); it may have been a "payoff" for Talbot for generating the idea for the promotion.[1] However it happened, it

---

1 For some excellent recent history on this, see Joe McClintock's article about the Lawrence promotion at *Bright Lights Film Journal*, https://brightlightsfilm.com/wp-content/cache/all/florence-lawrence-truth-behind-we-nail-a-lie-famous-ads-1910/#.XE4PYFxKhpg.

worked—Florence Lawrence is now considered the first "movie star," and it had far more to do with a shrewd and clever marketing campaign than it did with her on-screen talent.

As the studio system emerged in the 1920s and '30s and film distribution became more national than local, marketing and promotion fell more and more under the auspices of the studios, which developed campaigns and ideas that might work just as well in Reno, El Paso, Kansas City, or Tallahassee. Promotional books with ideas were sent to theaters, alongside standard posters and lobby cards and other advertising materials, to ensure that each theater was adequately equipped to promote the opening of that week's film. This continued well into the television era. Oftentimes, studios would strongly suggest promotional ideas that theater owners may or may not pursue. For example, to promote a teen dance film in the 1950s, the studio might suggest that a local theater team with a local radio station to host a "dance contest" directly before or after screening of the film.

On the most extreme level were producers such as the legendary William Castle, whose career is a case study for any independent producer, and whose book *Step Right Up! I'm Gonna Scare the Pants off America* is a must-read. Castle became famous for "insisting" that theaters hire a nurse or doctor to be on stand-by, in case any of the moviegoers watching his horror films went into shock or passed out from fear. He had audiences sign "insurance policies" to prevent them from taking legal action. For his film *The Tingler*, about a spider-like creature that shocks its victims to death with an electric jolt, Castle wired some of the seats in movie theaters with an electrical wire that would "buzz" unsuspecting patrons at key moments in the story.

It's very important to note that the promotional ideas by Castle and other smaller studios in the 1940s and 1950s were just suggestions—of course, it was impossible to install electric seats in every single theater that showed *The Tingler* only to have the wires removed the following week, and the various "insurance" policies and medical warnings were completely bogus. More mainstream Hollywood promotions include the kinds of things that we see today: a high-profile red-carpet premiere where a select few fans get to be invited guests; an "on location" screening, hosted where the film was shot (outside of N.Y. or L.A.) as a way to give back to the community that supported production of the film; and personal appearances by movie stars (or characters) in places where they can interact with fans, such as Comic-Con.

Since the 1970s, promotional giveaways in conjunction with other business entities have been another common practice: getting collectible cups or toys from Taco Bell or Burger King, or entering "official" contests with giveaway prizes related to the film, are often used to reach broader and younger audiences. Finally, there is the "schwag" that goes along with every film that gets into the theaters: buttons, pins, caps, slap bracelets,

T-shirts, stickers, and so forth—which offer everyone a little "piece" of the film that you can't necessarily just go out and buy in a store.

In the Internet era, promotions and connecting fans to films are often more likely to occur in virtual spaces: joining an online community fan page, following a film's (or even a character's) Twitter account, or participating in a hashtag campaign are ways of offering fans an "experience" above and beyond the movie or program itself. But the old-fashioned bring-the-stars out idea still can work wonders. One example is the documentary film *Anvil: The Story of Anvil*, about a long-suffering Canadian heavy metal band. A hit at film festivals, but obviously with a somewhat limited and specialized audience (heavy metal and documentary fans), the producers decided that one high-profile way of releasing the film was to "tour" the film with the band itself. Thus, the filmmakers and band launched a tour called "The Anvil Experience," with a screening of the film followed by a concert performed by the band. Although the immediate financial impact was limited to the local markets that hosted the band, the resulting publicity and notoriety made the film more visible and popular when it opened in other cities or became available on a streaming service. And they didn't even have to fake their deaths to make it work!

CHAPTER TAKEAWAYS

- Publicity, promotion, and advertising are all interrelated marketing strategies, but have distinct objectives, outcomes, and practices.
- Unit publicity generated during a film's production is often essential for a successful release campaign.
- A unit publicist is often the first point of contact, the person who can generate substantive ideas about potential feature ideas, and ensuring that needed marketing materials are produced.

EXERCISE 8A: CATALOG A CAMPAIGN

Wherever you are and whenever you might be reading this, it's pretty much guaranteed that a major studio film, or widely available television show (via network or streaming), is just about to open. What are you most excited to see in the next month? Here's a chance to familiarize yourself with a release marketing campaign as it emerges in real time.

1. Identify a film or television show that will **open wide** to the public in three to four weeks from the start of your project. This project may have been seen previously—perhaps an earlier season of a TV series, or a film that had a debut at a film festival earlier in the year. But you are only going to focus on the current release campaign.

2. Over the course of three weeks, find at least one example of **advertising** for the film, remembering the definition of advertising as *paid space*. Find examples of each of the following:

   a. A commercial aired on broadcast television
   b. An advertisement in print (newspaper or magazine)
   c. Digital advertisements, including paid Facebook/Twitter ads, banner ads, etc. (anything *not* on the project's "official" sites)
   d. A billboard (you can do a Google search—you don't have to drive around looking for one!)
   e. A one-sheet or teaser poster at a movie theater that will exhibit the film (for film release only)
   f. A radio advertisement, including sponsorship of a podcast

3. Find evidence of at least three **promotions** related to the film, keeping in mind that the most salient characteristic of a promotion is offering something of *value* to the potential viewer. Promotions may include:

   a. In-person appearances by stars or creators at events such as Comic-Con, charity screenings related to the film, etc., where they come into contact with filmgoers and the target audience.
   b. Contests or giveaways at either a local ("free tickets to the Mall Multiplex 16 screening of *Morons in Space 2* to the 10th caller) or national (Taco Bell collector cups) level.
   c. Social media campaigns/hashtag campaigns designed to get viewers to participate/share/like/retweet (i.e., "Which *Morons in Space 2* character are you?" or "#moronselfie," etc.)
   d. Schwag giveaways (buttons, wristbands, T-shirts, etc.)
   e. Sneak preview or other special invitation screenings prior to the film's release
   f. Special access to digital material (behind-the-scenes features, deleted scenes, interviews, etc.) in exchange for email/contact information; Official Fan Club goodies and giveaways.

4. Finally, see if you can find four or five different kinds of **publicity** that support the film/TV release campaign. Look for:

   a. Interviews with or appearances of stars or creators on broadcast television, including late night, morning, newsmagazine, afternoon talk show, game show, sporting events, awards shows, etc., where they explicitly promote the project
   b. Interviews with stars or creators on podcasts or digital platforms (YouTube, Buzzfeed, etc.)

c. Interviews with or profiles of stars or creators in traditional print media (newspapers, magazines), particularly *cover stories*

d. Critical reviews of the film in a variety of digital, print, and broadcast media

e. Features in any media about the making of the film focusing on *below the line* talent (such as costumes, special effects, music, etc.)

f. Features in any media about where and when the film was made, including *on location* stories

g. News stories in any media about the marketing campaign itself (i.e., stories announcing special promotions, stories about when the exclusive new trailer will drop, etc.)

h. Official production notes or other copy or images available on the project's official website, Twitter feed, Facebook page, etc.

5. With every item you find, make a document or spreadsheet that allows you to note the following:

a. Where did this material come from and where is/was it accessible to the public? (In other words, identify the source.)

b. What are some of the salient key words or phrases that you would immediately associate with this project as you first watch/read/look at/understand/experience each piece of material? (For example: comedy, sci-fi, Adam Sandler, sequel.)

c. What audience do you believe this particular material is trying to reach? From your perspective, who might this appeal to you? (If this is too complex of a question to answer, at least address why or why not this particular material works for *you*.)

6. Once you have everything collected, take a look at your notes, and jot down ideas (in either bullet point or "essay" form) that addresses any one (or more) of the following questions:

a. Identify the same phrases, key words, taglines, etc. that are common among most or all of the elements you found. Comment on how consistent (or not) these key points are delivered, and speculate as to how variations or anomalies in this "official" verbiage might be employed to engage a more specific or narrow audience.

b. Identify the images and visual design elements common to most or all of the elements that have a visual presence. Speculate or comment as to how these various design elements reinforce the key words and themes you have already identified.

c. Take a look at the elements presented in social media versus the elements presented in traditional print and broadcast media. Compare and contrast the ways in which the viewer/audience is asked to understand and experience the film. Do the social media elements seem *quicker* or more *dynamic*? Is there "more" information available via print or broadcast? Does one type of element favor stars and spectacle while the other favors story and theme? How does potential interactivity change the value of the viewer's interest in the project?

d. Consider only the *story* of the film. How is the story presented in various marketing elements? Where do you get *teasers*? Where do you get the "most" information about the story? How do each of the various elements avoid spoilers? Which element do you think intrigues *you* the most about the project's storyline?

Now, all of the just cited examples of marketing occur when a film is released. For the rest of this chapter, we will back up several months in the life cycle of a film project and talk about how publicity is managed during production, and the role of the unit publicist. Although unit publicity might seem arcane and uninteresting when compared to other forms of publicity that occur nearer the cultural spotlight, the techniques, methods, and approaches taken during production are the seeds that will blossom when the film is released.

EXERCISE 8B: REVISED LOG LINE

- Take your project and come up with *two or three* compelling 20–30-word log lines. If you are working with a group, you might want to anonymously share your ideas, and have the group vote on which is the best, or discuss the merits of each idea.

You did a log line in your script coverage exercises, and it's not too much different now: you need to condense the story idea/premise to one sentence. But this log line might be a bit "jazzier" or have a bit more "fun" than the coverage log line. Think of this as the Netflix (or, for older readers, *TV Guide*) description of the plot. One more difference: in this case, you'll probably want to include the major stars' names in parentheses.

SAMPLE RESPONSE 8B: LOG LINES

For *Soul on Da Ice*, here is a possible log line:

> A disgraced former hockey star (Bruce McFudd) seeks redemption when he inspires a group of inner-city nerds to take up the sport of curling.

If we want to play up another angle, we might try:

> A former hockey star (Bruce McFudd) tries to win back his ex (Caroline Crane) by proving he can coach a youth curling team to victory.

Or, there's this, if we want to go a bit over the top:

> The world of curling will never be the same when a ragtag group of inner-city kids upset a national competition guided by their desperate, has-been coach (Bruce McFudd).

LOG LINE HINT: IDENTIFY YOUR STORY'S SUBJECT AND ACTION. You'll notice that each log line has a slightly different *flavor*—one is focused on the main character, the second on the romantic storyline, the third on the team. All might be equally "accurate," but you can see how just some subtle differences in emphasis might frame someone's desire to see the film. Do you want the usual male-dominated sports fan audience to see it? Try the first. Want to appeal to women? Maybe the second is better. Want to focus on the ethnic/cultural makeup of the kids and draw more urban audiences? Then the third would be the way to go.

You'll notice, in particular, that the **subjects** (*who* is the log line/film about) and the **action** (personal redemption, winning back the ex, kids becoming famous) are what differentiate these three approaches.

EXERCISE 8C: NO-SPOILER SYNOPSIS

- Write a **no-spoiler** synopsis for your feature that is about 200–300 words long. This synopsis should include information about the main characters, and the key situation and action of the film; avoid any spoilers that aren't obvious from the film's title or other elements. (For instance, if the film is about an historical event in which the outcome is well known, then you don't have to "hide" that information.) Remember to include the actors' names in parentheses.

You'll also remember that you wrote a synopsis or two as part of your script coverage exercise. This time, the level of detail you provide is very different, the most important element being no spoilers. This can be difficult for films that have *surprises*, particularly those twists that occur in the early acts. Indeed, it might be impossible for you to do a successful synopsis without revealing something important.

For example, the main character has a parent who is reliable and funny and an essential part of the plot, but dies unexpectedly in the second act, forcing the hero to take a different path of action. You might want to consult with your producer about whether the filmmakers would like that information to be known in the synopsis.

Essentially, you want to remember that this synopsis is almost like a trailer in writing: you wouldn't want to give away any big surprises in a trailer, but you also want to prepare your audience to be surprised by what happens.

EXAMPLE 8C: ONE PAGE, NO-SPOILER SYNOPSIS

At the Winter Olympics in 2006, Canadian goalie Shane "Winger" Winston (BRUCE McFUDD) was leading his national team to victory when the distracting behavior of his unruly opponents led to a humiliating loss. Known forever as one of the greatest chokers in sports history, his ignominy includes a permanent suspension from the NHL, a long abyss playing minor league hockey in Europe, and now arrest for public drunkenness at his 20th high school reunion, prompting a painful split from his long-suffering girlfriend, Dierdre (Tony award winner CAROLINE CRANE).

At his sentencing, Winger is ordered to do community service at an afterschool facility in inner-city Detroit. The good news for Winger is that the facility specializes in ice sports, and as he enters, he has dreams of coaching hockey. But the hockey program is already successful, as rec center director Mac Stauffer (SAMUEL L. JACKSON) tells Winger. They don't need anyone for hockey—they don't need anyone for speed skating, or even ice dancing, for that matter. They need someone to coach curling.

And so, Winger is put in charge of six scrawny, disengaged kids who aren't exactly blessed with athletic ability. Unable to break through with them, and unable to teach them much except how to stand on the ice and fall gracefully, Winger remembers that the only one who ever consoled him about his misery was the coach of the Canadian national curling team, Ford McFrank (JOHN LITHGOW).

With that, Winger and his underdogs throw themselves into learning Canada's "other" national sport, bringing some street flair to the sweeps-and-stones set. But their unlikely success faces resistance from some of the players' parents, and an impending career move for Dierdre means that Winger has very little time to win her back. Will Winger and his "Wingnuts" ride their radical wave all the way to a prestigious youth championship? Or will Winger's rotten luck only guarantee him another encounter with failure?

SYNOPSIS HINT: WORK FROM YOUR LOG LINES. Obviously, depending on your project, you might find various ways to *frame* the action. This particular synopsis probably lines up best with the first log line idea, focusing on the central character and his journey to redemption. An equally compelling synopsis might more highlight the central love relationship, or shift focus entirely to the characters on the team.

EXERCISE 8D: START OF PRODUCTION ANNOUNCEMENT

- Create a press release that announces the beginning of principal photography. This should be in the standard journalist "5 W" style (who, what, when, where, why), and include:

  - A proper header with contact information
  - A clear headline and slug
  - A synopsis of about one paragraph (you can adapt/shorten this from your one-page synopsis—it should be more complete then your logline)
  - Identification of all key cast and crew members to date (include writer, director, producers, all main cast members not otherwise mentioned, perhaps a DP or production designer, particularly if those are notable/awarded individuals and/or coming off very popular projects)
  - A quote about the project from a producer or director
  - A quote from the project from the main star

EXAMPLE 8D: START OF PRODUCTION ANNOUNCEMENT

For immediate release:

Contact: Lillie Prescott, Rhein + Blacque, PR (555) 777–1800

CAMERAS SET TO ROLL FOR *"SOUL ON DA ICE"*
Bruce McFudd to star in inner-city sports comedy

Max Puffery Productions and Stick-em Pictures have teamed to produce the new Bruce McFudd winter sports comedy *Soul on Da Ice*. Production begins May 3 in Detroit, with further production scheduled for Toronto and release set for February 2022. MagniFilm will distribute in North America to coincide with the Winter Olympics in Beijing.

With an original script by Mark Meltzer and Paulette Wagner (creators of the Netflix comedy *Housebroken*), *Soul on Da Ice* features McFudd as a Canadian ex-pat who was disgraced after a spectacular failure as an Olympic goalie. A decade later, in trouble with the law, he agrees to community service in the form of volunteering at in inner-city winter sports program in Detroit. When he meets his somewhat sickly and unathletic charges, he realizes that the only ice sport where they might succeed is curling, which they take up with a flair and panache that make them the bad boys of the curling world. *Soul on Da Ice* will costar Tony award winner Caroline Crane as McFudd's long-suffering girlfriend, and Samuel L. Jackson as the youth program director, with a cameo by John Lithgow as a legendary Olympic coach.

Producer Max Pfeiffer picked up the script as a pitch after seeing curling during the recent winter Olympics. "It's an unusual sport, but I was surprised at how entrancing it was and how seriously the competitors take it," says the producer. "Mark and Paulette were able to capture that competitive element perfectly. It's a shaggy dog sports story with a lot of heart, and Bruce is going to be magnificent."

Award-winning stand-up comedian and Toronto native Bruce McFudd came aboard after Pfeiffer partnered with director Yvonne Bostick, who secured financing through her new shingle, Stick-em Pictures. "Yvonne is one of the truly hilarious directors, I just love her visual sensibilities," says McFudd. "Her shorts for bubbles.com make me spit milk through my nose every time!" Also a native Canadian, Bostick confesses to being more of a hockey fan, but is eager to shoot near her home in Windsor, where the film will replicate the Olympics by filming at the actual cite of the curling event.

"I know people might think youth league curling is a strange idea for a comedy, but it's really a great fit," says the director. "It's really a story about someone who gets a second chance at love and glory."

Extra Credit Possibilities

Frequently during a film's preproduction process, multiple press releases are issued. You've already done one for the start of production. Can you write a press release announcing:

- An Oscar-winning actor has agreed to play a key supporting part in your picture—announce the deal and his or her participation.
- Your project has found a distributor! Announce the details and include reaction from both the original producer and the new company involved.
- The director on the project has been replaced due to a family medical emergency that will require him or her to step away; a new director has been hired. Announce this to the press and be sure to include quotes from all parties concerned about the necessity and disappointment regarding this news.

EXERCISE 8E: PITCH MEMO

- Come up with at least five feature ideas for your project, in the form of a memo you draft to your team and your immediate superiors. You can model these ideas off of the categories above, or suggest anything in the spirit of generating positive coverage about the story. Be sure you suggest potential outlets for the pitches.

EXAMPLE 8E: PITCH MEMO

Memorandum

    TO: Studio Executive and Production Team
    FROM: Unit Publicist

As we begin production, I'd like to suggest the following feature ideas to be considered for possible coverage or a set visit during principal photography.

- America—Meet Bruce McFudd. He's the star of Canada's top talk show and a national treasure, and now he's making the big leap across the border to the states. What might U.S. audiences expect from this new comedy sensation?

  - Would like to pitch *Entertainment Weekly* for a possible set visit.

- Curling—Canada's "Other" Sport. What is curling? The cast and crew of *Soul on Da Ice* will get to know when they are coached by production adviser Stephan Le Martin, a three-time Olympic medalist, and they all will very likely find that what looks easy on screen is deceptively difficult.

  - Would like to pitch *Sports Illustrated* and include a set visit when Stephan is working with the kids in the film.

- That Olympic Feeling. How did production designers, location scouts, and a band of local carpenters turn a junior college hockey arena in central Michigan into a replica of the 2006 Olympic Center in Torino?

  - Would like to pitch Detroit papers and other local outlets for set visits.

- From Broadway to the Big Screen. You've seen Caroline Crane on Broadway and in a number of smaller dramatic roles, but this is her comedic "coming out" party. How does this classically trained performer known for her searing Shakespearean prowess find her way into a warm-hearted romantic comedy, while still managing to be a good mom to her twin toddlers?

  - Would like to pitch women's and lifestyle magazines.

- Meet the Wingnuts. Extended profiles on the six young actors who play the members of the underdog curling team, including interviews with select parents and teachers.

  - Would like to pitch to Nickelodeon for special "behind-the-scenes" pieces to be featured on their affiliated websites as exclusives.

PITCH MEMO TIPS: Try to use direct and dynamic language to *sell* these ideas; using alliteration, puns, or other "fun" forms of language is one way to accomplish this. At the same time, try to avoid too many obvious clichés—if they are substantive and related to the pitch, they can be a helpful way into the reader's mind, but be careful not to force it or simply employ a cliché out of habit.

EXERCISE 8F: PITCH LETTER

- Take *TWO* of your pitch ideas and generate letters to a specific outlet, encouraging a set visit, and highlighting the appeal of your pitch for that specific outlet.

These pitch letters should also include other relevant production information, which you can copy from the Start of Production Release, including key cast and crew/company information, a brief description of the plot (log line or slightly longer), and basic studio/release information if available.

EXAMPLE 8F: PITCH LETTER FOR FEATURE/SET VISIT

Dear Nickelodeon:

As you may know, Canadian superstar Bruce McFudd is starring in the latest Grandmaster Studios production, *Soul on Da Ice*. In this delightful underdog sports comedy, McFudd plays disgraced former hockey star Shane "Winger" Winston, who seeks redemption when he inspires a group of inner-city nerds to take up the sport of curling. Costarring Tony winner Caroline Crane as Winger's estranged wife, and with Samuel L. Jackson and John Lithgow rounding out the cast, *Soul on Da Ice* is currently filming on location in the Detroit area, and scheduled for a late-winter release. The movie is being produced by Jeremy Gluck and Olivia McMaster, and directed by Jenny Wilhelmsen (*Air Bud 5: Bud in the Sky*).

Soul on Da Ice also features six incredibly talented newcomers, all between the ages of nine and 13, as the loveable team of not-so-athletic inner-city kids who breathe life into Winger's dreams of redemption with their streetwise attitude and strong competitive spirit. We'd like to invite one of your producers to the set for a few days to create a series of short video profiles about these remarkable young performers and their own unlikely stories. With many of them pulled from local auditions and with limited professional experience, they very likely will steal the hearts of movie audiences with their authenticity and charm.

We believe that this series of personality driven short videos would be ideal for a number of your digital platforms, and a full-length version linking them together would be an ideal half-hour piece that you could program on the Nickelodeon network. We're sure that your viewers will not only identify with these rising stars, but also benefit from seeing them turn into professionals, from balancing their schoolwork with their newfound fame, to Olympic-level training in one of the world's most unique sports, to working alongside industry veterans such as Jackson and Lithgow.

We would also make several parents, friends, and teachers of these young people available for interviews, and would be happy to arrange a local production crew. We have identified two weeks at the end of September that we think might be ideal for a set visit.

Please feel free to contact me at the *Soul on Da Ice* production office at (555) 555–1292, or reach me via email at publicist@soulondaice.com. I look forward to hearing from you soon.

CHAPTER 9

Behind the Scenes

EPKs and Production Notes

Producing the materials that will be used during a film or program's release is the main part of a unit publicist's job; even when a project does not have a full-time publicist on set, most producers, studios, and networks will take the time during production to ensure that the materials needed for both EPKs and production notes will be generated in a timely fashion.

Since these two practices involve the same basic kind of information collecting—mostly in the form of conducting interviews and collecting images related to the project—I'm presenting them together here in this shorter chapter, which focuses on two exercises designed to walk you through the process. Don't be fooled by the chapter's length, as the Production Notes exercise (9B) is the most substantial one in this book, and very likely take the longest to conceive, organize, produce, and deliver.

THE EPK—ELECTRONIC PRESS KIT

The EPK has been a fairly standard part of major filmmaking production practice since the 1970s. While there is a longer history of studios revealing "behind-the-scenes" information that dates back to the earliest days of Hollywood, it wasn't until video technology and television broadcast distribution made the EPK an efficient and relatively affordable way of supplementing a film's marketing campaign.

For many years, the EPK was invisible to the general public. Much as its text-based counterpart, the **press kit** (or **production notes**, to be discussed later), the EPK was mostly intended for critics, magazine editors, talk-show producers, and others who might be suitable outlets for publicity. A typical EPK would most likely include a main "Behind-the-Scenes" segment; a very brief scene or two from the final film (to be broadcast when the talk-show host says to the star, "Let's take a look at a clip …"); brief, edited sit-down interviews with some of the principal cast and crew members; and, very likely, one or two *featurettes* that focus on a specific aspect of the film (the same kind of thing that you highlighted in the Feature Pitch exercise). Some EPKs might feature "B-roll" or "raw footage" of the film being made (with the director calling "action," etc.).

Supplied on commercial grade videotapes (or now via digital file sharing), an outlet would have everything it needed from a "video" perspective to publicize the film. For example, the EPK would be sent to a producer of a talk show; that producer would pick out the best clip from the film, then share the EPK with the host and writers, who can watch the various features (such as the sit-down interview with the star) and think of questions to ask for broadcast. That night, the host will say, "Now, I understand you did a lot of historical research to play this part, can you tell us a little bit about that?" This question is asked because it's known that the actor has a great story about finding just the right hat or figuring out just the right accent, because the actor was seen answering the question before, on the EPK.

Likewise, you might imagine an EPK sent to a local news channel. Our example film *Soul on Da Ice* takes place in Detroit and was filmed in the area, so the Detroit TV stations and news websites will be especially interested in helping publicize the film. One station might decide to simply air one of the featurettes on a news broadcast. "We've got a behind-the-scenes look at this new movie, which featured a few young Detroit actors with stars in their eyes," says the anchor, before tape starts rolling on the EPK segment. (One interesting note: When I was a working publicist, many EPKs were produced by the same people who produced segments for *Entertainment Tonight*, *Access Hollywood*, and other shows, ensuring that everything was made according to industry or even program-specific standards.) Or, the station could use the B-roll, behind-the-scenes footage, raw interview footage, and its own reporting (profiling the local restaurant that has a key scene in the film) to edit together its own "news report" about the film.

EPK production really ramped up in the '90s and '00s, as this previously unavailable content suddenly became valuable as "DVD Extras"; in fact, most major films, such as the *Lord of the Rings* and *Star Wars* films, had large video documentary crews, knowing that the deep secrets of how the films were made and the characters brought to life would have value to the film's hardcore fan bases. Even in smaller films, the materials produced for the EPK could be packaged with the DVD release of the film, whether that was simply a 10-minute behind-the-scenes documentary, a short interview with the director, or a few minutes joking around on set with the star between takes.

With DVD sales now going the way of VHS, Betamax, and Laserdisc sales of yore, there is the possibility that EPKs could recede a little in public consciousness[1]. For those who still purchase or collect hard media, the extras on the Blu-ray or 4K or next-generation discs still will most likely include EPK-type material, and official websites and other digital platforms might prove to be another space where EPKs will be shared. Regardless of how visible EPK material is to the public, it's still very likely to be a key source of information for the press (including print, television, and digital media), and an essential component of communicating the project's cultural value to an audience.

---

1   For a recent article about the fate of the DVD extra, check out this article by Fabrice Robinet of the *New York Times* (https://www.nytimes.com/2018/04/06/movies/dvd-extras.html).

I'm sure that someone could write a book on how to produce an EPK, so we'll focus for now on the publicist's role in helping bring the EPK to life (especially since the publicist would probably rely on EPK footage to generate the production notes). On most films, a publicist will not actually "produce" the EPK, but rather serve as a liaison between the film production team and the EPK production team. Usually, EPK crews are hired by the producer or studio to arrive on a film set for a few days—EPK crews on for the entirety of a shoot are not unheard of (see the *Lord of the Rings* example previously), but usually not necessary.

The EPK crew is lead by a main producer, who may also function as the writer/director of the EPK. If you are shooting in a major entertainment industry city (Los Angeles, New York, London, Atlanta, etc.), chances are that the EPK producer is local and hires a camera person, sound operator, and perhaps editor, or has a company with all of those people on staff. If you are shooting on location, it's possible that a producer from New York or Los Angeles (or wherever is near your set) will be hired, and then recruit a very local crew to produce the footage. Usually, camera operators and sound recorders from local news stations are available on a freelance basis.

The publicist will coordinate with the producer of the EPK the best dates for the crew to be on set. This is usually something discussed with the producers of the film early in the production process—it should be one of a unit publicist's first jobs, to look at the production schedule and determine ideas for when the EPK crew will work. You want to be sure that the work being shot on those days is *interesting looking*—if that day is a "second unit" day when a skeleton crew will be shooting footage of airplanes being towed, then the EPK crew probably won't get much except 90 seconds of B-roll. You also want to be sure the crew is there when all of the film's stars are available: sometimes a major star only works on a film for a few consecutive days, and there are many days where costars are not called to the set at the same time. Remember, the actors, director, and anyone else who might be interviewed as part of the EPK are working—they have restrictions on how many hours and days of the week they can work, and the publicist must factor that in.

Once the dates are determined, a publicist will then communicate all information regarding the schedule to all parties concerned, including the EPK producer and crew, the production office (who in turn inform all production personnel), the studio, the agents who represent the actors, etc. While the writing skills necessary for this part of the job are minimal—updated schedules and memos that should be easy to read and fit in with production workflow—careful attention to detail and strong management skills are required.

A good EPK producer will have read the script and talked with the producers about possible angles, features, and other ideas for the EPK. Sometimes the film suggests a fun theme—for example, the EPK for the film *School of Rock* uses a "school" visual motif with chalkboards, etc., and generic hard-rock music at key points of transition. As a publicist, your job is to be sure the EPK crew gets what it needs, but also that the EPK does the job it is supposed to do. Suggesting featurette ideas, informing the EPK producer about some really cool innovations being made by the special effects artist, or how the costume designer solved a last-minute wardrobe malfunction are all things a publicist might do to ensure that the EPK is as comprehensive and compelling as possible.

Probably the most impactful way a publicist can help make the EPK work is through constructing thoughtful and meaningful **interview questions**. Most EPK producers will ask the standard questions—"Tell me about your character," "Why do you think audiences will like this film." A publicist can possibly offer a bit more insight and get the interview subject to talk about things that go above and beyond the usual and make the project seem truly unique.

This is an especially important skill in the present day. As mentioned before, publicists are generally spending less time on the set during production. If a publicity firm or studio division is handling the unit publicity from afar, the actual publicist overseeing the film might not even be on the set the days the EPK is produced. As such, the interviews of the cast and crew members might be the only opportunity to get an interview done. This is key because, as we will see, these interviews are the life blood of the written production notes. In recent years I have been asked to generate increasingly more EPK questions for the projects I work on from a distance. The stars of the film will not be available to me seven months from now when the production notes need to be written and completed, so I rely on the interviews (shared with me digitally or via written transcriptions) to give me access to their perspective and insight on the filmmaking process.

In preparation for Exercise 9A, I suggest you take a look at a few EPKs; if you ditched your hard media collection and only watch films via the cloud, a local library (or heck, a $5 bin at a department store) will probably have some DVDs with plentiful "extra" material. Concentrate specifically on any sit-down interviews: you won't hear the question, but you'll get a sense of what was asked from the answer offered in response. Think about what makes each answer from the star, director, or crew members particularly "important." It's very likely there are about 20 minutes of total interview footage—why did the EPK producer, the studio, and the publicist ultimately feel that what is presented on the EPK is relevant, significant, or interesting?

THE PRODUCTION NOTES

Production notes are the written elements of what used to be called a press kit. A full press kit would also contain stills photographs, slides, or digital files that a press outlet might use in publicizing the film (those same stills a publicist helped cull from the hundreds or thousands shot by the set stills photographer). In earlier days, press kits might also include small promotional items, audio recordings of interviews, video copies of the EPK, or other marketing-related materials. It is usually the film's producer and distributor who work together to complete the elements of the press kit upon the film's release.

The written elements of a press kit remain the dominant framework by which the other materials are understood, and the most important way that a production team can communicate to the press about the project's value. All of the images and schwag are nice to have because they are almost like promotions—*pieces* of the film that connect the audience directly with the project (it's one reason why press kits complete with high-quality still photographs and can fetch a nice penny on eBay). But in terms of giving a critic, editor, journalist, or talk-show host the language and information necessary to properly appreciate the film, the written production notes are absolutely essential.

A typical set of production notes, almost always written, edited, and assembled by the unit publicist (or a staff publicist working on behalf of the producer, studio, or distributor), includes the following elements.

A COVER PAGE

Sometimes with an image from the film, an appropriate company logo, etc. The cover page contains the title, main stars, main crew (writer, director, producer), running time, MPAA rating, and contact information (usually the marketing or publicity executive in charge of the film's release campaign). There may be other information that producers wish to include, such as format, language, country of origin, award "laurels," etc.

A CAST AND CREW PAGE

Typically, a single page at the beginning of a press kit features character names, actor names, production titles, and crew names, in an easy-to-read format (see our examples for tips on how to format properly and effectively in Microsoft Word).

In many cases, a full **credit list** (such as what runs at the end of the film) is not yet available; if it is, some producers ask that the entire credit sequence be included in the production notes. That information is often supplied to the writer of the notes, but must be formatted properly so that it looks "clean" on the page.

LOG LINE (25–30 WORDS) AND NO-SPOILER SYNOPSIS (200–300 WORDS)

You've practiced and executed these already, and should be included on a single page in your production notes.

"ABOUT THE PRODUCTION"

This offers a narrative of how the project was made. This can range from six to 25-plus pages, double-spaced (2,000–8,000 words). This narrative will include quotes from relevant cast and crew members about the making of the film, culled from EPK interviews or other interviews with the unit publicist. Usually written in the same tone and style as a feature magazine article, these notes are positive and frame the project in the best possible light.

SHORT BIOGRAPHIES OF THE KEY CAST AND CREW

The publicist will often collect "official" bios from the talent representatives of the cast; lesser-known actors or below-the-line crew members may not have official bios. Since professional biographies are written in a number or formats, the writer of the production notes must ensure that all of biographies are more or less written in the same journalistic style.

(For example, one biography might put a film title "In Quotes" while another uses *Italics*. If you are writing notes, you need to pick one or the other and make the appropriate correction to the original text.)

OPTIONAL—SPECIAL FEATURES

Just as EPK featurettes or your feature pitches, these are more focused, specific elements that may or may not be requested or desirable. It could be something as simple as some historical background on the film's story; a dedicated Q&A with the director that is presented in an interview format; or an extended profile of a member of the cast or crew. These features can often be *beta-tested* as set visits or production pitch letters. As a professional, I usually try to suggest at least one "extra" feature when I contract to do work, though ultimately it is up to the producer or studio to decide whether an additional feature or features is desired.

You can find sample sets of full production notes online through official project websites; not all releases will share this information, but many will. Because these notes are the legal property of the producers, studios, networks, and distributors who own the rights to the projects in question, we are not able to provide "real-life" samples. I also link to several examples of production notes I have contributed to on my website, writeawayink.com, but you should be encouraged to seek out production notes or press kits for film and television projects that you find particularly compelling or interesting.

A NOTE ABOUT THE EVOLUTION OF PRESS KITS

For many years, press kits were considered something of a collectible not because of the written material, but because of the still images, original and "official" artifacts of the film that were not generally available to the moviegoing public, which could prove valuable as keepsakes or investments. In many cases, studios made not only these photos, but also negatives, slides, and later CDs and thumb drives with these images, so that print (and digital) outlets would have easy access to these materials for advertising, publicity, and promotional purposes.

Beginning with the television era, it became essential for these previously analog media to be available in more modern formats. Audio cassettes—essentially "radio" versions of EPKs—might be created to share with the country's radio stations, which could either pop in the cassette and play it in its entirety, or excerpt it. A media kit for the film *All the President's Men*, housed in one of the collections of my university's library, has cassettes that feature interviews with each of the stars, alongside a script that one could read along with. So if you were a radio-show host in Bend, Oregon, you could "host" an interview with Dustin Hoffman or Robert Redford. There were educational press kits made for schools that often included film strips, 8-millimeter or 16-millimeter films that were the available technology in most K-12 classrooms in the era before videocassette players. As satellite and digital communications became more available, these "hard media" offerings began to wane, as it became possible for stars such as Hoffman or Redford to be interviewed from a great distance as part of a **video junket**. As video technology became media industry standard, the creation of press kits fell into the current two-pronged system of the EPK/digital audio-video and the traditional "written" press kit handed out to critics, journalists, and editors at film screenings.

Throughout these initial changes, **special features** remained a significant part of a film's marketing package. Although electronic press kits have been available since the 1960s, for decades afterward, the major studios wanted to supply as much information as possible in print, to ensure the proper information was always available in "hard copy" for any journalist who may require it. Yes, it was great to be able to circulate an EPK that had several three-minute features about each of the wondrous technological advances in a blockbuster film, but that was very likely only available in an industrial videotape format. If you are a small-town newspaper reporter who wants to write a story about how model builders helped create the latest *Star Wars* movie, highlighting the local business that makes the modeling clay used in the movie, then you wouldn't have easy access to watch repeatedly that three-minute video so you could transcribe the quotes from the effects artists who are being interviewed.

That's why the full press kit with multiple features was so important. My father worked at 20th Century Fox when it released the third *Star Wars* film, *Return of the Jedi*, in 1983. This made me *very* cool at my suburban junior high, as I possessed early film "schwag" including posters and stickers that read *REVENGE of the Jedi*—the film's title was changed just six weeks before the film's release! So I still possess quite a few promotional items from the film, including the full "official" press kit, which contains the following:

- An "Announcement Story" (two pages), describing the release of the film, with "blanks" left on the page for a local writer to fill in the exact date and location of the film's opening.
- A set of production notes (58 pages, formatted to be about 200 words per page), with:
  - A title page with basic credits (the ones you would see on the film's one-sheet or print ads)
  - A full cast page
  - Two pages of production crew credits
  - An 18-page "About the Production" section

o A one-page "The Story" (in this case, not really a synopsis, just three short paragraphs describing the very basic "situation" of the film)
o "About the Players" section, in which bios also include quotes from the actors about their roles, and are framed in a feature-writing style. ("MARK HAMILL really is Luke Skywalker and his enthusiasm for his role and the STAR WARS Saga is quite contagious.") This section features eight actor bios and runs 16 pages.
o "About the Filmmakers" section: 25 pages covering more than a dozen technicians, producers, etc.

- Feature: "John Williams and a Musical Landmark" (five pages)
- Feature: "Designers Create Creatures for Star Wars Sequel" (five pages)
- Feature: "The Star Wars Saga on Location" (five pages)
- Feature: "Monumental Space Epic Reaches the Screen Through Teamwork" (three pages)
- Feature: "Mark Hamill: From Skywalker to Mozart" (four pages)
- Feature: "Harrison Ford as Han Solo" (three pages)
- Feature: "Carrie Fisher Returns as Princess Leia" (three pages)
- Feature: "Billy Dee Williams Brings Back Lando Calrissian" (four pages)
- Feature: "Anthony Daniels as C-3PO" (three pages)

If we are adding up those pages, that's 97 pages, nearly 20,000 words of writing—equivalent to about 23% of the length of this book! In addition, the kit includes 12 black-and-white stills from the films, each of which has an explanatory caption and full credit information (names of everyone in the photo, etc.).

With the Internet, of course, a digital "record" is much easier to create, access, and distribute, so the need for written-only feature material has fallen off. Likewise, PR firms and studio departments no longer have the need to develop, print, and mail hundreds of still prints, or even digital copies, since they can give their intended recipients easy access to those materials via secure online portals. Even the EPK no longer needs to be on a commercial-grade videotape, just a professional quality digital file that can be downloaded, edited, published, and shared online in a way that is accessible to anyone. Still, the ability to generate feature ideas and generate images and recordings that ensures every possible "angle" is exploited is something that must be at the front of any publicity professional's mind, whether they manifest themselves in production notes, personal bios, web-based interviews, or social media platforms.

CHAPTER TAKEAWAYS

- A critical and necessary outcome of unit publicity is creating materials for the EPK and press kit/production notes.
- Developing interview questions that are both generic to the creative process and also specific toward the project will provide substantive quotes for use in both digital and printed "about the production" information.
- Production-based publicity such as set visits and feature pitch ideas can be expanded and developed in special features sections.

EXERCISE 9A: EPK QUESTIONS

- Generate three general questions about the film that you would ask of all of your interview subjects. This can be "tell the story of the film," "tell us about why you wanted to do this film," etc.
- Generate three specific questions for *five* of the people working on your film—two or three cast members, a producer, a director, and/or a writer. Try to make these questions a bit more substantive than the general ones. Think of your feature pitch ideas—can you get your subjects to talk about those aspects of the film? What are the answers you might want to hear and how can you craft a question to get that answer?

EXAMPLE RESPONSE: EXERCISE 9A

Three general questions:

1. What interested you in making *Soul on Da Ice*?
2. Why do you think stories about sports underdogs are so popular?
3. Are you a fan of the Winter Olympics? What is your experience with winter sports?

Cast member questions (Bruce McFudd)

1. Can you explain the popularity of curling in Canada?
2. What makes Winger such a unique character?
3. How did you train/study/prepare for the role?

Cast member questions (Samuel L. Jackson)

1. What do you think you bring to the character of Mac?
2. How is it working with Bruce McFudd?
3. What is it like working with so many child actors?

Producer questions

1. What do you hope audiences take away from this film?
2. Tell us about working with Yvonne Bostick—how is she handling her first major directing assignment?
3. American audiences don't know much about Bruce McFudd—why is he the ideal person to cast in the role of Winger?

Director questions

1. This is your first feature film assignment—what has the experience been like?
2. You're a Canadian, so can you give us any insight into the sport of curling and why it is so popular?
3. How has it been working with Bruce McFudd?

Production designer questions

1. Most of this film takes place during the winter: how did that affect the choices you made to bring the film to life?
2. What kind of director is Yvonne Bostick? How has she been as a collaborator?
3. Tell us about the unique uniforms that were created for the youth curling team; who designed that "Wingnut" logo?

EXERCISE 9B: PRODUCTION NOTES

- Assemble your own set of production notes for a sample project. Begin by making a template that contains space for all of the elements indicated previously (cover sheet, cast/crew page, etc.). I suggest that you use real names for the cast and crew, keeping it believable (a couple of A-list celebs as leads, lesser-known performers for the supporting roles, etc.).

  o **Biographies** can be taken from the talent's "official" websites, or you may write them based on an actor's IMDB page or other sources. Try to write bios for at least five actors, and also the film's writer, producer, director, director of photography, and editor. Be sure to format bios consistently (see below for tips).
  o The "**About the Production**" section should be at least 2,000 words long, and include quotes from members of the cast and crew. Go ahead and make up those quotes, or partner with someone and do a mock interview in which they play the part of the person you are interviewing.
  o Your **special feature** idea should be at least two or three pages (700–1,000 words), and should include relevant quotes and information.

SOME TIPS FOR THE CAST/CREW PAGE

Learn to use the "Tables" function on Microsoft Word. I use a fairly simple system, which is demonstrated in the instructions that follow:

Create/insert a 3 × 3 table:

On the line above your table, center your cursor and type the word "Cast":

Cast

One at a time, "inner" vertical lines so that it lines up on either side of the word "Cast" (you are "narrowing" the middle column):

Cast

Highlight the LEFT column and change the paragraph orientation to RIGHT JUSTIFIED. Highlight the LEFT column and change the orientation to LEFT JUSTIFIED. When you type in text, you can verify the correct orientation.

Cast

Character		ACTOR NAME
Character 2		ACTOR NAME
Character 3		ACTOR NAME

Fill in the character name on the left, and the actor's name on the right. I like to put actor names in ALL CAPS, but that is purely a stylistic choice. Hint: If you "tab" after you type

"Fisher" in the example below, you will automatically "build" a new row as seen, with your cursor in place to type the next character name.

Cast

Luke Skywalker	MARK HAMILL
Han Solo	HARRISON FORD
Princess Leia	CARRIE FISHER
Lando Calrissian	

When you are done, highlight or select the entire table. Then, select "No Borders" from the "Borders and Shading" option.

Cast

Luke Skywalker	MARK HAMILL
Han Solo	HARRISON FORD
Princess Leia	CARRIE FISHER
Lando Calrissian	BILLY DEE WILLIAMS
See Threepio (C-3PO)	ANTHONY DANIELS

Copy and paste the "Cast" title and a few rows; change "Cast" to "Crew" or "Production Crew" and fill in as appropriate. Note: it is personal preference as to whether you want to list credits as "Director" or "Directed by," "Etc." You'll see that in some cases I use the "label" (noun) rather than the "action" (verb), but with some practices, one "sounds" better than the other.

Production Crew

Director	RICHARD MARQUAND
Producer	HOWARD KAZANJIAN
Screenplay by	LAWRENCE KASDAN GEORGE LUCAS
Story by	GEORGE LUCAS
Executive Producer	GEORGE LUCAS

SOME TIPS FOR 'ABOUT THE PRODUCTION'

- One of the easiest ways to structure this section is to tell the story of how the project came to be: begin with the writer's original idea, how the script got the attention of the producer or director, when the cast came together, and then the details of going before the cameras.

  ○ The writer: Where did the idea come from, why is it important to you, why did you "believe" in this story?

- The producer and director: Who first showed you the script, what was your reaction, how has it been collaborating with the writer on developing the script?

  - Frame everything from a positive perspective: sometimes a script has multiple writers, went through casting changes, even studio changes (such as the *Good Will Hunting* example discussed previously). Although these may have created some conflict, minimize the negative and accentuate the positive.

- Finding the cast: Why are they appropriate, what do they bring to the project? (Ask the cast the same questions you asked the writer and producer, such as how they first become aware, and how it's been working on the film prior to production.)
- Production details: Where did they shoot, how long, what challenges did they face (both practical and unexpected)?

  - This is a good time to bring in quotes from technicians working on the film, such as the cinematographer and production designer.

- I also find it helpful to frame this narrative in the context of the film's themes. Thus, I try to have an opening and closing paragraph in which the people involved are talking about the meaning and value of the film—what it means to them, and what they hope it means to audiences. Those themes can then be interwoven throughout the notes, giving the history of the making process a unique angle.
- Be wary that some stories or quotes play better when the person telling them is live (recorded for the EPK interview) rather than typed out. Make sure you are correcting grammar, turning the quotes into complete sentences, and minimizing excessive words. It's perfectly acceptable to slightly rewrite a direct quote: use the subject's exact words as much as possible, but if they say "terrific" seven times in one paragraph, it's usually okay to change, elude, or replace that word so that it reads more efficiently. Remember: your producers, directors, and other subjects (and their reps) are very likely to read this for approval.
- Try to find the balance between formulaic—the things that every press kit covers (What are the themes? What is it like working with so-and-so?)—and the unique (the elements that make this film different than other films). If you read enough press kits, you'll see a formula that more or less works, but try to take time to find the things that are presented that could *only* be relevant to that particular film. Often, those elements are the best frames to examples by which to present the more generic and expected materials.

SOME TIPS FOR FORMATTING BIOGRAPHIES

- Be sure that all title formatting is consistent; I put movie titles in quotes, and italicize plays/books, but you can make any choice you want as long as it is consistent from bio to bio.

- Be sure that each bio follows a similar narrative structure. Some bios go from present-to-past; others start with biographical details, then go from past-to-present. Some bios feature film credits first, then television, then stage; others will simply move in chronological order.
- For new talent with fewer credits, it's okay to include lesser-known works (independent films, shorts, etc.), particularly if those projects won awards.
- For veteran talent, keep the focus on the major films, roles, and accomplishments. For example, Samuel L. Jackson has more than 175 credits as an actor on his IMDB page; a reasonable bio would focus on his five or six most recent notable efforts (starring roles), then perhaps 10–15 more of his memorable titles from previous years. Be sure to indicate nominations and wins for major awards such as Oscars, Emmys, Tonys, Golden Globes, etc. Also, if the actor previously worked with the same director as the current project, those titles should also be included and highlighted.
- Many "official" bios contain personal information about an actor's charitable work, outside businesses, and personal life. My practice is to minimize or eliminate this information in a project press kit unless it is truly exceptional (i.e., given a Presidential Medal of Honor, married to an equally famous person, etc.).
- Try to keep the length of the bio somewhat in proportion to the size of the role in the film. If the film has a newcomer as a lead and a veteran such as Samuel L. Jackson in a cameo, that might be difficult, but do your best to keep things relatively consistent. If it means including a few more credits or information on the lead, and a few less for the cameo, that is understood.
- Make sure any credits you list are substantive: many actors appeared as extras in films or television shows decades ago, and you want to be sure you don't overvalue or mistakenly estimate their contributions. Don't say, "He starred in the series *Miami Vice*," when in fact he just appeared in one episode as "Bartender #2."
- If you are using an official bio, be sure you adapt it so it's up to date. If a bio is only six months old, it might say that the actor's "next project" is something that came out three months ago. Adapt accordingly, and check IMDB or the trades to see if there are other "upcoming" projects that you might want to highlight.
- Some official bios will give lengthy descriptions of an actor's previous roles. For example, for Harrison Ford: "He starred as the iconic 'Han Solo,' mercenary pilot of the Millennium Falcon, in George Lucas's beloved *Star Wars* franchise for 20th Century Fox and later Disney." You could shorten that to "Ford is best known for the *Star Wars* franchise" or something to that effect. Again, make sure all your bios are consistent in this regard: Don't list one actor's credits with director/studio/name of character/description of film, while another actor's credits are just a list of titles.
- Remember, in this case, you are not *selling* the actor/crew member—you are simply giving a bit of brief, notable context about that person's career. We'll teach you how to write a more *pitchy* bio in a later chapter.

CHAPTER 10

'You Gotta See This!'

Hype, Word of Mouth, and Writing for Release and Distribution

U ntil now, almost all of the writing exercises we have engaged in have been intended for a very limited and most likely "friendly" audience. Script coverage, story notes, even production notes, are documents that will most likely be circulated among various people you work with and/or work for: everyone is ostensibly on the same team and has the same desired intentions and ambitions for the project. The exceptions to this have been the pitch and solicitation letters, which are tailored to very specific people or entities (an agent or manager, a specific outlet for a feature story, etc.). And even in those cases, so far we've been asking people to "partner" and collaborate on some element of the creative production. You need someone to help you <u>make</u> something.

Now, however, the production is finished (or, in our timeline, very nearly so). The cameras have stopped rolling, the footage has been cut together and only the finishing touches in sound and postproduction need to be completed before the project is locked. As a producer or executive concerned with the project's release to the public, you no longer need anyone's help getting the film *made*. Now, you need help getting the film *seen* and *sold*.

So while you'll be writing more pitch letters in this chapter, you now need to pitch effectively enough to persuade someone to watch your film. Invariably, that someone will very likely be a person who is *not* part of your immediate "work family," someone with no invested interest in whether the project succeeds or fails. It's also very likely that someone besieged by invitations from dozens of other studios and producers and networks and agents and managers and publicists will also want someone to take a look at *their* movie or TV show or web series. Not only that, but you will also very likely ask that person to not only watch the project, but also to publicly "like" it and affirm its value by spreading word about the film to others. Finally, with some exceptions, it's rare that your writing is going to be directed at a single individual: now you have to create materials that can be used in multiple situations with multiple audiences.

From the professional industry writer's perspective, this shift in what you are writing about and how that writing functions is equivalent to the difference between **narrowcasting** and **broadcasting**. The production notes might be seen as a theoretical bridge between those two slightly different practices. When a publicist or studio writer creates and completes a set of production notes, they are typically approved by a series of producers, marketing executives, and others: those in power are the ones who ultimately have final say about the content of the notes, and they are the writer's most important audience in that respect. And, obviously, these are people closely connected to the project and deeply invested in its ultimate success.

Those same written materials, however, are intended to be used for much wider distribution to critics, editors, and other industry professionals, who need the basic information about the project made available to them. These are people who know nothing about the project, and could potentially engage in a wide manner of practices with different intended outcomes (a photo shoot, an interview, a personal appearance, etc.). Thus, the production notes must meet the needs and approval of the smaller, internal reading audience (the producers), and it does so by effectively communicating key information about the film to a potentially much more diverse, less informed, and less invested reader (a potential outlet).

That's going to be the key thing for you to remember as you complete the exercises in this chapter—and because you very likely will be working on an "imaginary" project (whether you are working alone or in a group/class situation), at this point it's going to require more leaps of imagination on your part to complete some of these exercises.

As with previous chapters, the very important caveat is that in the professional world, every project has its own completely unique conditions. Briefly, these differences are often due to the circumstances of a project's distribution, which is by necessity connected to the realities of a constantly shifting marketplace, a subject far beyond the scope of this book and my own expertise. As with production, big budgets and ambitious thinking are encouraged in some campaigns, frugality and minimal effort in others. But even using your own knowledge of how projects become available to the public, and some critical thinking, you can probably imagine drastically different scenarios for how a film's release campaign might play out, and you may have noticed this in the cataloging exercise in the previous chapter (particularly if you compared your information with others).

For example, one film might be an independent film made in a very specific location: films I've worked on in this regard range from Victor Nunez's *Ruby in Paradise* (filmed on the Gulf Coast of Florida and Ashley Judd's breakout film) or *Lowriders* with Demian Bichir (shot in Latinx neighborhoods in East Los Angeles). It's very likely that during such on-location filming, local press will write stories about the production, and will remain interested in supporting news of the production's eventual release. Perhaps a film is exhibited at a major film festival, where publicists help generate "buzz" for unsold films, ultimately setting the ground for the film to get a wider distribution deal. Perhaps then the distributor decides to do a limited release in New York and Los Angeles for awards season, followed by a mid-January release in arthouses in 25 markets, and an on-demand/streaming premiere six weeks after that. In our example, an audience member living in one part of the country might become aware of and/or get to see the film months or even a year before the wide public has access to it, and marketing teams need to know how to conduct a **rolling campaign** that hopefully builds as time goes on.

On the other hand, the project might be a **tentpole** blockbuster franchise that will be released on thousands of screens with a special midnight Thursday opening, and simultaneous releases in Asia, Europe, and Australia the week after. *Everyone* is going to know that this film is coming out May 25 and television, radio, billboards, and Internet ads and memes will be entirely focused on the fate of Superhero X or the adorable new sidekick in the new Disney princess musical. The project might be a "very important film" by a "very important filmmaker" that must be discussed on the news by serious people who talk about very important things. Or, the project might be just another stoner comedy about three idiots who get more than they bargained for when they inherit a dilapidated food truck, starring that guy from that show and that other guy from that stand-up special on Netflix. Each of these projects is going to require communicating with different audiences at different times, and finding allies in the industry who are willing to assist in that effort.

So the particulars of each campaign will be different. For this chapter, as mentioned, use one of the projects your group has worked on so you will have some familiarity with the property and the selling points of the project. At least one person in your group will have written production notes for the project, so that is always a good place to start.

Complete Exercise 10A:
END OF PRODUCTION
ANNOUCEMENT

SCREENINGS AND CRITICS

One of a publicity team's most essential jobs is to ensure critical coverage for a film's release. There are literally hundreds of well-established professional film critics in the United States (nearly 100 in the National Society of Film Critics alone), along with hundreds more amateur critics, fan organizations, gossip columnists, and other potential outlets where someone is willing to publicly praise (or condemn) your project. Successful publicity also means being connected to the editors, publishers, and staff of each of those critical outlets—not just the people with the title of *critic* or *movie reviewer*—more points of contact essential to getting good work done. The publicist-critic relationship is a necessary component to the job—and if both parties are passionate about their work and looking to present the project to the public in the best possible light, then this is a relationship that can be quite productive and supportive for all parties concerned.

Obviously, a publicist can't force a critic to like a film or to write a positive review, and both parties have to develop somewhat thick skin about negative reviews, because that same publicist will have to get a review from that same critic the following week on a different film. A good publicist will know how to maintain an honest and professional relationship with a critic regardless of that critic's opinion about a specific film, and a good critic will rely upon a good publicity and marketing team to provide compelling and useful information and access to projects of value. Just because a critic might not like a particular film doesn't mean that the website he or she writes for won't be interested in a feature article about the subject or photo shoot with the star.

Furthermore, the presence of critical reviews—good, bad, or in-between—helps legitimize any project that is newly available to a viewing public. Whether it is a high rating on Rotten Tomatoes or Metacritic, or a specific favorite reviewer's "five-star" rave, or a spot in the "Top Ten New Docs to Stream This Month" article from *The AV Club*, seeing critical reviews reminds audiences that the film is "out," available, and part of the current cultural landscape.

And, as mentioned, those reviews are often presented alongside or in close proximity to other publicity and marketing efforts about the film. One hopes there is some unanimity and consensus between the *hype* of the release publicity and the evaluation of the critics and tastemakers (and, ultimately, the moviegoing public). Creating that consensus—"The critics agree, it's the best animated musical since *Frozen*"—is something that can be designed, planned, and engineered by a shrewd marketing team, and put into action in the various written materials that support the film's release.

Remember, the production notes, the screening invitation, or anything conveyed by the studio or producers to the press and the public, is a chance to essentially air another commercial or trailer for the film in the imagination of the reader or potential viewer. This needs to be an ongoing process, as the description of the final film evolves and certain aspects of the film emerge as more salient, interesting, or compelling. Some of the creative decisions proposed in development might have changed the tone or meaning of the film; maybe a new actor gave an unexpectedly brilliant performance that has producers considering a push for an Emmy or Golden Globe award. Quite frequently, the project's title has changed, or a new studio or distributor has gotten involved and wants to ensure that the film is successful in a particular marketplace or with a particular demographic.

You have your own experience being a target of marketing as an audience member, and anticipating the release of a film you are eager to see. You may read about the film being in production with a favorite star, with a somewhat vague but tantalizing description of the plot. Perhaps part of the way through production, the studio releases a "first look" behind-the-scenes interview with the star in costume, with some pre-CGI clips of them in action. As the film wraps, the studio releases a **teaser** trailer and a "Coming Soon" poster in the multiplexes, adding a few more details. Two months before the film is due out (and most likely complete enough for the studio to begin showing to select critics), the studio releases a full two-minute trailer, launches an official website, starts sending out production notes and stills, eventually circulating short preview clips, 30-second TV ads, and visual and virtual advertising. The week of the film's release, you'll see the stars on the talk shows with even more specific and newer scenes, and stories on social media "buzzing" about the film's secrets.

We can also think about this from the perspective of an indie/outsider film that takes the cinematic world by storm—anything from *sex, lies and videotape* to *Little Miss Sunshine* to *Moonlight*. Those films—at least initially—had far less visible, but carefully targeted, marketing and publicity campaigns. An independently financed film from a determined young filmmaker from far away gets into a film festival not only because of the quality of the film, but because the film's producers already have professional-looking marketing and public relations materials available; those same materials make the film a festival "must-see" and attracts the attention of potential distributors. Those distributors focus on key markets and seek the support of the highest-profile critics to heap early praise on the film, eyeing awards-season voters and sending them free screeners, and placing the stars on high-profile outlets where awards voters and tastemakers are expected to be (such as local public radio in Los Angeles and New York). It's probably at that point when the film pops up on the radar of a reasonably avid moviegoer, who starts becoming aware of the "hype" of the film just before it is made available to them, despite the fact the film may have been in the pipeline for several months.

Of course, not everyone follows film as closely as a "reasonably avid" moviegoer or film industry professional; most moviegoers most likely only experience one or two of these marketing elements. But remember that the person you must first connect with through your writing is an industry professional, and you need to be sure that as soon as you have a distribution plan, you are ready to reach out to these people and get them to agree and act quickly. We've got an opening date—all systems are go.

Complete Exercise 10B: Critic's Screening Invitation

PLANNING A CAMPAIGN

You've gotten the film to the critics, editors, tastemakers, and potential partner outlets, and let's assume that at least a significant number of them react positively to your project. You probably won't get a specific yes/no reaction from critics or reviewers, who may prefer to express their opinions only in writing, but usually people who attend advance screenings expect to be asked about their reactions and the possibility of some sort of outcome tied to the film's release.

The digital era has radically expanded and shifted the ways in which entertainment projects are marketed and publicized. In the heyday of feature film marketing (really until about 2006), a typical feature film would probably have a marketing life of about four to six months, from the initial outreach to long-lead outlets to the film's initial opening in specified marketplaces and exhibition platforms. As consumer-based home video options have grown from VHS to DVD to VOD, additional marketing strategies and campaigns may be deployed, but those are usually driven by advertising and paid space. The major publicity work is usually finished a few weeks after the primary release date, with subsequent releases to new markets repurposing previously created marketing materials (updated press kits, recirculation of celebrity interviews, etc.).

Digital distribution has destabilized the old model somewhat. Some films go straight to on-demand or streaming with great fanfare—those outlets used to be seen as "dumping grounds" for failed feature films, but now it might be the place where a veteran filmmaker premieres a controversial new work, or where a Sundance favorite in January can be on your home TV screen in February. There might be less time to build an effective campaign: even if you have a couple of months, the director of your little indie film (who may have completed shooting the movie a year ago) might be unavailable to promote it on a moment's notice; meanwhile, your glamorous international star won't be in any fashion magazines since those pieces are usually planned months in advance.

You're usually going to maximize your chances of coverage by writing a specific pitch letter to a strategic outlet. You did this a little in Exercise 10B, in which you suggested a feature idea in conjunction with a screening. In exercise 10C, you have the chance to create more pitch letters tailored to specific types of outlets. Let's define some of the terms used in both publishing and public relations to give you an overview of a typical campaign.

LONG LEAD

This is an outlet that plans more than two months before publication date. Although there are fewer monthly magazines than ever, those that remain have a powerful position in the cultural marketplace—anyone who shops in a supermarket will see who is on the cover of *Cosmopolitan* or *GQ*, or on the cover of a year-end "Best of" publication or mid-summer "What's Hot" special issue of a major magazine. There are also prestigious film journals, senior freelance critics, and other industry professionals who might have longer turnaround times for their articles or profiles. Long-lead outlets usually prefer to see films eight to 12 weeks before release, so that they can assign writers, designers, photographers, and project managers to approved articles, segments, or features.

SHORT LEAD

Conversely, this is an outlet that features more frequent product, from weekly magazines, television shows, podcast, etc. Weekly magazines and major television outlets might be considered **medium lead**, as they will usually want to be pitched a month or more before distribution, but even they often have last-minute changes and can work with a condensed timeline.

IMMEDIATE LEAD/IMMEDIATE RELEASE

These outlets are essentially instant, and include websites, programs produced and aired daily (such as *Entertainment Tonight* or even the regular evening news), and newspapers. It's highly unlikely you would be approaching an **immediate lead** outlet at the very last minute about an idea, but it's also very likely you would be providing it content or information right up until the moment it publishes or goes live or broadcasts. For example, if you want *E! Entertainment News* to cover your project's red carpet premiere, then you might pitch the project two weeks before, follow-up with confirmation the week of, and then the day of to make sure the *E!* cameras are well-placed on the welcome line, and that the film's stars and director take time to say a few words before entering the theater. That footage might air within hours of the event. In another circumstance, it's possible that real-life events make your film instantly relevant—perhaps someone associated with the film has died, or a prominent politician has spoken up about some controversial subject the film covers. As a publicist or marketing executive, you want to be able to call up a columnist, reporter, or editor and say, "Let me put the film's director on the air to comment about the controversy" or "I can get you a quote or two from the deceased star's fellow cast members that you can include in their obituary." (Note: It might seem crass to exploit someone's death or a real-life situation, but oftentimes it is the press that approaches the star or studio about making a comment, and it is considered completely appropriate to make sure that such material is handled sensitively and properly by all parties involved. I'll talk a little more about "emergency" publicity in the next chapter.)

EXCLUSIVE

This brings us to another important term that, in typical show business fashion, has no fixed meaning. Offering an outlet something unique and special—an **exclusive**—is obviously a big deal. If Robert De Niro, famously impatient with doing publicity, has agreed to do *one* major interview in support of the project you are working on, then offering that one interview to a huge outlet such as the *New York Times* or *60 Minutes* is a big deal.

Marketing professionals and outlets alike, however, will fudge on exactly what is meant by truly "exclusive." Maybe it's the only interview that the star will give in that particular country, region, city or state; or, even more likely, the interview isn't "exclusive," just unique to the outlet. (As in, "Robert De Niro sat down with an exclusive interview with our own Channel 8 entertainment reporter, Victoria de la Cava." The actual interview with Victoria de la Cava won't air anywhere else, but De Niro also did "exclusive" interviews that day with reporters from channels 2, 11, and E!)

For major outlets, such as high-profile magazines and talk shows, exclusivity, or at least having an understanding of the same star's publicity schedule, has some importance. It might take quite a bit of expense and effort for a local television or radio station to produce an interview with a major star, and the station doesn't want that expense undermined or compromised because the star is doing seven very similar appearances at competing local TV and radio stations. If a long-lead magazine wants to feature your star on the cover and in a special fashion shoot, then it is far more likely to do so if it knows it is the only outlet to get that "special" treatment, and that a similar cover story/photo spread won't be seen in a competing magazine. This is an example where clear, honest communication (and a functional status report) will prevent professional relationships from going awry. It's easy enough for a segment producer or magazine editor to forgive a publicist if a film isn't very good or a star turns out to be kind of a dud interview; it's much more difficult to work with someone who promised you something special but ended up offering that same "special" opportunity to everyone else.

MARKETING/PUBLICITY STATUS REPORT

Maintaining an accurate and dynamic status report to summarize all of the various marketing and publicity strategies is key for any successful marketing campaign. While there are literally dozens of ways of collating, sharing, and updating such information, whether it is the responsibility of a single executive office or something shared via cloud-based file-sharing, the important thing is that everyone associated with the campaign has access to understanding what is going on with various outlets at any given time. In the pre-Internet era, publicity departments would circulate (via fax or courier) a weekly update for the first part of the campaign, followed by daily updates for the campaign's final two or three weeks. Included in this distribution would be all relevant marketing and production executives, and the project's producers.

It is the *status* part of the **status report** that is most important. Yes, we all agree that we should pitch the star of the series to appear on *Carpool Karaoke* with James Corden, but what's going on with that? When was the last time we talked to the show's producer? If the show has agreed to the segment, have we contacted the star's manager about a time to produce the segment? Has the star picked out the appropriate karaoke song? Does the producer know that the star needs to be done by 4 p.m. that Thursday because she or he has an evening flight to Paris? Are we awaiting approval or a decision on another late-night interview before we commit to this? Certainly, contacts at Corden's show and support staff will help run down some of the details, but the status report helps keep all of those targets in focus as release continues.

The other essential function of a status report is to ensure that the publicity and marketing campaigns are coordinated and working *with* and not *against* each other. This seems kind of obvious and logical—*of course* a campaign should be unified—but sometimes proves to be more complicated than expected, especially where there is a lack of communication and current status.

For example, your big star might have a personal publicist, someone the star pays $20,000 per month to take extra care with their public relations and public image. That publicist might be trying to arrange special coverage about the star that coincides with the release of your film, and neither party wants to work at crossed purposes. Your star might have a high-profile charity that has just won a prestigious award of some sort, and wants to talk about it in a special interview with *60 Minutes*. Meanwhile, the film's producer has a special relationship with the producers of *20/20* and has promised them an "exclusive" sit-down with the star for the week the film opens. This is far from a disaster as long as people realize there is a conflict, and *60 Minutes* probably doesn't want to air an

Complete 10C: Pitch Letter with Invitation, and 10D: Sample Status Report interview with the star just days after *20/20* does. A status report identifies these various efforts, and ensures there is no confusion about where the studio and producers place their priorities as final decisions are made.

FINAL THOUGHTS ABOUT A RELEASE CAMPAIGN: 'HYPING THE HYPE'

While this might seem absurd on the surface, it's mostly true: One of the key functions of publicity is to publicize the publicity. This has become even more true in the age of social media, and speaks to larger issues about how marketing works and the value of various marketing practices in relationship to one another.

One of the more obvious ways you might be familiar with this practice is in the collection and distribution of critical quotes that praise the project. We've discussed this briefly before, in considering the importance of the publicist/critic relationship. It's the publicist's (or publicity department's) job to screen a film or make it available to critics early, so that the reviews can be published the week or day of the film's release. But of course, you've undoubtedly seen hundreds of television and print advertisements that contain quotes from critics. Some of these quotes might even be printed before the reviews themselves have been published; others are "collected" and immediately inserted into advertising that is released within days after the film's release into the theaters.

From a marketing perspective, this makes sense. For weeks, commercials and trailers (advertising/paid space) have called this film "the most highly anticipated drama of the new year" or "the film that everyone will be talking about." Then, in time for the Sunday evening TV commercials, the film that came out on Friday now has commercials that scream "the critics agree ..." or " ... #1 comedy at the box office." What was collected and distributed by the publicity departments (the positive reviews) has been reappropriated to itself become "news" and part of the new phase of advertising.

As a young staff publicist, one of my jobs was soliciting comments and feedback from critics and reviewers immediately after they saw a film. As mentioned before, for most major outlets, getting a major critic to go on the record with an opinion before the review came out was impossible, and I learned quickly not to ask. If a positive review was published, then I would make sure the review was circulated to all parties concerned, and I might highlight specific phrases or comments that might be effective in immediate and future advertising. (Examples: "Susan Sarandon gives her best performance in a decade," "A winning combination," "It's laugh-out-loud funny," etc.).

But there were other critics who were only too happy to provide an early quote that might be fashioned into an advertisement or marketing campaign. In fact, I had one major, nationally known critic tell me he liked providing early quotes that were favorable to a film because his mother liked to cut those advertisements that featured his name out of her local newspaper and put them into a scrapbook. As a film scholar and someone who cares deeply about the quality of films and television, this was horrifying—this major film critic was essentially admitting to me that he publicly "liked" something so that his mother could be proud of seeing his name in the paper. Because of this critic's stature, his opinion was very likely placed very high in an ad campaign, and this critic was perfectly happy to say something vaguely nice about a performance (e.g., "Andrew Dice Clay like you have never seen him before") to get his name in the paper, only to publish a very negative review of the film as a whole at a later date.

Similarly, there is a long and sad history of unscrupulous publicists either misquoting or simply making up quotes to generate positive "buzz" on a film that needed it. For example, in the early 2000s, Sony Pictures got in trouble for attributing quotes to a critic named "David Manning" from an actual publication (*Ridgefield Press* in Connecticut). "Manning" was enthusiastically quoted supporting otherwise poorly reviewed films, and some investigation lead to the revelation that no one with the name "David Manning" worked at the *Ridgefield Press*. Sony was actually forced to set up a $1.5-million "refund" fund to offer $5 to any patron who had seen one of the movies that "Manning" had "reviewed"![1]

There are many other examples of publicists publicizing publicity, or lending support to spread the word about other marketing efforts that are more common, slightly less visible, and it's hoped not nearly as problematic. For example, consider a movie promotion, such as connecting a film's premiere to a prominent charity event or other cultural event (such as the Super Bowl, World Series, New York Fashion Week, etc.). Let's say that your studio has decided to tie the project's release to one of these major events, hoping to attract major corporate partners and generate additional coverage that extends beyond the usual entertainment circles.

For example, let's assume that the subject of your film is an athlete connected to the Olympics (such as our *Soul on Da Ice* project), and the studio partners with the U.S. Olympic Committee to have a contest in which fans win tickets to a high-profile Olympic event, where they will share a suite with the stars of the film. As someone in the marketing department, you might find yourself pitching and promoting not only the film, but the contest giveaway as well. You'll want to be sure that the film's stars mention the contest promotion when they appear on the various morning shows, and that the announcers/broadcasters in all of the other related sports events are given up-to-date information about how people can enter the contest. Written materials—in the form of the contest description, details, etc.—help in the dissemination of this information.

But let's extend this a bit further. Imagine that this particular contest gets an unusually high response. It was expected that 10,000 people would enter, but instead the contest has gone viral. As with the "ice bucket challenge" or other social media phenomenon, for some reason this promotion is "hot" and people want to know more about it. Now, as a publicist

---

1   https://web.archive.org/web/20010609225327/http://www.msnbc.com/news/581770.asp?cp1=1

or marketing person, you have to manage the publicity and public awareness of this event. You want to be sure that the outlets writing about the contest know the details of how many people are entering; you'll want quotes from people at the U.S. Olympic Committee and the movie studio to talk about how happy they are with the participation; you'll want to "build up" the excitement as the contest closes. You didn't sign up to be a publicist for a promotion, but suddenly that's your job: you are hyping the hype.

THE HISTORICAL MOMENT: CONNECTING TO 'NOW'

"Hyping the hype" is one example of how a publicist, marketing executive, or project producer has to remain "in the moment" with a campaign. It's an example of perhaps the most unique skill that someone can bring to a product that is available in the marketplace—the ability to answer the question of why a project has value *right now*. Not in a general sense—here, *right now*, literally means as close to this second in time and this location in space as possible. In a world where people are bombarded with information, requests for action, and opportunities for engagement and interaction, the difference between getting a result or not getting a result often have to do with the relevance of any action to a very specific moment.

Just consider your own activity and how you choose to spend your entertainment dollar or invest your time watching a film or television program (or rock concert, festival, etc.). Certainly, there are the things that you plan for days, weeks, or perhaps even months in advance, and in those cases, you are very likely to be dissuaded to cancel or change your plans. But most of your entertainment decisions are based on whim and immediate value, particularly when it comes to what movie you want to see. Odds are, you're going to choose the movie that seems "most important" to you. It's as simple as deciding that in mid-December, you're going to take your family to see a new animated Christmas film, rather than wait and watch it when it comes out on cable or VOD in mid-March. It might mean wanting to see that art-house film that got amazing critical reaction in December, but isn't available in your town until early February, and you want to be the first among your friends to see it. It might be that you are interested in a political or social movement (such as #metoo or #blacklives-matter) and choosing to pay to see the film that has a female filmmaker or more minority artists represented as your preference over the generic, white-guy-protagonist, would-be blockbuster; and it also might be that the following week, politics have tired you out, so you go to see the mainstream blockbuster to "escape."

Take a look at this chapter's sidebar for some examples of publicists and studios having to respond creatively to outside events that affected the release of films.

Of course, connecting the film to *now* might also be a difficult challenge for other reasons. When a prominent actor or filmmaker dies unexpectedly, marketing unreleased material poses a particularly vexing problem (which I will talk about in a later chapter). Death isn't the only concern, as unexpectedly bad "personal" publicity can also easily undermine and upset a well-planned campaign. When Mel Gibson was involved in a high-profile incident where he drunkenly insulted a female police officer in 2006, it affected his value as he tried to promote the release of his film *Apocalypto* later that year. More recently, when allegations of misconduct surfaced against actor Kevin Spacey, the marketing team for the film *All the Money in the World* (where Spacey's scenes were reshot at the last minute with actor Christopher Plummer) had to scramble to come up with new material that explained the change in actor, the logistics involved in replacing Spacey, and the "positive" spin that might be had from the incident overall.

It should also be pointed out that not all *now* publicity has to be defensive or only in reaction to events. For example, the film *Ocean's 8* is set partly at the annual Met Gala, which takes place in May, and the film was released in early June. While the Met Gala doesn't "need" the film for publicity purposes, nor does the film exactly "need" the event, the film's marketing team strategically made sure that mentions of the 2018 event identified the film's impending release as a way of connecting what was going on "today" with what will be out in the theaters shortly. One article from *Bustle* breaks down the stylistic and logistical connections between the film and the event, a very shrewd piece of publicity that would capture the interest of both the fashion and moviegoing worlds.[2] As the world of social events and fashion casually tuned in to the Met Gala coverage in May, they were most likely also exposed to some medium- and short-lead coverage such as the article in *Bustle* that reinforced the impending release of the film.

The real opportunity when you are thinking about the *now* aspect of publicity, whether it is anticipated or simply a reaction to events, is to think of it as a chance to expand your audience and your reach. There is always an entertainment-based press that will be happy to partner with you to promote and publicize your movie—that's why they are in business. But remember that the target aim of publicity is to make your project seem *newsworthy*, and getting into the *actual* news (however that term is defined) is going above and beyond what your bosses and clients might expect. Thus, think about the *now* as your chance to reach out to new outlets, different journalists, and unique ways to spread the word about your project. If your writing is solid and clear, you'll very likely find yourself engaging with high-impact people who aren't usually "approached" by the entertainment industry. The final exercise (the "Think Piece" pitch) will stretch your knowledge and instincts and give you an opportunity to envision a campaign that capitalizes upon the moment in the most interesting and compelling way possible.

Complete Exercise 10E:
'Think Piece' Pitch

---

2   https://www.bustle.com/p/when-did-oceans-8-film-at-the-met-gala-the-movie-even-has-anna-wintour-cameo-9246633.

PUBLICITY AND TIMING

Marketing campaigns are planned for months and sometimes years in advance, and yet they can be undermined, altered, or changed at the last minute to accommodate the *now*. Three examples here will suffice for an overview. A generation ago, an excellent film called *The China Syndrome*, about a meltdown at a nuclear power plant, got some decent reviews and praise for stars Jane Fonda and Jack Lemmon when it was released in March 1979. Obviously, the film had been in development and production for a couple of years, and while the subject matter was timely—the nation was debating the value and safety of nuclear power—it was only generally so. Then, just 12 days after the film was released, the nation was gripped by a crisis at the Three Mile Island nuclear power facility in Pennsylvania, an event that still ranks as the most dangerous incident at an American nuclear facility. Suddenly, the film wasn't just "generally" important, but was literally offering perspective on a real-life, life-or-death story. As a result, a second wave of publicity, totally unanticipated by the studio and filmmakers, was necessary as the film became a point of discussion far beyond entertainment circles.

"I remember *The China Syndrome* well," says veteran studio publicist Rob Harris, who was then at the beginning of his career. "The question there wasn't how to leverage the event to benefit the movie, but rather—importantly—how not to appear to be exploiting the tragedy for crass commercialism. The real-life event carried the unintended consequence of making the movie appear opportunistic."

Just two years later, a comedy film called *First Monday in October* was produced starring Jill Clayburgh as the first woman appointed to the U.S. Supreme Court (where she comically butts heads with a veteran justice played by Walter Matthau). The film was based on a play produced in 1978, and was scheduled for release in February 1982. In the summer of 1981, however, newly elected President Reagan said he was going to nominate Sandra Day O'Connor to be the first woman on the Supreme Court. As a result, the studio (Paramount Pictures) decided to release the film early: Reagan officially announced O'Connor's nomination on August 19, and the film was released just two days later (O'Connor was confirmed about a month after that). While the film received mediocre reviews and did "okay" at the box office, it's undeniable that world events helped frame and influence the marketing of the film and who might go to see it. (I certainly remember the film. It was rated "R" for some profane dialogue and brief nudity, but my parents approved me seeing it as an 11-year-old because I was asking a lot of questions about how the Supreme Court worked, why there had never been any women nominated before, and so on, and they probably felt that the film would be appropriate learning material given the cultural moment.)

Then, consider the unusual case of the 2005 film *Fever Pitch*, a romantic comedy about a lovelorn fan of the Boston Red Sox. As with the film *All the Money in the World*, real-life events not only influenced the off-screen marketing campaign, but the on-screen product as well. Based on a British film (which was about football/soccer in the U.K.), the script for *Fever Pitch* had been in development for a few years, and one of the central elements of the plot was that the protagonist found his way to love and happiness, even though his beloved Red Sox remained "losers." Eventually, the project was given a green light to star Jimmy Fallon and Drew Barrymore (a coproducer) and to be directed by the Farrelly Brothers. Using the Red Sox home ballpark of Fenway Park for some scenes, the film was shot in the summer of 2004, with the production team shooting the ending as written: the good guy wins but, as usual, the Sox lose.

But as the film was being edited in October, real life flipped the script, as the Red Sox improbably beat their rival foes, the New York Yankees, in the American League playoffs, and took a commanding lead in the World Series against the St. Louis Cardinals. While the sports world was reeling with the possibility of the Red Sox winning a championship for the first time in 86 years, the Farrelly Brothers and the film's producers realized that if the Red Sox won, their film would have a weak ending. As a result, they quickly wrote a "postscript" scene, summoned the two leads and a skeleton crew to St. Louis, and shot Fallon and Barrymore "in character" as the Sox won the final game of the series, incorporating their long-awaited win into the film's love story. While this experience undoubtedly was a nightmare for the film's producers, it was a blessing for the publicists, who had a juicy, "once in a lifetime" opportunity to show art imitating life, and a great idea for a well-placed feature.[1]

My colleague Dave Fulton, a veteran publicist who often works on sports-related films, also recalls a situation where the sports world provided his project with some unexpected lift. "We were very fortunate on *The Blind Side*," he remembers. While the film was in production in the spring of 2009, the film's real-life subject, football player Michael Oher, was drafted by the Baltimore Ravens in the first round of that year's amateur draft. Although the movie wasn't released until late fall, there was already some knowledge of his accomplishment. "Michael Oher had a great story, from being homeless to playing football at the University of Mississippi," Fulton says. "When he was drafted, the media jumped on *The Blind Side* bandwagon. Even though Oher didn't personally support the movie, his adopted family did, and we were able to create a national phenomenon."

---

3   You can read one of the articles generated in support of this film's unusual production history at https://ew.com/article/2004/11/12/fever-pitch-ending-changed-after-red-sox-win/.

CHAPTER TAKEAWAYS

- All release campaigns are unique, requiring producers, filmmakers, executives, and publicists to work together and agree on a strategy and schedule that serves the purposes of the individual project; there are very few "cookie-cutter" campaigns.
- New forms of digital distribution have disrupted the traditional long-lead/short-lead model that was in place during the era when print communication dominated marketing practices. Publicists will often be tasked with providing materials and support for a longer period of time and across more diverse platforms than previous generations.
- The highest-value publicity is the publicity that helps connect the film to the present moment, and to highlight why it is important for audiences to see the film *today*. Often, such connections cannot be anticipated months or even weeks in advance, requiring open-minded thinking and quick decision making when reacting to unexpected events.

EXERCISE 10A: END OF PRODUCTION ANNOUNCEMENT

This is a simple exercise—it's essentially the opposite of the Start of Production Announcement exercise, and is designed primarily for industry trade magazines. Once upon a time, this used to be a fairly standard routine in a studio or unit publicist's job (e.g., *Soul on Da Ice* Wraps in Montreal), but with postproduction schedules having changed so much because of digital technology in the past few years, the time between a film's "end of production" and release is not as cut-and-dried as it used to be. A producer or studio might choose to forgo this announcement until the film is actually finished and ready to be shown, or there is other news related to the film's release or distribution. Regardless of exactly when this release might be issued, including all of the up-to-date information about the film's availability is essential. (Example: "With postproduction being completed at studio facilities in Hollywood, the film is scheduled to debut at the New York Film Festival in September, with a wide release to follow in October.").

Write an End of Production release that contains the following information:

- A brief synopsis/description and key cast/crew information (can be same as Start of Production)
- A quote from two primary creative or production entities on the film (star, writer, director, producer, studio executive)
- Information on the currently planned release schedule or debut/premiere/exhibition information

EXERCISE 10B: SCREENING INVITATION TO CRITICS

A screening invitation seems like a simple thing—and, in fact, it only has a few required elements—but creating an effective one is always a challenge. Remember, the people receiving these invitations might get two or three dozen of these in a busy week. Given that most feature films run 90–120 minutes, and many television series will ask a critic to watch two to four episodes, one can see that it's impossible to respond "yes" to more than a small handful of films, most of which are scheduled to screen after regular work hours.

In recent years, with secure online screening becoming more common, there is a new practice of making projects available online for people to watch at their leisure, which has decreased the demand for in-person screenings. Many producers and publicists, however, still prefer to have "official" in-person screenings for press whenever possible, at least for feature films. Obviously, filmmakers hope that all audiences have the "big-screen experience," and a critic reviewing a gorgeously shot period piece or raucous comic-book adventure on a cell phone or tablet screen is hardly an optimal viewing experience. Furthermore, because of matters related to security, privacy, and piracy, a potential viewer might be discouraged when his or her home computer or new laptop doesn't have the right software to view a particular film, or wherever there's not enough Wi-Fi bandwidth to stream the film effectively. The other advantage about an in-person screening is that you can guarantee that the person you invited has shown up, and follow up appropriately. Sending that person a link means you'll have to check in every day or two to see if she or he has seen the movie yet.

And regardless of whether you are sending a snail-mail invitation via the post to attend an in-person screening, or just emailing a secure link to someone hoping that person makes time to watch the film on his or her own, you still need to have that "something" in the invitation that guarantees they will want to attend, watch, and respond. Of course, if you have the latest Marvel Comic Universe film, or the film that just won the Palm d'Or at Cannes, or the long-awaited big-screen version of a hit Broadway musical starring last year's Best Actress Oscar winner, then the sell might be a bit easier. But if it's an indie film that is just about to premiere at a film festival, or a movie that the studio isn't sure how to market because it has no known stars, your challenge could be a bit larger.

Create a screening invitation for one of your sample projects—this is a generic invitation that would invite a professional critic to attend an in-person screening. Your letter should contain:

- A generic salutation ("Dear …")
- An invitation paragraph with key credits
- A short-paragraph length synopsis/preview of the story. This should be longer than a log line, and might run three or four sentences. Ideally, it would set up the situation, introduce the main characters, and hint at the conflict/key story points, without giving away any spoilers. (Feel free to recycle or adapt previous synopses that you may have written for either development or production notes.)

- An informational paragraph that indicates when the film is due to be released; this paragraph might also include supplemental credit information that was not included in the "key credits" paragraph. If available, rating information, running time, etc. should also be included.
- A list of available screenings with locations, times, and RSVP information.

EXERCISE 10C: PITCH LETTER WITH INVITATION

Sometimes, you'll want to take extra measures to ensure that a very specific person attends an advanced screening. This might be a major critic, editor, or perhaps even an important celebrity or cultural figure who could have a strong role in supporting the project publicly. Above and beyond the generic screening invitation from the previous exercise, this invitation includes a more direct pitch to suggest specific action beyond attending the screening.

For the purposes of this exercise, consider your potential invitation recipient as someone who works primarily in the entertainment industry and is used to responding to pitches and invitations regarding film, television, and entertainment. (We'll focus on getting the attention of people outside that circle in Exercise 10E.)

You can begin this exercise by repeating the basic information from the screening invitation; however, you want to include in this invitation—directly after the synopsis paragraph—a specific suggestion for an article, segment, feature, or other specific outcome that is tailored toward the specific outlet you are inviting.

To do this, look for a real-life outlet (even a specific individual) you believe would be an ideal invitation recipient. For example, if your goal is to get the star on a major late-night talk show, pick out a specific show, with a specific host, and suggest an idea that will make your pitch rise above the usual "chat-show" model (i.e., suggesting something for *Carpool Karaoke*, or a possible parody sketch for your star to host *Saturday Night Live*.)

EXERCISE 10D: SAMPLE STATUS REPORT

If you are working in group, challenge yourself (either individually or collectively) to create a template for a publicity/marketing status report. You can do this by creating a shared document, or by delegating one group member to collate and coordinate all of the various pitch ideas for your project.

Whether you are working individually or as a group, set up your status report in a manner that conveys information in the most efficient and effective manner. Are you going to arrange your report by listing outlets alphabetically? Are you going to divide them into long lead, short lead, immediate lead so that they are organized by a deadline? Who is responsible for updating the report as new potential outlets are added, and editors respond to pitches? How do you make sure that action items are highlighted so that people reading the reports know what is important to respond to immediately?

EXERCISE 10E: 'THINK PIECE' PITCH

This exercise asks you create a pitch letter that is intended for someone who might not typically be "pitched" a film or television project, and intended to create an opportunity for a high-profile feature from a major outlet. For example, trying to get a segment on a show such as *60 Minutes*, or an extended profile of someone in a magazine such as *The New Yorker*, or a long feature interview (equivalent to a cover story) in a major newspaper or magazine that doesn't necessarily put "show business" front and center.

As with Exercise 10C, you should try to pick a real-life outlet to target so that you can assess what kind of features it likes to pursue, and even to suggest possible writers, interviewers, photographers, or other creative talent already employed by the outlet.

Again, you may borrow the paragraph synopsis you used for your screening invitation and elsewhere, but in this case you should be sure that it is angled specifically toward your pitch. For example, if your project is a true-life story about an outdoor survivalist and you are pitching a nature magazine for a cover story, you want to be sure you emphasize that part of the project (rather than focusing on the main character's relationship with a parent seen through flashbacks).

Most important, you want to offer a pitch paragraph that gives your reader some thoughtful suggestions about why this particular project is so important and interesting that it needs *special attention* and not just the usual critics' review buried in the entertainment section. In this case, you might be competing for space in print or on the air that is normally taken by political and international news, stories from the worlds of sports or music, and other major cultural and historical events that are considered important. Often, one angle to use is suggesting that the project is a lifetime achievement or symbolizes a key moment in someone's career, such as a major actor's first attempt to direct or produce, or signifying a well-known filmmaker coming "out of retirement" or working in a new genre or format.

CHAPTER 11

Following Up

Post-Release, Personal, Corporate, and 'Long-Term' Publicity

Thus far, we have been focusing on what we might call *event*-related publicity—the event in this case primarily being the release of a feature film or television series to the public, and tied to a specific date that is also framed in such terms as *premiere, debut, opening, drop, reveal*, etc. We've focused on the "first time" that something becomes available to an audience.

But there are other ways that publicity and the writing that goes along with it is not necessarily tied to a specific date, event, or even project. This chapter covers two common practices: post-release campaigns (including awards campaigns); and personal and corporate publicity. These may fall under this secondary category, though to dismiss these practices as less important overall is a mistake. Rather, they are companion or ancillary practices that complement and expand the initial event-focused marketing work.

POST-RELEASE AND AWARDS CAMPAIGN

The first common practice is what we might call **post-release** publicity for a project that has been made available to the public. As we have previously suggested, projects obviously have a commercial and cultural life far beyond their initial release. Feature films, after a few weeks or months in exclusive theatrical release, almost always develop a secondary market through the sales of hard media home video (DVD), premium cable broadcast (HBO, Showtime, Starz), on demand through cable services ("pay-per-view"), Internet portals (iTunes or Google Play) or streaming (Netflix, Hulu, Amazon Prime)—or a combination of all of these over time. Sometimes these post-release markets involve a new and coordinated campaign designed to raise awareness and increase sales or downloads, and often the materials used to support the initial release of the film—production notes, visual advertising materials, behind-the-scenes interviews from the EPK—will be recycled or adapted. It's important to note that even if there is no "big" campaign or effort (i.e., the studio's just going to drop the film on Amazon Prime without any fuss or fanfare), those specific marketing materials still need to be provided, and updated if necessary. That includes perhaps creating new written material that is platform-specific: a log line describing the plot on Netflix might require fewer words than what is allowed for the description on a cable VOD service, or a contractual agreement might indicate that the star or director's name always be included in the project description so it can be easily found doing a search on the chosen platform.

Another very common, but often less visible, post-release strategy is an awards season campaign on behalf of a particular project or individual. This involves focusing all efforts on targeting the members of various voting bodies, including critics associations (which can be regional, national, or international in scope), trade unions and organizations (Directors Guild of America, Screen Actors Guild, etc.), and the traditional "golden statue" organizations such as the Hollywood Foreign Press Association (which produces the Golden Globe Awards), the Academy of Television Arts and Sciences (ATAS, or the "Emmys") or the Academy of Motion Picture Arts and Sciences (AMPAS, which hosts the Academy Awards or "Oscars").

The feature film industry's awards season is in January and February, recognizing achievement for the previous calendar year, so "awards season" typically starts in October and November, as studios and producers start to position their films as worthy through a variety of means (to be explained in a bit). You've certainly noticed how many of the films that receive the bulk of the awards circuit attention are the ones most likely to be released in theatres in the last two months of the year. This is not a hard-and-fast rule—when *Silence of the Lambs* dominated the awards circuit in 1992, it marked a highly unusual case of a film that had been released the previous February collecting major awards. But in the 26 years since, just looking at "Best Picture" Oscar winners, 19 of them were released in the United States after October 1, with 15 released in November or December. Of the seven exceptions, five were high-profile summer blockbusters that were released in May or June, while two (*Unforgiven* and *American Beauty*) were released in August and September. It's important to remember that even though the awards are revealed in January and February, the nomination process usually concludes by the end of December or earlier, so the work of the publicist has to be in advance of these less visible deadlines.

For television, it's a bit more complicated: the SAG awards and Golden Globes honor television from the previous calendar year, while the Emmy awards are held in September and honor the shows from the previous "television season" (which ATAS defines as June 1 of the previous year to May 31 of the current year).

Imagine then a publicity campaign for a miniseries or program that airs in early spring of a certain year—for example, the limited series *Feud: Bette and Joan*, created for FX by Ryan Murphy, about the longtime professional and personal relationship between actresses Bette Davis and Joan Crawford. The show debuted to the public in March 2017, running for eight weeks. That meant the long-lead press campaign probably began in December 2016. Indeed, the planning was in place then for Ryan Murphy to start talking about the show at the winter (January) press tour of the Television Critics Association. A standard release campaign was executed between January and March, with stars Susan Sarandon and Jessica Lange appearing on the cover of *Entertainment Weekly* in late January, the same week that FX dropped teaser trailers of the show. When the series finally aired, more visible and dynamic publicity came in the form of television interviews, such as Jessica Lange appearing on *Live with Kelly and Ryan* in mid-March.

Then, probably no more than a week or two after the last episode aired, a campaign was launched for Emmy consideration, and running through the summer. In early August, there are separate interviews with Lange published on deadline.com, indiewire.com, and hollywoodreporter.com, three major trade outlets where Emmy voters would most likely have their eyeballs on a regular basis. This campaign proved successful, as the program earned 15 Emmy nominations, eventually winning two awards at the ceremony in September. Shortly thereafter, the publicity and marketing team then turned to the SAG and Golden Globe awards. Both organizations' nominees were announced in December (meaning the ballots were due in mid-November), with the awards handed out in January 2018.

Add to that less prominent awards—such as the Television Critics Association (nominations June, awards in August), the Critics Choice Television Awards (December/January), the Writers Guild of America (December/February), Producers Guild (Early January/late January), etc., and you can imagine that it becomes imperative to keep your status report up to date. Also remember that there had been preproduction and unit publicity prior to all of this, dating back to at least May 2016 when the project was officially greenlit by FX. Therefore, execution of that entire campaign ran from the summer of 2016 through January of 2018, and required the continued participation and involvement of the principal talent (Murphy, Sarandon, Lange) for the entirety of that time, even though they "finished" principal photography in November of 2016!

Because so many of the films nominated for awards tend to come out at the end of the calendar year, most studios and producers will fold in their awards campaigns with their regular release campaigns. This means some extra work for the marketing departments, as they must prepare screening invitations, pitch letters, and advertising material that will be micro-targeted to very specific groups of voters, most of whom live in Los Angeles and New York. The rest of the country, for example, might see a billboard by the side of a freeway, or a banner ad on the side of a municipal bus advertising a star-driven film; in Los Angeles, that same film might also include a prominently placed "FOR YOUR CONSIDERATION" ad, a reminder to all eligible voters that they can do more than simply "see" the film.

Awards season is also a boon time for the trade publications, whether they are online or in print. Studios take out multiple "For Your Consideration" ads—you can even "buy" the front or back cover of the weekly print edition of *Variety*. There are similar ads placed in major newspapers such as the *Los Angeles Times*. The increased advertising also allows space for more substantive content that might be focused on a very specific craft or interesting off-screen talent. You see more "Best of" articles at the end of the year, a chance for a film that was released a few months ago to get a prominent mention alongside the hot new films that are receiving Oscar buzz. The major trades will also often provide analysis and handicapping of awards show odds. Obviously, there isn't a lot of hard science that can go into exactly what might happen with nominations and awards. But a shrewd publicist will ensure that when Critic X analyzes the possible candidates for a Best Supporting Actress nomination, they include a mention of the performer who "wowed" critics in her role as the lead's alcoholic mother in an otherwise unremarkable indie drama that was in theaters six months ago and now is on-demand.

The trades also often publish specialty features about cinematography, editing, sound design, production design, costume design, and other "technical" areas of motion picture production, where they will highlight the best of the work done in those areas that year. That might be an occasion for a publicist to pitch a short interview with a film's director of photography, or to suggest that the film's editor take part in a roundtable discussion of the state of new technology in the industry. It should be pointed out that "below-the-line" talent (basically anyone who is not an actor, producer, writer, or director) rarely is the subject of a wider publicity campaign. You've probably never seen an editor or camera operator or costume designer as a guest on a talk show, talking to Terry Gross on NPR's *Fresh Air*, or serving as a celebrity guest judge on a cooking show. Awards season is the rare time when those behind the scenes might get a little time in the spotlight, where the press and public can better appreciate their talent and efforts.

Complete Exercises 11A and 11B

CORPORATE PUBLICITY

As you have probably ascertained by now, one of the delicate balances of entertainment publicity is the ability to simultaneously promote a project (film, television series, album, stage play, etc.) while also promoting individual entities (studios, producers, actors, filmmakers) that are part of that project but also exist *beyond* the project. This is one of the unique things about the entertainment industry—it is a place where you build a career by moving from project to project. In that sense, many people in the profession who consider themselves makers or creators often finds themselves in the position of pitching both "*what* they have made and want to make" and "*who* they are" at various points throughout their career.

Everyone who studies film and media making (and certainly who work in the profession) knows that the process is inherently and by necessity collaborative. Still, the distinction between promoting the collective accomplishment of *the film* and the individual achievement of *the people who made the film* can be difficult to navigate. Suppose, for example, that you have a film that has two A-list stars in it, and a high-profile A-list director. As critical reaction begins to come in a couple of weeks before the film is released, everyone at your studio or production company realizes that this is just an "okay" movie. Reviews are mixed; some people are pointing out how maybe the casting didn't work, or maybe it's still too slow in the middle, or just maybe no one can get too excited about another romantic comedy that ends with someone running through an airport, or a spy thriller in which the hero's spouse turns out to be working for the enemy.

But among the so-so responses, everyone agrees there is one thing that makes the film memorable—for example, a brilliant performance by a very young child, in a difficult and substantive supporting role. Consider the publicity challenge for a studio publicity team: it needs to do its best to get people to support the film as a whole, but everyone wants to talk about "the kid." Your studio has paid two A-list stars several million dollars and enlisted a high-profile director, all of whom (for the sake of argument) think they are brilliant. So when you make your call to Jimmy Kimmel's producers—who do you pitch? When *Entertainment Weekly* says it wants to give the kid the cover, do you try to talk it into including at least one of the other stars on the cover as well? Is the director going to be prepared to answer endless questions about the child's performance while most likely feeling that their other contributions to this project are being overlooked? How do you limit access to the young actor (which involves significant legal and logistical concerns) while still maximizing the child's value?

Ultimately, of course, these questions can only be answered on a case-by-case basis. But one can see how publicity and marketing must function not only for projects and events surrounding the release of projects, but also as part of an individual entity's career. By "individual" entity, I mean not only specific people, but specific companies, corporations, studios, networks, etc.

As to this latter category, it is well beyond the scope of this book or my experience to offer substantive insight into the world of brand-building, corporate identity, and data-driven marketplace analysis that often drives decisions in terms of how corporate entities and individual artists manage their public image and public relations. But I can point to a few common practices that require substantive writing skills, and often fall to someone already in the field of entertainment public relations.

First, it's important to appreciate how the value of a corporate or studio "brand" has shifted and developed over time. At every point in the history of filmed entertainment, studios, production companies, and television networks have exercised control over their product by presenting each new release as part of a larger entity. This might not be as all-pervasive as it once was, but it still holds true today. Just as we might anticipate a new film from a legendary director, we also might anticipate a new project from Pixar, or from the Marvel Comic Universe, or a new *Star Wars* film, or the latest offering from the Muppets. And yes, it's not a coincidence that all of those entities are part of the same corporate empire, Disney, which dominates entertainment culture as a brand that primarily speaks to younger viewers and family audiences.

That's not unusual in film industry history. A couple of decades ago, Disney also became the corporate parent of Miramax, a company that had dominated the American "indie" scene for nearly a decade and was itself a brand that had a certain cultural and commercial value to people within the film community. In the golden age of studio filmmaking, movie audiences would know that RKO pictures had a distinct art deco look; Paramount films often represented solid, middle-class values; MGM films had the biggest stars and most lavish production value; Warner Brothers films were gritty and realistic; and Universal made the "guilty pleasure" genre films (westerns and musicals) with lesser talent and budgets.

Television networks, meanwhile, aim to speak to different audiences over time, and often brand themselves accordingly. CBS has typically presented itself as aimed at older and better-educated viewers; ABC built itself much as Disney, aimed at family audiences; while NBC often presents itself as hip and irreverent. Cable and premium outlets are now fully engaged in public relations wars in which they brand themselves as "above and beyond" in terms of the creative imagination ("It's not TV, it's HBO"). Thinking beyond just content creators, consider how entities such as the Sundance Film Festival, the American Film Institute, Creative Artists Agency (CAA), the Screen Actors Guild, or the Television Critics Association all must engage in broader public relations practices. Those are just a few of several dozen such entities that play key roles at many points in the creative process of making and distributing film and television, among the hundreds of individual businesses and corporate entities that see themselves as players in a constantly shifting creative marketplace. All of these entities require professional public relations and marketing executives who are going to rely on consistent and effective writing to maintain the business public image, just as the studio executives who work on a project-by-project basis.

Thus, most corporations and entities must have an up-to-date and comprehensive **corporate bio**. This bio is often posted on company websites, but is also distributed to other entities on an as-needed basis. For example, a unit publicist who is assembling production notes for a feature film might be asked to include bios (or "profiles") of all the various production companies involved in the making of the film (in a similar way in which the publicist might collect individual talent bios). Many businesses also develop a **corporate description**—or what we might consider a log line—that condenses what is important and relevant about the company in a single sentence. A **slogan** (or what we might have called a *tag line*) would be another written element, often influenced by ideas from marketing and advertising, which might have a variety of ideas or suggestions they would want to see in conjunction with the other written materials.

Later in the chapter, I'll discuss the difference between a bio and a **backgrounder** in the context of individual publicity, but know that an extended corporate profile or backgrounder-length piece is another option for corporate public relations. For now, I'll just focus on what might be required for a simple, shareable, and effective bio. This is a bio designed to be available at a moment's notice to anyone who might need it for a news story, research, or other phase of the production process.

For corporate bios, the goal is to be as efficient and informative as possible. While strong writing can always help identify what makes a company unique, the point of this bio is not to *sell* the company so much as describe what it is and what it has accomplished.

A corporate bio should begin with an introductory paragraph that describes the company's business/work product, and includes information about the latest/newest/most currently notable project or endeavor. Subsequent paragraphs—the order of which can vary—should include:

- Identifying key individuals in leadership/ownership. Some companies will prefer to keep individual names out of the bio (and very likely include all necessary individual information in separate personal bios). In other cases, primary stakeholders, executives, and other invested parties may require legal recognition. Obviously, be sure to get all titles correct and correct spelling of all names.
- A brief history of the company that includes origin/establishment dates, key corporate acquisitions or partnerships, and major accomplishments. How you define "major" depends on the company: if you are an independent producer who has gotten two short films nominated for Academy Awards, that's a major accomplishment. If you are a multibillion-dollar studio that only had one film earn more than $50 million at the box office last year, you might want to emphasize other accomplishments.
- A sentence or two that summarizes the corporation's vision or articulates how the entity sees itself and measures its own success. This can often be distilled from a longer corporate vision statement. There are various places where this might be integrated into the bio: it works well as either an introduction or conclusion, or as a founding principal that can be worked into the origin/history paragraph.
- Paragraphs that provide a more detailed history of accomplishment and output, moving either in forward or reverse chronological order. I have never found a consensus on whether a bio or list of credits should go from present-to-past or past-to-present. Most publicists and writers probably agree that it's best to *open* in the present, so that the first paragraph highlights what is most current; but where in time a bio might go from there varies. Do you want to emphasize current projects and what people most immediately remember? Start from today and go backward. Do you want to show off the historical evolution and development and growth of the company? Then maybe you start at the beginning and move toward the present. Similarly, as we will see with writing an individual's bio, there is not a consensus on how various categories of activity might be organized. If a production company has produced both film and television programs for more than 20 years, do you list all of the films first, then the TV shows?

The other key element required for corporate publicity is something that you have already practiced, and that is a **general press release** to announce relevant news and provide quality information for public dissemination to news outlets. Too, there might be times when a corporation wants to promote or publicize itself above and beyond its projects—perhaps to a trade magazine or publication oriented toward business and economics (i.e., to get on a list of the "Best-Run Corporations in America"). In that case, a **pitch letter** might be needed, along with the aforementioned backgrounder to deliver a workable angle that will prompt a response from a press outlet. You'll most likely also need to provide **individual bios** to the key members of the executive and perhaps even administration of the company, which themselves can be of varying length and depth (see section that follows).

Complete Exercise 11C: Client Bio and Backgrounder

If you'd like to practice some of these skills specifically for a corporation, then perhaps your instructor will consider it potential extra credit. You'll be practicing them specifically in the next section's exercises, so feel free to adapt those assignments to reflect a collective or corporate interest, rather than simply a personal one.

PERSONAL PUBLICITY

A project-based client list is nice to have, but it is essentially "gig work," only lasting a few months or perhaps a year, as the firm covers the life cycle of a project's initial release. Billed weekly or monthly or regulated by a dated contract, the producer or studio engages the outside firm the same way a prop house might be hired to manage a film's properties on location or rent a high-tech postproduction facility to accommodate the project's extensive special effects. Nice work if you can get it, but with a limited time frame.

Thus, most independent publicity firms serve individual clients. A corporate or personal client might represent years of income and productive professional work as the publicist works with the client to create long-term public relations strategies that transcend any single project or event. Even if an individual client is only on the books for a few months at a time, both the publicist and the client share an interest in the ongoing success of the client, not just how well their next project does. (Of course, for most high-profile talent, agents and managers are the central figures in career building; but the shrewd and effective use of a publicist has always been an asset to a professional's long-term development and improving his or her value and visibility.)

One key question that I am often asked, particularly by young artists, actors, or filmmakers who believe they might be taking a "next step" in their early careers, is why and/or when should someone hire a publicist? The answer to the question of why/when to hire a publicist is the same: you hire a publicist when you have something specific to publicize, at least at the beginning of your career. If you become mega-famous and require a "defensive" publicist (discussed later), then so be it, but the first publicist you work with will need something specific to sell as "news." You're talented? Great! You won an award in college last year? That's awesome! You're super charming in interviews and photograph well? What a bonus! But you aren't in something that's coming out in theaters next month? You didn't write anything that is debuting on Netflix, and you don't have any projects in production, and the next thing the public is going to see is a year away? Come back in about nine months, and we'll talk. This is why project-based publicity, on behalf of a film or television show, is such a dominant practice: it has a built-in "clock" that involves deadlines, decisions, and dates. An individual client needs to fit in to that deadline-based schedule somewhere, and if the client doesn't have something specific to promote over a specific time frame, it's difficult to engage with the public relations process.

Another determining factor of when or whether one needs a publicist might have to do with what kind of public relations and marketing efforts are already being made on behalf of the project. Sometimes a publicity staff is charged with pitching only the project's biggest stars; at that point, someone who is lower on the PR totem pole might consider working with a separate publicist or public relations professional. If that's the case, it's important that the personal publicist and studio project publicist are talking to each other about coordinated marketing strategies, so they aren't working at crossed purposes (for example, pitching "exclusives" to rival outfits). There are also times when clients are doing something "new" in their personal or professional lives where there is less of a public relations infrastructure. If a famous actor decides to write a book, open a restaurant, or establish a new charity, it's very unlikely there would be a "studio" to back him or her up, and a private PR firm is best handled to support campaigns on behalf of more personal endeavors or projects.

In addition to helping a client prepare an up-to-date bio, a good personal publicist will also generate pitch letters that support a specific, focused PR campaign related to an upcoming release or event. For more developed campaigns or longer-term publicity efforts, many publicists will also write what is called a **profile** or **backgrounder** that serves to highlight significant biographical facts in a more dynamic written context. In a way, you might consider a backgrounder the equivalent of the "About the Production" section of production notes. Written in the style of feature journalism, a backgrounder often highlights the subject's current work; is centered around an *angle* that makes the client seem unique and interesting; and features quotes from the client to make her or him seem appealing as an interview subject.

Hopefully, the client's current work dovetails nicely with the angle that the publicist wants to pitch. As someone who has worked with individual clients at firms on both coasts for more than 25 years, I've helped craft bios, backgrounders, and pitch letters for a whole host of actors, screenwriters, directors, and other professionals (including chefs, architects, book authors, theater companies, and television hosts). Regardless of what stage they were at in their careers, their work with a publicist was invariably connected to a specific new thing that they were doing, which helped add a new "chapter" to their story that someone might find interesting or compelling.

A few examples might help demonstrate what I mean. In the early 1990s, one of my company's clients was an up-and-coming actor named John C. Reilly, who had appeared in smaller parts in some high-profile films that were released within a couple of months of each other (*What's Eating Gilbert Grape?* was a breakout film for Leonardo DiCaprio, and *Hoffa*, which starred Jack Nicholson). Before that, his few film credits included small roles in films made by major directors such as Woody Allen (*Shadows and Fog*) and Brian De Palma (*Casualties of War*). He also appeared in two other films starring Sean Penn, and one starring Tom Cruise, so every role had been in was a highly visible, but lesser-sized role. Thus, with his emergence from a bit actor to a major supporting actor, his roles in *Gilbert Grape* and *Hoffa*, along with his upcoming appearance in the high-profile adventure drama *The River Wild*, positioned him as a young star on the rise. Because most of his roles were dramatic and he had a background in Chicago theater, he was a serious actor capable of working alongside some of the great dramatic talent of the day. Now, of course, Reilly would be pitched as a versatile veteran, capable of doing comedy as well as drama, and known as a leading actor and a great supporting cast member when necessary. Although he has continued appearing on stage, we now think of him as a "movie star," well-known and respected throughout the industry.

A couple of years later, one of our company executives worked for a time with the actor Jerry Orbach. By that time, Orbach was a well-respected performer who had three decades of successful work on stage, in film, and on television; but he'd never been a magazine-cover star or awards season favorite. In bigger films, he'd have smaller parts; he'd guest star on legendary TV shows, but shows in which he was the star didn't last long. He'd been on Broadway in major musicals (*Chicago* and *42nd Street*), but was a straight dramatic actor for the most part on screen. He was also about to begin working on a television series called *Law & Order*, about to enter its third season. For a veteran character actor, taking a lead role on an exceptionally popular franchise was a "feel good" story about Orbach finally finding a platform that would showcase his talent to millions of people on a regular basis. His bio reflected that change in status in his career from "reliable familiar face" to "accomplished television star."

Many of the other individual clients I have worked with were very likely about to make a transition in their career—from unknown to known, from working to famous, from "where are they now" to "comeback of the year," from "former child actor" to "successful adult entrepreneur," from one media form to another, even from one career to another. The current project you are pitching for an individual client will most likely contribute to or represent that career transition, and thus your angle and subject for the pitch letters should be fairly easy to imagine.

A backgrounder, then, combines the various other elements—biographical facts, current projects, and personal story—into a single narrative. Backgrounders are designed to be generic, and they don't have to be pitchy—the pitch letter will always carry the weight of offering a specific outcome or response from the potential outlet. For an individual client with an active career, it should be updated quarterly for basic facts, and substantially rewritten every two to three years. These backgrounders can also be developed with the input of agents or managers (though as always, it is important for the client to feel entirely comfortable with how he or she is being represented).

I approach writing a backgrounder or profile much the way I approach writing production notes, getting most of my guidance from conducting an interview with the subject. Depending on whether I have worked with them before, or if I have previous bios or profiles available, I tend to ask just a few questions, looking for quotes about their life and their work that are conversational, funny, and personally authentic (even if they do come across as a bit clichéd). I always assure my subjects that they will be able to review how they are quoted, and I tell them to not worry about speaking in complete sentences or using perfect grammar. (I am not in the practice of recording my conversations, though some writers might find that useful and/or necessary.) Some of the standard questions are:

- Where they were born, grew up, how they came to their current career, relevant personal details.
- How does the current project represent an interesting creative, personal, or professional challenge?
- Who (or what experience) do you credit with your ability to be creatively successful at this moment in your career?
- What are you working on that might be something we can see in the next six months or year?
- What are your current hobbies, interests, or guilty pleasures? (Here is when talking about charity efforts, sports loyalties, or other pop culture connections might be made. If your client is an expert chess player, noted anime expert, black belt martial artist, classically trained pianist, or NASCAR enthusiast, there's a potential niche audience to reach out to during a campaign.)

DISASTER, NEGATIVE, EMERGENCY, AND 'DEFENSIVE' PUBLICITY

There will inevitably come a time when a publicist will have to publicly speak about and account for something negative regarding a project, client, or event. Indeed, oftentimes in news stories involving the entertainment industry going awry or celebrities behaving badly, you'll see a quote from a spokesperson or representative, or an official statement from one of the people in question. A publicist or manager often serves as that official outlet for an apology, explanation, denial, or acknowledgment.

In an earlier chapter, I mentioned the cliché, "There's no such thing as bad publicity," and indeed, a shrewd publicist or marketing professional will understand that every chance to talk to the press about a client or project represents a unique opportunity for more cultural visibility. But of course, one can only be positive to a limited degree when the news is particularly grim or upsetting.

There are essentially three categories of negative publicity that one might anticipate—personal, professional, and death (the last one obviously having a profound influence on the first two). Negative personal publicity has traditionally been the purview of gossip that may or may not have a basis in fact: perhaps a celebrity couple had an ugly breakup at a posh restaurant, or a director has quit a project after a nasty quarrel with a producer. Gossip-based outlets such as TMZ might call a publicist for a reaction or official statement, but these events rarely have long-term effects unless they are repeated or chronic.

Recently, of course, far more serious and consequential behaviors have had a more profound influence on people's careers and the industry as a whole. Once upon a time, rumors about a powerful person's abuses of power remained internal to the industry, the kind of open secrets that seemed to be part of the way things were done. Whispers of producers or directors who demanded "casting couch" auditions, lower-tier employees forced to endure verbal abuse, or discriminatory hiring and promoting practices seemed too daunting to address except in rare isolated incidents. With the #metoo and #timesup movements, many previously respected figures have been called out publicly for their recent (and not-so-recent) behavior. What's important to recognize is that regardless of how those individuals have chosen to explain their behavior and account for their transgressions, there is also an effect on those who have worked near the person in any substantive way. In other words, it's possible that your client once costarred on a television show with a big star now accused of terrible behavior, and you may be getting calls inquiring if your client wants to go on the record with a statement about what he or she knew or what was experienced. Of course, your client may always choose to say absolutely nothing (which in most cases would probably be the wisest choice), but circumstances might dictate that a written statement or carefully managed interview is necessary.

Negative professional events are the kind of things that are probably of less interest to a gossip-seeking press and public, but are just the things that might require a response or statement from a client regarding his or her roll on a project. A common occurrence is a high-profile project falling through for one reason or another. In most cases, industry professionals pay little attention to the details, but every once in a while, it's important to set the record straight, and to do so in a positive light.

For example, a star might leave a project, for whatever reason, just before cameras are due to roll, and someone else has to step into the part at the last minute. One example is a project I consulted on a couple of years ago, a courtroom drama called *The Whole Truth*. My work on the film was in support of the film's release, so I was not part of the process at the beginning of production. Just a few days before filming was to begin in Boston, star Daniel Craig dropped out of the lead role. This meant that shooting had to be put on hold until another actor became available. Eventually, Keanu Reeves took the part, but in the meantime, the producers had lost some of their locations in Boston, and made the decision to reset the film in Louisiana (where they could get the right type of locations). On the surface, of course, this feels like a disaster—the star and the location changing at that last minute! But by the time the film was finished, the filmmakers were prepared to turn the disaster into a positive event. Reeves was bringing new ideas to the character, and resetting the action in the Deep South created new resonances for the themes of the film and how other actors approached their roles.

My colleague Dave Fulton has been a publicist and associate producer on a number of projects, and held those positions on the film *Waterworld*, which generated reams of negative publicity before it was released due to the film's high budget and rumors of behind-the-scenes problems on the film set between the star Kevin Costner and director Kevin Reynolds. While most of the rumors about the film's troubles were overexaggerated or just plain incorrect, the film also had to deal with natural disasters and unexpected production issues that went on throughout the filming process, making Fulton's job exceptionally challenging. "The key to 'defensive publicity,'" he says today, "is having good media relationships who will take an objective approach to your crisis. There are always two sides to any particular story, and you must work extra hard to get someone in the press to give a fair overview before the rest of the media start to gang up on your film. That strategy would include giving full access to both on the set and behind the scenes. You also need a person of authority (producer, director or actor) to face the tough questions and defend the project to the media."

Other potential professional negatives might include an endorsement contract expiring and not being renewed (so your client is no longer the spokesperson for a major product), or a high-profile creative or business failure that has a disproportionate influence on an individual's career (for example, the client puts all of his or her own money into a failed restaurant, or the client's self-funded production company doesn't produce anything). Again, each situation and circumstance is different, and clients often work with managers and other personal consultants to decide how to publicly *own* the negative attention. Longtime personal and corporate publicist Lori DeWaal knows that the key to handling those moments is being strong, capable, and professional at all times. "I think the fact that I have already established credibility with the press helps in those chaotic situations," she says. "They aren't out to destroy my clients, but there's always that delicate balance that needs to be walked between what the press wants to know and what the client needs to protect. Ultimately, I respect the press, and in times of need, I get that respect back."

In my own experience, I have always advised clients to acknowledge known truths in their backgrounders ("Yes, I struggled with addiction" or "I had a lot of confidence in that project, but it ended up costing me a lot of time and money"), particularly if the behavior was further in the past. I remind them that they may be asked about it by the press in an interview, and leading the conversation about the negatives from the past makes it easier to end the conversation after a sentence or two and move on to more important subjects. It should be pointed out, however, that most of my work is far removed from that moment of crisis: immediate responses to negative events must be much more measured and disciplined.

The final category of negative attention is indeed final—and that is when someone important has died. This might be your client, someone working on a project you represent, or someone a client (or even you yourself) may have once worked with. Sometimes one can anticipate a passing—someone is very old, has been sick and hospitalized, and is calling their loved ones to say goodbye. But there are also unexpected deaths that can be tragic, traumatic, and horrifying.

I was fortunate enough to work with two esteemed actors—one known for film, one in television—who died while they were clients at one of the firms I consult for. The film actor had a five-decade career and was semiretired; the televison actor was in his sixties and still working regularly. In both cases, within a day of their deaths (and still slightly ahead of the news cycle), I had crafted a short statement declaring the facts of their deaths and any statements the family or close associates wanted to make at that time. Personally, I have always chosen to minimize what is said; however, it was important to point out in my release that the deceased was an award-winning actor, and a decades-long professional, devoted husband and father, etc. That statement was then often circulated with the actor's bio and backgrounder, so that such information was available to anyone who might be writing an obituary or memorial article. I have heard of publicists who write extensive obituaries of their own for circulation, but a proper obituary (in my opinion) probably is best written by those who do so for a living (i.e., an entertainment or news journalist). In the cases of both actors I worked with, within 24 hours a nice obituary was published on CNN.com (which then was circulated to other outlets)—and each obituary liberally quoted (or simply copied and pasted) several sentences from the backgrounders I had written for them. For example, quotes from the actors about their careers, which I had collected in the interviews for the backgrounders, were reprinted word for word in the obituaries.

While in both cases the deaths of those actors was unexpected, they both fell into the category of *sad* rather than *awful*. For the latter category, I often think of unexpected events that go beyond just the loss of a well-known person, but end up affecting the projects they may have been involved with and the lives and careers of those around them. This can even occur far from the actual project itself. My colleague Rob Harris, for example, remembers the unfortunate timing of one project he worked on, the film *Space Camp*, a youth-oriented film about kids enrolled in a youth astronaut training camp who accidentally find themselves launched into space via a space shuttle. It seemed like a great idea, but in January 1986, the *Challenger* explosion made any chance of marketing a story about the space shuttle an immensely difficult proposition. "It was a kids' movie, and audiences stayed away in droves," remembers Harris. "It reminded everyone of Christa McAuliffe, the school teacher killed in the explosion. Short of pulling the movie from distribution, there was no way to avoid the backlash on that one." Indeed, in his pan (negative review) of the film, Roger Ebert wrote, "The time is not right for a comedy thriller about a bunch of kids who are accidentally shot into orbit with their female teacher. It may never be right again." In the ensuing years, *Space Camp* has been well received by secondary audiences, long removed from the context of that tragedy.

Harris also had the unfortunate experience of working on the Oscar-winning film *Gladiator*, when one of the film's stars, Oliver Reed, died on the film's location in Malta before all of his scenes were completed (Rob documents much of this in his excellent memoir, *Unexposed Film: A Year on Location*, which is a must-read for anyone who wants to be a publicist). In that sense, he and I share a unique badge of honor, as I had my own experience with "awful" when I had to manage the media frenzy surrounding the death of Brandon Lee during the filming of *The Crow* in Wilmington, North Carolina, in 1993.

You can imagine your own feelings when you read about tragic and terrible deaths—drug overdoses, car accidents, suicides, plane crashes—and magnify that a hundred times if you have known or worked with the person. As emotional as those times may be for either yourself or the people you are being asked to represent, using your writing skills becomes more important than ever, as it is through written language that most people feel most comfortable communicating. The importance of being efficient and effective with your words never seems more critical, and trusting your critical and technical skills will very likely allow you to successfully navigate negative attention.

CHAPTER TAKEAWAYS

- Publicity efforts that follow the initial release of the film often rely on release materials, such as production notes and EPKs, but also require platform-specific elements that must reflect the film's current value and profile.
- Awards campaigns are directed to very small audiences of award voters, often in trade magazines or outlets in Los Angeles and New York; they provide an opportunity for lesser-known or below-the-line talent to promote themselves, and for reminding viewers of projects that came out earlier in the year.
- Corporate and personal publicity rely on a variety of up-to-date materials including bios (brief and factual), backgrounders/profiles (longer and more feature-driven), and pitch letters (to highlight current work).

EXERCISE 11A: NEW PLATFORM LOG LINE

Using your sample project, create new log lines that will support distribution on the platforms listed:

- A foreign sales package (up to 50 words)
- A DVD "box description" (up to 100 words)
- A log line for an on-demand portal (one sentence)

Some tips about a "post-release" log line:

Keep in mind that earlier in the process, a log line had different functions: it had to explain the plot to someone unfamiliar with the project, along with giving an *angle* or hint about the project's tone. Later, as the script became a film, a log line may have become more *pitchy* and emphasizing not only the story, but the stars or other interesting elements of the project.

Development log line:

> Young girl stuck in the middle of nowhere is carried away to a magical land full of adventure and danger.

Production log line:

> Judy Garland stars as a young Kansas girl who is whisked away to a magical land full of music, adventure, and danger.

Release log line:

> Up-and-coming star Judy Garland stars as Dorothy, a young girl from Kansas who finds music, adventure, and new friends when she is whisked away over the rainbow.

Post-release log line:

> In her star-making performance, Judy Garland stars in this MGM classic featuring flying monkeys, singing munchkins, and a memorable musical score featuring "Over the Rainbow."

Can you see how all of these effectively capture the story in a scale appropriate to the development of the project?

The project you are selling to a secondary market has now previously been sold to the public, so there may be some general awareness of the story, genre, etc. On the other hand, the project may have faded from view somewhat, and audiences will now be reminded of it in your description (as opposed to "introduced" to it). In addition, there has been public and critical reaction to the film that may add value to the property. Was the film a blockbuster? A critically acclaimed hit? Award-winning? Was there a breakout actor who may not have been as famous during the initial release? Feel free to pitch a bit more so that you are highlighting the value of the project overall, not just the story.

EXERCISE 11B: AWARDS PITCH LETTERS

This exercise asks you to create two separate pitch letters. The first targets a member of a critics or awards organizations; the second targets a media outlet that you are hoping will feature your client in a special profile or interview in which the client can discuss their "award-worthy" performance.

You can pick a current or recent film project that you know well and choose a performer, writer, director, or craftsperson that you think is award-worthy, or you can make up a situation based on your in-class projects or your imagination. For the purposes of this assignment, I will be imagining an independent project that made a debut in an early year film festival such as Sundance and was released to theaters in April. In particular, a veteran performer who has been out of the spotlight for a couple of years earned some unexpectedly enthusiastic reviews for the performer's supporting role. In the ensuring summer months, some voters and critics may have forgotten about that performance, and the producers are hoping to support a DVD/on-demand release with news of the film landing on a few "Top 10" lists and earning a smattering of high-profile nominations. "Best Picture" might be out of the question, but a "Supporting Actress" nod is a distinct possibility.

Your letters will want to remind voters of the role the performer played, and also include some of the important critical reaction that focused on the potential nominee. You might also include some very brief biographical material about the person. Finally, it's important for the reader to know the current status of where to view the film again: perhaps there are awards-season screenings, or you have a secure link for awards viewers, or the studio is sending out a DVD screener.

For the first letter, the pitch is just a "reminder" and is in the mode of the "For Your Consideration" ad: in fact, you can feel free to supplement your letter with visual material if you are working with an already produced subject. The intended response is that you hope the reader includes the pitched subject when he or she submits nominations and ultimately votes. (Note: In the professional world, many awards and critics' organizations have regulations or restrictions on how their members may be approached or targeted by studios, producers, or publicists. As such, you might not always be producing this written awards-promoting material in the form of a "pitch letter." It might be disseminated, for instance, in a brochure or "year-end" roundup that highlights a number of potential award winners from the same studio.)

The second letter is designed to get a response in the form of featuring the subject in a new piece of publicity that has high visibility among awards voters. This could mean an appearance on a major late night or early morning talk show, or a special outlet such as a newsmagazine, as was done with the initial campaign. It could also mean an interview or profile in the trade magazines, as they assemble their special issues about awards season. At this point, it might have been several months or more since the person you are pitching has thought about that project—which also means they might have something new to promote/publicize, and/or have limited availability. You'll need to have some element of what is going on with them *now* besides just the awards season buzz.

EXERCISE 11B: SAMPLES

Dear Awards Season Voter:

In his recent year-end roundup of the year's best films, *New York Times* critic A. O. Scott cited Melissa Chen's portrayal of the duplicitous Dr. March in the indie thriller *Child of the Cloud* as "one of the most effective screen villains of the year." Other critics have called the performance "groundbreaking" (*Boston Globe*), "powerfully disturbing" (*Variety*), and "riveting" (Peter Travers, *Rolling Stone*).

Now, you have the chance to experience that performance again, and consider nominating Melissa Chen as "Best Supporting Actress." Screenings of *Child of the Cloud* have been scheduled at the Dobbins Screening Room in Beverly Hills and at Magno in New York, and the film will begin streaming on Netflix on December 1.

Melissa Chen's strong performance is no surprise to those familiar with her work in last year's Sundance hit *Street Talk* or her guest-starring arc on the latest season of the hit NBC series *Play Time*. She'll be seen next year alongside Robert Downey Jr. in the latest *Iron Man* film, and is currently in rehearsal to costar with John Malkovich in the New York Public Theatre production of *King Lear*.

Screening information for *Child of the Cloud* is available at www.childofthecloudmovie. com/screenings, or please let me know if you'd like a link to a secure screener to watch at your convenience.

Sincerely,

Dear Features Editor:

Right now, there is no one more interesting than Melissa Chen, who has critics buzzing and handicappers betting that she'll be among those nominated for "Best Supporting Actress" for her scene-stealing performance in last summer's indie thriller, *Child of the Cloud*. Described as "groundbreaking," "disturbing," and "riveting" by the nation's top critics, it's just the latest in a whirlwind year for Chen, who is in demand on both stage and screen.

In addition to her accolades for *Child of the Cloud*, Chen will also costar with Robert Downey Jr. in the next *Iron Man* film, and is sure to dazzle New York audiences when she appears as Cordelia alongside John Malkovich's *King Lear* in next year's Shakespeare in the Park production by the Public Theatre.

Currently, Melissa is available for interviews in support of the Netflix release of *Child of the Cloud*. Her story as a Southeast Asian immigrant who studied theatre in London before relocating to America is inspiring, and she has a lot of stories to tell about her work in the Sundance hit *Street Talk* and costarring on the NBC hit series *Play Time*.

I'd love to set up a time for you to talk to Melissa for your "Spotlight" feature in the December/January issue. If you'd like to see *Child of the Cloud* again, we have some screenings set up this month (www.childofthecloudmovie.com/screenings), or I can arrange to get you access to a secure online screener.

Thanks as always for your attention, I hope to hear from you soon.

EXERCISE 11C: CLIENT BIO AND BACKGROUNDER

Write both a short bio (suitable for production notes) and a backgrounder/profile for an individual or corporate client. I suggest working with a person or individual who is already established and well known enough so that basic facts are available to you.

Write the bio first (an example follows), and then use your imagination to create a series of questions that you might ask while doing research for a backgrounder. You can then make up answers to those questions in the voice of your subject. If you are working with a group or partner, you might even consider role-playing as each other's subjects, and practice your interviewing skills with a "live" respondent.

Depending on your subject, the basic bio might be anywhere from one paragraph to more than a page long (more experienced subjects obviously need more length in their bios). The backgrounder, however, should be restricted to three to four pages total.

EXERCISE 11C: SAMPLE

John C. Reilly—Backgrounder

Chicago-born John C. Reilly is a Golden Globe nominee for his performance as legendary screen comedian Oliver Hardy in *Stan and Ollie*, costarring with Steve Coogan. That marks the end of a successful 2018 that also saw Reilly costar with friend Will Ferrell in the comedy *Holmes and Watson*, and reprise his role as Wreck-It Ralph in the animated sequel *Ralph Breaks the Internet*.

Reilly's screen career began with a supporting role in the Brian De Palma film *Casualties of War* in 1989. He made his mark on audiences in films such as *Days of Thunder*, *What's Eating Gilbert Grape*, *The River Wild*, and *Boys*, before breaking through costarring with Mark Wahlberg in Paul Thomas Anderson's acclaimed *Boogie Nights*, which earned Reilly and his cast mates a SAG award nomination. Major roles in hit films followed, including Terrence Malick's *The Thin Red Line*, Anderson's *Magnolia*, and again with Wahlberg in *The Perfect Storm*. He's also worked with the likes of Martin Scorsese (*The Aviator* and *The Gangs of New York)*, and brought his talent to acclaimed indie films such as Miguel Arteta's *The Good Girl*, Mike White's *Year of the Dog*, Stephen Daldry's *The Hours*, and Lynne Ramsey's *We Need to Talk About Kevin*.

Although he began his career in dramas, Reilly has also become well known as a comedian, through is collaboration with Ferrell on such films as *Talladega Nights* and *Step Brothers*. He also starred as the title character in the Judd Apatow-produced *Walk Hard: The Dewey Cox Story*, and in 2017's medieval comedy *The Little Hours* with Aubrey Plaza.

In addition to *Wreck-It Ralph*, Reilly lent his voice acting talents to films such as *9*, produced by Tim Burton, and *Sing*, produced by Illumination Entertainment. Recent roles also include *The Sisters Brothers*, *Kong: Skull Island*, and *The Lobster*.

A veteran stage actor who trained with the famed Steppenwolf Theatre Company, Reilly drew critical acclaim in 2000 when he appeared alongside the late Philip Seymour Hoffman as they alternated roles in Sam Shepard's *True West*. He also starred in major productions of Paddy Chayefsky's *Marty* and as Stanley Kowalski in the 2005 Broadway production of *A Streetcar Named Desire*. Reilly also wrote and coproduced the television special *Bagboy*, and produced and lent his voice to the series *Stone Quackers* on FXX.

CHAPTER 12

Writing for a Career

Just as many people who dreamed of working in the entertainment industry for a living, both my father and I initially were attracted to the industry as potential creatives. Falling in love with the movies and television as a storytelling-based art form, we found ourselves moved by the characters, situations, moments, classic lines, and happy endings that dominate the conventional Hollywood approach to narrative. My dad identified with the young narrator of the John Ford classic *How Green Was My Valley* and was bedazzled by the lightning-fast dialogue and good-guys-win, behind-the-scenes bonhomie of *Singin' in the Rain.* I found kindred spirits in suburban-raised Elliot from *E.T. The Extra-Terrestrial* and Marty McFly from *Back to the Future*, and was inspired by the unusual cinematic language suggested by Richard Linklater's *Slacker* and the gender-bending glam rock bedazzlement of Todd Haynes' *Velvet Goldmine.* Who wouldn't want to be part of an industry that was so personally moving? A type of work that seemed to reward the ability to make people laugh, think, and explore their imaginations? A chance to create something that might inspire a young viewer to do something bold, brave, different, and unique with their lives, just the way we ourselves had been inspired?

While my father and I never lost our passion for films and television, we also both found, in our own way, that there was a lot more to the business than being *creative* in the traditional sense of the word. Obviously, we both knew from experience that establishing a career as a **filmmaker**—someone who writes, directs, and essentially serves as the primary **storyteller**—was statistically a very daunting proposition. According to an analysis of the membership of the Writers Guild of America West (WGAW), there were about 8,700 union screenwriters in Hollywood in 2016—but only about 60% of them actually found employment as writers. Furthermore, of those 8,700, fewer than 400 were under the age of 31 years old, with less than 40% overall under the age of 40. (The percentages of female and minority screenwriters in the guild, while improving, is still woefully low, suggesting the prospects for those populations are even more discouraging.)[1]

---

1   Hunt, Darnell M., et al. WRITERS GUILD OF AMERICA, WEST, THE 2016 HOLLYWOOD WRITERS REPORT https://www.wga.org/uploadedFiles/who_we_are/HWR16.pdf

Similarly, there are 16,000 members of the Directors Guild of America, but the vast majority of them are assistant directors and second assistant directors: the studios only distribute between 600–700 films per year. Run down the list of the top films at the box office at any given moment, and you'll also very likely realize that very few films are written and directed by the same person: Of the top 20 films at the box office in 2018, only two films had the same person credited as both sole writer and director (Chris McQuarrie for *Mission Impossible: Fallout* and Brad Bird for *The Incredibles 2*). In a handful of other films, directors were co-credited on the screenplay, but in every case (except for the original horror film *The Quiet Place*), those films were based on franchises, sequels, or other previously established material.[2]

Thus, the market for original material and artists who create those stories is shrinking in the feature film world. There are far more writers employed in television, but most of those writers are working on series or ideas created by other people. And while we all respect the amazing output of artists such as Shonda Rimes, Dan Fogelman, Jenji Kohan, Joss Whedon, Dick Wolf, and the other excessively prolific "show runners" and producers, it took those artists many years of experience to get to a point where they could get their series ideas to broadcast.

So, as many of my colleagues and students who I've seen discover new pathways into the field they care so much about, my father and I realized that despite whatever writing talent we had, despite the originality or novelty of our ideas, we were very unlikely to succeed in such a competitive marketplace. Fortunately for both of us, the value of our writing skills meant that we could still be a part of this industry.

In fact, I discovered that while I had a passion for movies, I also had a great passion for *talking* about movies—communicating about them both in conversation, and also in my writing. I wrote reviews of films I saw in theaters in my junior high notebook. I watched every episode of *Siskel and Ebert* to see how those two intelligent and thoughtful men discussed the value of the movies that were currently in theaters. As a college student, I found more joy and productivity in the Cinema Studies Department at NYU, literally immersed in film and media culture day and night, while not having to toil away with light meters, splicers, f-stops, and the seemingly endless stages of postproduction that my filmmaker colleagues were required to learn and master.

So while my writing has not been "creative" in the traditional sense, it's still offered me hundreds (if not thousands) of opportunities to contribute to the creative process, and in support of things I found interesting, important, or just plain wonderful. The writing that I've introduced in this book is important not just because it's a way of greasing the wheels of the big bad entertainment industry factory machine. It's important because in almost every case, it allows *you*, the writer of these materials, to participate in the absolutely essential work of explaining why a particular piece of work is valuable (or not).

---

2   In fact, of the top 35 films at the domestic box office in 2018, only *four* films could be considered totally "original"—not based on any previously published material or real-life story. In addition to *A Quiet Place*, the others are *The Meg*, *The Nun*, and *Rampage*. Six films were from the Marvel Comic Universe, 13 from other franchises, four were remakes or "reboots," six were based on books, and two from real-life stories.

In that sense, it has functions that might be equated to very different kinds of practices elsewhere in our lives. Imagine, for example, visiting a car lot where all the cars basically look the same—the differences are in the size of the engine, the gas mileage, and other less visible features. You'd need someone there at the lot—perhaps a salesperson—to provide some guidance and advice about the vehicle that might best fit your needs. At the very least, you'd need to have some type of information—a brochure or catalog—that offers some detail to provide you with the proper information. Theoretically, "any" car might work for you and get you from place to place, but you don't want any car, you want the car that's right for your budget, your overall transportation needs, your family's needs, and so on.

The writing that you do in the industry on behalf of other projects is in many ways that sales process. After all, when you go to the movie theater, you probably aren't going to ask the 19-year-old selling you tickets whether *Ant Man vs. The Wasp* is a better date-night movie than *Widows*. If you are a busy executive who has to recommend that your company spend $500,000 buying an original script that will give your movie star boss a chance to step into the director's chair, then *any old script* won't do, it has to be the *right* one. If your job is to figure out who to book for a *Good Morning America* appearance on the Friday before the Super Bowl, then you aren't just going to take the first celebrity you are pitched simply to get that part of your job over and done with. You need guidance, suggestions, and to be persuaded, actions ultimately supported by those written materials that allow you to examine, measure, and quantify each decision.

In that sense, it's important I convey that the value of these materials is not secondary to the value of the screenplay or the storytelling: it is, as I said in the first chapter, the clothes your baby will wear when he or she first goes out into the world and starts to "grow up." Your baby can't be naked (at least, not for long without prompting some question as to why the baby never wears clothes), and you can't just stuff the baby in a pillow case with a hole in the top and call the infant "dressed" and have people take it seriously. Being able to use your words to explain why something is valuable is indeed part of the act of creation, and offers those of us who are passionate about movies *and* well-versed in the use of the written word to find a place of solid employment and productivity.

So, to wrap up, I'd like to offer professional writers a few points that I believe are essential for success. They also have some value to anyone involved in the creative media or entertainment industries, but are of particular importance to writers. I've mentioned a few of these along the way, but hope by reiterating them here, at the end of this book, they'll have some extra resonance and context.

READ, READ, READ

If you are going to make a living as a writer in any form—creative, technical, whatever—you have to be familiar with the standards of professional writing in your field. In the Internet age, when we are used to processing written language in a number of different formats, modalities, platforms, and circumstances, it's very easy to dismiss poor writing as simply a circumstance of time. It's annoying to have to hit that "shift" key on your phone before you use an apostrophe or a quotation mark, so you let it go when a friend shows the same sloppiness in a thank-you note.

But professionals in any field have to hold themselves to a higher standard, and that standard can best be measured by looking at those who are paid money to do what you want to do. Regardless of what kind of writing you are doing, the craft of building strong sentences and paragraphs, the artful use of precisely descriptive words, and the technical precision of effective punctuation, proper formatting, and correct spelling help communicate meaning clearly to your reader.

And the best way to develop good muscle memory is to continually read and get your eye and your brain used to what works and why. If you are in the entertainment industry, as mentioned before, you should be reading the trades every day. Screenwriters, producers, and directors should find time to read screenplays on projects that don't belong to them; if you know someone working on a film or TV show that seems interesting, ask if you can see a copy of the script just so you can ascertain for yourself what got that project sold. Take time to read broader cultural commentary about the entertainment business in the form of op-eds and think pieces, alongside substantive interviews and profiles of important people in the industry. Find four or five film critics whose opinions you find interesting (regardless of whether you agree with them) and compare how they review the same film. Read published biographies, memoirs, and histories so that you can appreciate how scholars and authors utilize their research and place it into an effective and original context.

It's very easy to consume informational and entertainment media in other forms when we want to relax or check out—we can stream hours of a new TV series when we have a day off, or download podcasts and audio books to keep us engaged during rush-hour traffic. And to be fair, those media have linguistic components that can also help improve your internal language processing mechanisms. But we see words differently than we hear them, and giving your eyes plenty of page-based exercise will undoubtedly improve your own ability to put letters and symbols into effective combinations.

WATCH AND LEARN

As film programs move toward the instruction of hands-on mediamaking—a welcome advance in education that is the direct result of more available and affordable technology—the study of film, television, and visual media from a critical and cultural perspective has dimmed in importance. When I went to film school, I was involved in programs that required two, three, or even four semesters of film history or other deep-dive studies into the aesthetic and industrial traditions that inform mediamaking practices. Today there are programs—including one employed at my current university, which I helped design—that can only afford one semester of required history (with the hope that students will use electives to supplement that requirement). Throughout our extensive community college system in Arizona, which features some outstanding, innovative, and successful media production programs, there are very few courses in film and media history or studies, since the emphasis is (justifiably) on preparing students for in-demand technical careers. It's completely understandable that the educational institutions have found this generation of students more interested in making film than studying its history, but it leaves many students without the same critical language and appreciative skills as previous generations of serious filmmakers.

Other factors influencing our understanding of previous eras in storytelling media involve the availability of digital, streaming, and on-demand platforms that offer literally infinite material, much of it brand new. Take a look at the website http://www.everysecond.io/youtube to see how much material is being uploaded to YouTube at any given moment (65 hours every 10 seconds when I checked). What this means is that if you are looking for something to entertain you or inform you about your chosen field, you are allowed to dive deep into whatever you want and ignore the rest. This began with the era of home video cassettes, when you could buy a copy of *Star Wars* or *The Godfather* and watch it over and over again; it's hard to remember that before then that you could only watch something when someone (a film distributor, movie theater, or television network) made it available to you, with no promise that you'd ever be able to see it again in the future.

The result is that increasingly more people involved in the film industry seem to have much more focused and narrow memories or understandings of their profession. If you are a Joss Whedon fan and can quote his oeuvre chapter and verse, then that's a great skill; but if you don't know the names and work of John and Tom Whedon (Joss's grandfather and father, respectively), then you're robbing yourself of understanding the legacy of incredibly successful writers that Joss derives from and how it might inform or shed light on the kinds of stories he tells, and why he tells them the way he does. The legacy does not even have to be literally bound by blood: I'm continually astonished at the number of students who claim the "originality" of Quentin Tarantino, when the director himself constantly speaks about the many generations of global cinematic practices that inspire him and which he frequently employs in his own films. Whether one considers such imitation and appropriation as effective or not is a matter of critical perspective, but to claim it as "original" or "unique" to Tarantino is to rob one's self of the knowledge of the history of the art form that may be a key framework for meaning and enjoyment. It is far less important that we value a particular artist or work of art as original, particularly in film and television, where so much emphasis is placed on developing material that is already familiar to audiences. Developing an appreciation for the way stories, characters, situations, and conventions are "recycled" will give anyone who wants to succeed in the industry an advantage over those who ignore the past 100 years of cinematic history.

I'm not necessarily suggesting that you need to take three years to study the history of film, or that you need to develop an "academic" appreciation of materials that were made before 2010 (let alone before 1980 or 1948 or 1927). But it is important to open yourself up to materials that are not necessarily "hot" or purely within your own comfort zone. Some recommend working through a list such as the AFI 100 Greatest Movies List, or watching all of the Best Picture winners, and that's a good start, though such lists are often dominated by American/Hollywood-style films that were financially successful and already widely seen. Just as you seek out "new" material, seek out material that is new for *you*, whether it's watching a dozen silent comedy shorts; binging three or four of the great "social problem" films from the 1930s; taking a look at John Wayne movies that aren't necessarily his "iconic" roles; or appreciating the innovations in independent filmmaking that happened long before the Sundance era. It should also mean developing an appreciation for the filmmaking traditions of at least one other national or ethnic culture. No matter your taste in American-style films, I can guarantee there is a great filmmaking or television tradition out there that you will love once you find it. Take advantage of the breadth of the digital libraries at your disposal, not just their depth.

BE A PROFESSIONAL

Most college and university programs offer what is called **professional development** either in class form, or perhaps as a function of a career services program. The presence of these courses in an educational setting might send the message that such information is *only* required at the beginning of someone's career. In fact, a professional profile and reputation is something that must be managed over the long term, and must evolve along *with* you as your career develops and new opportunities emerge.

Thus, checking in with yourself as a professional on a regular basis is imperative for you to be prepared for success. Do you have a resume that you could send to someone *right now* that can land you your ideal job? Do you have business cards in your pocket in case someone introduces you to a potential employer at a social event? If someone in your field mentions a new technology or application that you are unfamiliar with, are you able to research it and understand it right away? If you have a contract dispute, do you have an immediate resource or contact that can help you navigate that conflict?

In addition to professional self-care, there's also the simple matter of how you treat other people and how you earn their respect. I often tell my students how I define success. Success is not *having what you want* or *doing what you want to do*; success is *earning the respect of others by embracing every opportunity you can to demonstrate good work*. Earning that respect is what opens doors to advancement, investment, and creative innovation.

It should go without saying, but that means showing up on time for every appointment; dressing appropriately; not staring at your phone (or your computer screen) when someone else is talking or presenting unless absolutely necessary; making reasonable and consistent eye contact; and asking thoughtful, substantive questions when given the opportunity to do so. Recognize and embrace every interaction with a professional colleague as an opportunity to show her or him that you respect the time you share together. If you find yourself lacking in a certain professional ability (I can suffer bouts of extreme social anxiety to the point that maintaining eye contact is a struggle), then find creative partners and associates who have those abilities and ask them for tips on how to improve. Most of what is expected from professionals is simply a certain kind of external presentation and level of behavior and it is easily achievable: it won't guarantee any specific kind of success by any means, but it will help you find more opportunities to demonstrate good work.

I also want to add that as a professional writer, you have a real advantage when you write to request a meeting, and especially when you write the "thank-you note" or email after that meeting (which you absolutely must do). You should have the skills necessary to not just write a perfunctory and obligatory "Thanks for coffee" note, but should be able to effectively and efficiently let your words specifically influence that person and provide him or her with a *lasting memory*: "It meant a lot to me that you took the time to talk to me about my career, but it was even more of a delight to discover that we were both fans of Australian rules football." I once had a colleague at a new job remind me of a note that I had sent her after a failed job interview four years prior, down to the specific words I used: I myself had no memory of what I wrote, but it had an effect on her and put me in very good stead in that new position from day one.

In an industry that is so competitive, and one in which we are so often told that we need to be *true to yourself* and to *look out for number one*, the opposite side of that coin—of presenting yourself as part of a team and ready to "meet" someone (literally or figuratively) and work with them—can be overshadowed. The truth is, no one wants to work with a jerk or someone who seems as though they don't want to be there—and especially early in your career. Being liked, in fact, is sometimes far more important than being talented—and obviously, it's best to be both. Do your best to make sure you are putting appropriate emphasis on creating a positive working relationship with others as you are into the work you actually do.

VALUE YOUR TIME, EFFORT, AND ABILITY

At some point, you will very likely get a position that prompts people to ask you for favors. It might be your boss who needs you to work extra hours, run a personal errand, or fill in for someone else who is on vacation; it might be a start-up company that hopes you can do some work pro bono for a few weeks until it can get its budget together; perhaps a prospective client who needs you to go the "extra mile" on providing feedback, or asking for yet another meeting in which you can talk about a future collaboration; it might be a stranger—or a dear friend or close relative—who *really* wants you to read her or his "amazing" script, even though that person has no professional experience or training.

Early in your career, you are far more likely to want to say "yes" to this extra work—and I will be honest: saying "yes" to a lot of those things in my early career *did* pay off, and very handsomely (both financially and creatively). But it also meant that I was often overworked, had little time for myself or a social life outside of work, or felt I was being undervalued. I was getting a salary for a 40-hour per week job that was decent, but when I ended up actually working 70 hours per week, including quite a bit of time for other people, it didn't quite seem fair.

Be prepared to wrestle with this for the rest of your professional career. Defining strong boundaries for yourself is a good first step. For example, when it comes to my professional writing, I do not work for free. I have a standard hourly rate—one I am happy to offer a great discount on if necessary—but when someone asks me if I can help create new marketing materials, I say of course, but I have to be paid. Now, if someone were to ask me to write a series of television commercials, or to develop a screenplay with that person, I might choose to work without guaranteed pay, as those are spaces where I do not regularly work as a professional. But my "bread and butter" is something I need to protect.

In addition to the financial value of your time, value your experience and knowledge by not treating favors any differently than you treat paying work. When I was doing coverage, it would have been easy to write simple but bland and ineffective "sample" reports for friends or colleagues—reports they could have then used to try to get an agent or manager. There are people out there who will "pay for good coverage," which isn't against the law, or anywhere near the top of the list of the ethically worst things that people will do to get their projects made. But for me, I would turn down any such offer not because it was inherently unethical or unfair, but because it completely ignored my value as a story analyst. Knowing how to write good coverage from a technical perspective made me a good story analyst, but ultimately I was also being trusted for my honest opinion. I told the story earlier about my boss's entreaty to provide a positive second read for *Bring It On*, but that was in the context of a team-based professional relationship—it's different from your boss asking you to do something versus a friend who might be offering to buy you dinner if you read his or her script and write coverage that makes their script sound like the second coming of Shakespeare.

Sure enough, there was one time when someone I didn't know, an actor who was referred to me to write a bio and backgrounder, also asked me about doing coverage on a script that he insisted was hot and that people had given him great feedback on. He wanted coverage from a "real" studio-based story analyst he was hoping would help persuade a producer to option the script. I told him I'd be happy to do it under two circumstances: first, that he include a check for payment when he sent the script along (I advise this when you deal with individuals; companies are usually okay to bill); and second, that he accept my opinion and analysis as an industry professional.

The script was awful. It was confusing, improperly formatted, filled with clichés, and trying to be a modern Indiana Jones-type adventure. The lead role was clearly meant for the aging actor to portray, with a suspiciously young female costar as a love interest as they bounce around the globe. It was a struggle to read, and a struggle to produce coverage that did not go into great detail about the script's weaknesses. I did my best to suggest potential positives ("something compelling about the film's ambitious scope") and tried to minimize the horror ("the characters function well in action sequences, but dialogue seems to fall flat"), but it was poor coverage.

The "client" was livid: he had paid (I believe) $45 and expected to get coverage he could use to sell his movie, and screamed at me over the phone. I reminded him that he had hired me as a professional, and that he would have to accept my opinion. He remembered, but he said, "I didn't know that you wouldn't like it." He only ended the conversation when we "agreed" that maybe I just didn't like the kind of film he was trying to write, that it was purely a matter of taste, and not execution. I was happy to concede that may be the case (it wasn't), but I felt good that I had stood my ground on this issue.

You don't have to wait for professional success to treat your own work as serious, mature, and professional, especially when you are in collaboration with others or working on other people's projects. Making sure you are compensated means making sure you are paid both in currency and in respect and acknowledgment of the value of your ability to do the work you do.

ACCENTUATE THE POSITIVE

The story of the bad actor's bad coverage also suggests that even when we are most "down" on something we encounter in our professional career, one of the best skills to employ is to try to see the positive in everything. You're going to not only hear "no" quite a bit in your career, you're also very likely to have to say it a lot of times, or be part of the process that communicates "no" to aspiring artists, "no" to new kinds of storytelling, "no" to underserved and underrepresented audiences, and "no" to all but the slowest and most incremental change.

The film and television industries are a weird combination of fast and very, very slow. It often seems as things "happen" by accident and that blind, stupid luck can be more important than the best laid plans. Great ideas from great minds linger for years in obscurity; well-intentioned passion projects turn into laughable failures; and poorly made, derivative dreck produced by talent of questionable moral character earns billions. "Nobody knows anything," wrote William Goldman, and that can easily put an intelligent, thoughtful person into a very cynical mindset.

But the neutrality of fortune also means that every person involved in the process has a way of contributing toward the positive value of the work. The film project you are developing, or the television series you are promoting, or the music video you hope launches your musical friend's career, those things may or may not be successful. But what you are more likely to remember is that the people who created those things all had a great time doing it because they were all passionate about the projects. By the same token, you might be on a project that's just another slash 'em up horror film that will probably go straight to an on-demand horror site and only consumed by the tiny (but quite fanatical) horror film community. But you might remember that the film provided 100 people with five weeks' worth of good salaries and a chance to do their jobs well, and establish professional credits and connections that gave them a leg up on getting the next gig.

You undoubtedly will have a job interview for a position you need, or a meeting with a producer who can literally make your dreams come true. It's most likely such a single meeting won't fulfill its promise: someone else will get the job, the producer was unimpressed. But you needn't consider it a failure. Was there something about the meeting you made memorable (in a good way)? Would you feel comfortable meeting that person again? Can you remember other people you may have met at that interview—assistants, colleagues—who you might encounter at a later interview or social event?

If indeed more successful projects happen by "accident," it's also because the people involved are probably looking for ways to take advantage of the unexpected positives. I hope you can see how most of these writing practices take that perspective, of being able to look at something creative and then produce and present, in a more or less honest way, an assessment of the value of that creation. Although script coverage and development-based writing practices might have to largely function in a negative capacity—"no, this isn't good enough"—it can do so in a way that builds the creative consciousness of the creative writers, challenging them to do better. Publicity and marketing practices are built around ways of explaining to audiences, viewers, consumers, and fans what makes a project special and unique, even if it is "really" just the same-old, same-old.

The words we use help shape the world around us by suggesting spaces and possibilities in the mind of a reader that can have a powerful influence on the way he or she understands and processes the many stories, texts, and experiences that stimulate that person's imagination. It is hoped you have developed and refined some skills that will help you foster your writing skills and allow you to suggest and discover a lifetime of success, creating professional opportunities for yourself that are both rewarding and fulfilling.

Index

treatment, 35–36
Twitter, 21. *See also* social media

U

*Unexposed Film: A Year on
    Location* (Harris), 181
unit publicist, 39–41, 111–114, 172
unit publicity, 111–114
Universal, 88–89

V

Variety, 13–15
Velvet Goldmine, 82
verbs, 69
video junket, 141
Voight, Jon, 110

W

Waterworld, 179
Wayne, John, 192
Whedon, John, 191
Whedon, Tom, 191
Wicked, 88–89
*Wicked: The Life and Times of
    the Wicked Witch of the West*
    (Maguire), 88
Witherspoon, Reese, 21
words
    count, minimizing, 53–54
    process, 68
    value, maximizing, 53–54
working group, 5
Writers Guild of America West
    (WGAW), 187

writing
    as career, 187–196
    as selling, 32–33
    bio (biographical informa-
        tion), 8–11
    samples, 84–85
    Three C's, 30–32
    value of, 6–8

Y

Yankee Doodle Dandy, 15
Young, Loretta, 20

Z

Zukor, Adolph, 80